D1320838

BARBARA STANWYCK

BARBARA STANWYCK

Al DiOrio

W.H. ALLEN · LONDON

COMET

Copyright © 1983 by Al DiOrio
First published in America by Coward-McCann, Inc.
First British edition, 1984

Printed and bound in Great Britain by
Mackays of Chatham Ltd, Kent
for the Publishers W.H. Allen & Co. PLC,
44 Hill Street, London W1X 8LB

ISBN 0 491 03373 7 (W.H. Allen hardcover edition)
ISBN 0 86379 072 0 (Comet Books softcover edition)

ACKNOWLEDGMENTS

Inevitably, in preparing a book of this sort, assistance comes from many sources and in many different ways. First, I would like to express my deepest gratitude to those co-workers and friends of Miss Stanwyck who were generous enough to share their remembrances with me. I am especially grateful to the kindnesses shown me by Anne Baxter, John Ericson, Glenn Ford, Joel McCrea, Gilbert Roland, and Robert Young. Additionally, I would like to thank Eve Arden, Jim Backus, Bruce Bauer, Ralph Bellamy, Joan Bennett, William Conrad, Pat Crowley, Robert Cummings, Francisco Day, John Dehner, Andrew Duggan, Chester Erskine, Donald L. Fapp, Nina Foch, Vincent Gardenia, Arlene Golonka, Harold Gould, Peter Haskell, George Kennedy, Gavin McLeod, Maureen O'Sullivan, Walter Pidgeon, Irwin Rapper, President Ronald Reagan, Barry Sullivan, Gay Talese, Phyllis Thaxter, Regis Toomey, Susan Kohner Weitz, Robert Wise, Keenan Wynn, and, especially, Mrs. Alfred Santell for sharing her late husband's papers with me.

Additional courtesies, for which I am grateful, were extended by the Screen Actors Guild, the Lincoln Center Library for the Performing Arts, the Academy of Motion Picture Arts and Sciences and the Margaret Herrick Library, the Motion Picture Country Home, the American Federation of Television and Radio Artists, the American Film Institute, the Directors Guild, and the Producers Guild.

Other individuals to whom I am indebted include George Beach, Louis F. Cappelli, Vanina Cassotto, Jack Costello, John Fricke, Marie Herman, Al Herzer, Jan Jeffries, Joe Lauderdale, Bob Lindsey, Louis Martinaitis, Doug McClelland, Steve Metz, Chris Mitchell, Dan Oldrati, Bob Reno, Rick Santella, John Stalzburg, Liz Smith, Jim Spearo, Tom Stuto, Gary Walden, and Ken Young.

A few deserve special thanks. First, to my agent Mitchell Douglas of ICM for his constant encouragement and support, not to mention his patience, and to Alida Becker for her generous guidance and friendship. I am grateful to my editors, Tom Miller and, especially, Deni Auclair, for helping to make this book such an enjoyable endeavor and to both Sarah Hofman Giller and Terry Cimilluca for their willingness to help with typing and other tedious bits of business and for always doing so with a smile.

Lastly, my most heartfelt thanks to those who continue to surround me with their unending support, love, and encouragement. Not only do they deserve my gratitude but my devotion. They include Anita Buonasorte, Lois Carita, Anthony Catalano, Jim Iannarella, Pamela and George Karsona, Karen and Terrance Regan, Betty Santoianni, John Santoianni, and Barbara Vena.

Lastly, I must thank my mother, Mrs. Martha DiOrio, and my sister, Mrs. Barbara Iannarella. They, more than anyone else, have helped me in all ways. I couldn't do it without them, and I wouldn't want to. There are really no words to tell them how I feel.

For Karen Heuser Regan, whose friendship over the last seventeen years has been an incredible source of love, strength, and comfort. She lives the true spirit of friendship every day of her life, and I am lucky to have her as part of my own.

CHAPTER 1

Chelsea, Massachusetts, was a fishing town no different from a score of others that dotted the coast of Rhode Island, Massachusetts, and Maine. Dominated by wharves of salt-aged wood and rotten pillars, the towns were inhabited, for the most part, by fisherfolk and their families.

Often of Irish descent, these were strong-willed, hardworking people whose spirits were made even more indomitable by the ever-present challenge of the bitterly cold and chillingly damp New England winters and the inescapable smell of rotten wood and fish. A drab existence at best, life in Chelsea was far from a dream come true. The women remained in the home raising a multitude of children while their husbands spent their days on the sea and their nights, more often than not, in the oceanfront bars.

The life of Catherine McGee and Byron Stevens was no better and no worse than that of most of their Chelsea neighbors. Byron and Catherine, children of Irish immigrants who had settled in Chelsea, were married.

Catherine McGee was a native of Chelsea, born probably around 1870. A beautiful colleen with long raven-black hair and violet eyes, she had a voice described as soft, gentle, and low. She was still a girl when she met Byron Stevens. Byron had been born and raised in Chelsea, too, of Irish and English parents. He was a handsome man, with red hair and a rather tall and gaunt form, whose many moods could fluctuate from a Black Irish temper to a somewhat quieter and more pensive demeanor that left those around him wondering if there wasn't a good deal more to Byron Stevens than met the eye.

Byron and Catherine were wed at an early age, probably around 1890, and started a family immediately. Two daughters, born in quick succession, were named Maude and Mabel, respectively. A few years later, another daughter, Mildred, was welcomed into the family. Finally, in 1905, Catherine gave her husband a son, who was named Malcolm Byron.

Byron was a skilled fisherman, but like so many others on the New England coast, he had to be ready to support his family in any way he could, and through the years he worked as a laborer doing roadwork and construction, and even developed into a skilled bricklayer. Just as had been suspected, however, there were hidden turmoils boiling in Byron's mind, and, eventually, on a dark and stormy night, in a scene reminiscent of Poe or Dickens, Byron ran away, leaving his wife and four children to fend for themselves.

Whether or not Byron ever intended to return or send for his family is unknown. Catherine didn't wait to find out. As far as she was concerned, she couldn't afford to wait. She had four mouths to feed, and come hell or high water, it was Byron's responsibility. Without hesitation she packed up the family's possessions, and with the four kids in tow, went to find Byron Stevens.

She eventually caught up with him in Brooklyn where he was working as a bricklayer. Catherine's power of persuasion must have been something to reckon with because, before long, Byron and his family were settled en masse at 246 Classon Avenue, and Catherine was pregnant with their fifth child.

The winter of 1906–1907 was a harsh one in Brooklyn. Catherine and the children spent months taking turns with bouts of influenza, and to make matters worse, in January, Byron found himself out of work. The prospect of another mouth to feed did not engender a great deal of joyous anticipation in the Stevens household, but still there was the hope that with the spring would come better health and some work for Byron. Little had changed, however, by July 16, when Catherine gave birth to another daughter, this one named Ruby.

Over the next two years the Stevens family went about their lives much the same as before. Byron worked whenever there was work to be had, and Catherine did her best to see that her children were fed and at least knew the togetherness only a large family can bring. The oldest girls, Maude and Mabel, were married but visited often, and along with Mildred they took turns wheeling little Ruby in her carriage. Often they would push her, with little Malcolm tagging along, up and down Classon Avenue, never going farther than the railroad tracks that served to fence them in on one end. The waterfront wasn't far, however, and sometimes they would take her there to watch the ships come into the docks for loading. It was the only escape they had from an atmosphere pungent with the steamy smells of the poor: strong soap, dirt, babies' wash, and cooking. Years later Ruby would admit that as a child she could seldom associate women with anything but washtubs, kitchen sinks, and the perpetual squeak of clotheslines outside dingy windows.

When Ruby was two years old, Catherine Stevens found that she was expecting her sixth child. Byron, undoubtedly, accepted this news as he had each previous announcement of impending fatherhood; it meant more work to be done and more responsibilities to be shouldered. Walking home by the waterfront each night, weary with fatigue and feeling older than his years, Byron often would let his mind drift romantically out to sea.

In the early, wintry months of 1910, Catherine Stevens was still awaiting the birth of her sixth child. She was stepping off a trolley car one afternoon when a drunk unexpectedly lurched forward, knocking her onto the ground where she struck her head soundly against the curb. A concussion resulted, and within the week Catherine was dead.

Byron was devastated. His spirit broken and his health weakened by years of hard living and hard liquor, he gave in to the irresponsible yearnings he'd fought off with the help of Catherine's strong will. Two weeks after his wife's funeral he joined a gang of laborers heading for Panama to work on the canal. He left behind a family he would never see again.

Perhaps the years of struggle had bred a selfishness in Ruby's oldest sisters, Maude and Mabel, or perhaps it was just the fact that they were married with problems of their own, but they did not offer active participation in the rearing of their two-year-old sister or Malcolm, then five. Mildred, the third child and known as "the beauty of the family," was already actively pursuing a career on stage as a chorus girl and couldn't fit the children into her freewheeling life-style either.

Nevertheless she was determined that her brother and sister would not be put into an orphanage. Money was hard to come by for everyone in days prior to World War I, and it was not uncommon for many poor Brooklyn families to offer room and board to homeless children whose families would pay for their care. After Catherine's death and Byron's desertion, Ruby was placed immediately into one of these paid homes. Unfortunately, the family didn't have room for both brother and sister, so Malcolm was placed in another home just a couple of blocks away.

It was a painful arrangement for the children, and Malcolm later recalled that even at so early an age, Ruby missed her mother. Inevitably, each afternoon, he would be summoned by the family watching over his baby sister and asked to find where she had wandered off to. Malcolm knew just where to look because he knew why Ruby was running away. She was too young to understand what had happened to rip her family apart. Patiently, Malcolm would walk to the old Stevens home at 246 Classon Avenue, and gently he would set himself down on the step next to his two-year-old sister who was "waiting for Mama to come home."

CHAPTER 2

Ruby and Malcolm Stevens clung to each other dearly for the next ten years. Life, in its own cruel manner, had left them virtually alone in a world full of strangers. Their oldest sisters, Maude, Mabel, and Mildred, only made time for them when it was convenient. Meanwhile Ruby and Malcolm were shifted from one boardinghouse to another. There was seldom room for both of them in one home, but nevertheless the children formed a close bond between them.

This was not the normal childish affection found between a brother and sister but a relationship in which each became the other's everything. They clung to each other as orphans in a storm, and each evening they parted company and returned separately to a house full of strangers with problems of their own.

Malcolm never teased or taunted his sister as some big brothers might. They never had scraps. Even as children they were too old to engage in such pettiness. Childish battles are unimportant when you face daily battles with loneliness. "We never played games so far as I can remember," Ruby would recall later. "I never cared for games anyway. The only game I can remember playing on the streets is the game of fighting."

There was little affection in the lives of Malcolm and Ruby Stevens except that they showed for each other. They became extraordinarily protective of one another. Malcolm later recalled one occasion when they met to play somewhere between their separate homes. They played all afternoon and suddenly found that they had lost track of time and it was dusk. They were both scared of the secrets nightfall held. Malcolm, then six or seven years old, volunteered to walk four-year-old Ruby home only to find when they got to Ruby's house that he was too frightened to walk home alone. At that point they turned around and Ruby walked Malcolm home.

Ruby was a very quiet child who found it much easier to make friends with adults than with children her own age. Things reached their dismal worst when Mildred gathered little Ruby and her brother together and told them as gently as possible that she had received word from Panama that their father had died on a steamer en route home to his children. For Ruby it was the final blow. In her little girl's mind she had at least been able to convince herself that she was different from the orphans of the world because somewhere she, at least, had a father. Now little Ruby had no recourse but to jut her chin out a little farther to face the world.

Later, when she was on different ground and could speak her mind to those interested in listening, she would confront the public with her childhood sense of abandonment. "Did you ever notice the expressions on the faces of orphans?" she'd demand. "They're all alike. There's a deadness, a dreariness about them that to anyone who has ever lived as an orphan marks them at once. Their eyes are lonely as if they're searching for a companion or friend. Searching for someone to belong to. It's a terrible thing to feel as if you haven't anyone in the world to go to with your troubles."

When she was five, Ruby made her first real friend in an alley behind one of the boardinghouses she lived in. He was the officer on the beat near the house, and he would ride through the alley each morning on his horse. One morning Ruby was emptying the garbage pail as he passed and he called, "Hey, girlie, wanna take a little ride on the back of my horse?"

Ruby's face lit up as she joined him atop the animal. From then on, and as long as Ruby lived at that particular home, she began each day clutching the belt of her officer friend as she sat behind him on the horse and they rode up and down that bleak alley in Brooklyn. Soon it became a familiar sight around the station house to see Ruby playing house in a corner of the room. She and Malcolm ran through the halls playing hide and seek, with Ruby's favorite hiding spot the kneehole of the captain's desk. It was her officer friend who began to teach Ruby that there is always something to be grateful for. "Youngster," he told her, "you're sure pretty enough and you're sure enough bright. There isn't anyone in the world luckier than you. Better remember that." More often than not, it was hard for little Ruby to take these words of wisdom seriously.

When Ruby was six years old, it was time for her to start school, but she resisted all attempts to discuss it. For years neighborhood kids had jeered at her as an outsider and taunted her by calling her "orphan." "You're right," she'd respond, challenging, "I'm an orphan and I'll always be an orphan. So what!" She learned early that if she cried she would only encourage their teasing, so tears were something Ruby Stevens kept to herself. But she wasn't as sure of herself as she would have the other kids believe, and now she dreaded the thought of having to go to school with these same brats and to spend the day with them. She begged to be allowed to stay home, but the response to her pleading was a whack on the side of her head. Ruby went to school . . . and wept all the way there for her Uncle Cap'n.

Another lesson Malcolm and Ruby learned early was to forget their birthdays and to try to forget Christmas. There was no assurance that their sisters would visit, and the families Malcolm and Ruby were living with were invariably too poor to do anything for their own children, let alone the little urchin sleeping on the cot in the dining room. On occasion, again, when it was convenient, one of their married sisters, Maude or Mabel, might invite them over on Christmas Day, but these were usually bittersweet occasions at best. Malcolm once recalled such a Christmas when they were invited to Maude's house. After dinner

Maude announced that she would be going out and that it was time for the children to go home. As she said good-bye and ushered them out, she handed each of them a package. Eagerly Ruby and her brother sat on the step to unwrap their treasures, but the sparkle in their eyes soon went dull as they stared at their gifts. They'd each gotten a black raincoat.

Through the years Mildred continued to pay for their room and board. She did care about her younger brother and sister, but she was living the life of a chorus girl and that meant traveling from New York to Boston, Philadelphia, Baltimore, and Chicago. This left time for little more than a long-distance acquaintance during the years when their need for family was most urgent.

Inevitably, when Ruby was eight, her world was turned upside down again when Maude decided that eleven-year-old Malcolm was old enough to be of minimum bother and therefore could come to live with her. What seemed like a great opportunity for Malcolm seemed like the end of the world to his baby sister, because this meant they wouldn't be living close enough to each other to be together very often. The final day of separation was one that would stay with Ruby for a long time. Years later her eyes would cloud with tears as she relived it. "I thought I would lose my mind. I screamed and I cried as though my heart would break. I fought and yelled at them. I tried to lock Malcolm up so they couldn't get him. We were so close, we had been through so much together. I couldn't believe they were taking him, and that I was being left behind. I promised that I would be easy to look after if they would only take me, too. I promised everything . . . if they would only leave us together. But they took him away, and we both cried terribly." That was the beginning of a scrapping Ruby Stevens.

CHAPTER 3

By the age of eight, Ruby Stevens had grown scornful, not necessarily of people, but of the things life did to people. She approached any relationship gingerly, always afraid that she was setting herself up for another fall. Even friendships with her school-mates were luxuries she couldn't allow herself. After all, on any given day she could be uprooted from one boardinghouse and placed in another, and this meant, more often than not, a change in school as well. Not only was such an existence inconducive to any sort of lasting friendships, but it was also extremely harmful to Ruby's education. Later she was to admit, defiantly, "I was the stupidest little brat in school, but I didn't care."

The fact that Ruby could not, or would not, make friends with the other children made them suspicious of her. She, in turn, was wary of them. She particularly disliked the prissy little girls and the silly games they played. She had no time for dolls, probably because she had never really been mothered herself. It is far from surprising that when

Ruby briefly considered writing her autobiography years later, her working title was "I Never Had a Rag Doll."

Aided and abetted by her brother, she managed to work herself into the boys' circle of sports. But they only tolerated her up to a certain point and then threw her out of their games because she was a girl. This would only get her back up, and she'd yell at them, "I can tackle as well as any one of you." The boast didn't help though, until, when being punished for a minor infraction of school rules, she was made to sit on the boys' side of the room. It was only then that she was accepted as a pal. Throughout her life Ruby Stevens would always feel more comfortable in the company of men.

When she was eight, however, love came into Ruby's tomboy life for the first time. At eight she had a crush on a blond youth, aged nine. His name was Claude. She tried her best to attract his attention. She even went so far as to wash her face carefully every day. When that didn't do any good, she wrote him a note stating her affection quite frankly and offering to be his girl. The note earned her a surly look from Claude at recess, and his continued disdain would have done credit to an about-towner of thirty. Then came the bitter awakening at a kids' party in the form of a game of "Kiss the Pillow." The idea of the game was for the girls to sit in a circle, and a certain boy would walk around in front of them and drop the pillow at the feet of his chosen sweetheart. The girl was then supposed to bestow a slight kiss on the cheek of the cavalier.

Ruby had made elaborate preparations for ensnaring Claude into this act. She had even sprayed herself with half a bottle of cheap "Lily" perfume, swiped from the dresser of a female boarder at the house. She had combed her hair and scrubbed her ears. It seemed too good to be true when Claude started walking toward Ruby and seemed to drop the pillow at her feet. She was dizzy with excitement as she rose to wrap her arms around him and bestow a maidenly kiss. All of a sudden Claude began backing away. "Naw, not you," he griped. "I meant Sally." He had chosen the simpering little girl next to Ruby, and she had been rejected again.

During the summers when Ruby was eight, nine, and ten, her sister Mildred took her on the road with her. Those summers fed Ruby's belief that she was being cheated. They gave her the hope that even a woman can escape. Mildred was one of John Cort's show girls, and John Cort was the Ziegfeld of his day. He was good to his girls. They would open in a show in New York, take it on the road, return to New York, and open in another show. Ruby spent those summers standing, for hours on end, in the flies. She met Hal Skelly and Maude Groodie. She lived in crowded dressing rooms, on trains, in railroad hotels. She learned the jargon of the trouper and the tenets of the trouper faith.

When Ruby was eleven, Mildred got a job in the chorus of *Glorianna*, a musical revue playing at the Liberty Theatre on Broadway. A beau of Mildred's, James Buck McCarthy, was half of a song-and-dance team in the show, Miller and Mack. At the time Mildred and Ruby were living at the Palace Hotel, and Buck was living down the street at the Princeton Hotel. The three of them spent endless hours together, and Buck became unofficial godfather to the "funny little gal with shining shoe-button eyes and brown pigtails."

Ruby watched each show from the wings, and whenever he had a free moment backstage, Buck would teach her a dance step or two. Invariably, when he would arrive at the theater, Ruby would be waiting. "Hey, Uncle Buck," she'd call, "watch this." Then she'd knock herself out with a tap routine or some other kind of dance.

"That's great, kid," Buck would call back as he hurried into his costume. "Gonna be a dancer when you grow up?" he'd ask.

Her pigtails would fly up and down around her face as she bobbed her head and replied, "Yep! I'm going to be a star. I'm going right to the top and nothing is gonna stop me!" Little did Buck realize at the time the single-mindedness that had already developed in Ruby Stevens.

Shortly after the reign of *Glorianna*, Mildred had to go on the road again, which meant it was time to put Ruby in yet another boarding-house. Mildred had high hopes this time. She had found Ruby a home with a family in a nicer neighborhood of Brooklyn known as Flatbush. Mildred had met earlier with the couple, Mr. and Mrs. Harold Cohen, and all the way there she filled Ruby's mind with wonderful stories about the darling children the Cohens had. She told Ruby that Mrs. Cohen kept her house so clean you could eat off the floor!

But Ruby didn't bat an eyelash. She'd heard all these stories before.

She simply held her shoulders straight and jutted her chin out defiantly. The Cohens were Jewish, but that didn't bother Ruby. Her unhappiness stemmed simply from her innate distrust of most adults. She knew their games. You did their dishes, and they paid you a nickel. You let down your guard, and they kicked you around.

Finally Ruby tried one last pitch. Once off the streetcar and walking down the sunny street, she shifted her little cardboard suitcase to the other side and begged Mildred to take her along on the road again, as they'd done all summer. All she wanted to do was dance. Why bother with any old school? Who needed it? She'd already been to practically every school in Brooklyn, and they were all alike. She hated arithmetic. She hated reading. She hated teachers. "You know what the last one said to me?" And she imitated the thin nasal whine: " 'You keep reaching for the stars, Ruby, you're bound to get bumped.' And she's right, Millie, I get bumped damn plenty."

"Don't swear, Ruby," Millie said, sighing. It was a useless pitch for both of them, and Ruby knew it. Mildred was doing her best to see that her little sister and brother got proper upbringing. She was a hardworking show girl, lucky to have a job, and she was doing her best. They walked up some steps, and Mildred pushed a button. Ruby stared straight ahead. She wouldn't even look up when the door opened and Millie said, "Mrs. Cohen, this is my little sister I told you about."

"Why, hello, dear, come in," Mrs. Cohen said. She had a baby with her. "Come in, Mildred. Here, give me the suitcase." She led them into the parlor and then into the dining room and showed Ruby the couch where she would sleep and gave her a place in the bureau drawer in the bedroom where she could put her clothes. She put the baby down— Buddy, he was called—and let him crawl around.

Millie had to go; she had a rehearsal, and the company was leaving the next day. Mrs. Cohen told her not to worry, they'd watch over Ruby and she would be just like a part of their own family. Would you like to bet? thought Ruby. She'd heard that line before. Forget it. You were never part of anything. You were the fifth wheel on the wagon, the outsider, the one who was always in the way or in trouble.

20

But the Cohens were different, and it didn't take Ruby long to realize it. In the mornings Mrs. Cohen would brush Ruby's hair and tie it with a ribbon. "You're a pretty little girl, Ruby," she'd say.

"You kiddin' me or somethin'?" Ruby'd ask, afraid to let her defenses down. Soon, though, she warmed to the Cohens and began to feel like part of their family. It was a feeling she had never had before, and years later she would recall those early days with the Cohens warmly: "Mr. and Mrs. Cohen were the first people ever to ask me if I 'felt good.' I didn't know what they meant. They were the first people ever to brush my hair, to care how I looked. They tried to teach me nice manners. They even tried to stop me from swearing! I'd been playing with some pretty rough youngsters on the streets. I'd learned manners and language that were not pretty at all. Their home was clean and decent. The food was plain but good. They were poor, but they knew how to 'pretty' poverty up a bit, stick a ribbon in its hair. And they were the first to give me affection—something which must be given and can't be bought."

At Flatbush and Church avenues, not far from home, stood a quaint old Dutch Reformed church with a little graveyard beside it, and that became Ruby's church. She went tentatively at first, but the minister, William Carter, was the handsomest man she'd ever seen, and she not only fell in love with him, she decided to become a missionary because he talked about missionary work so much, about the gallant women who made such sacrifices for the heathen.

She told the Cohens and they never laughed. They were seeing a great change in this little girl. She'd marched into their house with a chip on her shoulder, and now there was no chip. She still swore on occasion, but she looked you in the eye now and she was willing to confide her dreams. When Mildred was in town and took her to a vaudeville show, Ruby would come back and imitate everything she'd seen. She'd dance and sing, imitate the comedians, have the Cohens in stitches.

They liked the theater, too, and once in a while, when she'd helped with the dishes or with the little boys, Mr. Cohen would take her along with his kids to a Sunday matinee at a stuffy little movie house in the neighborhood. The other kids enjoyed it, but Ruby was transported. Pearl White was her goddess: "Her courage, grace, daring, and spirit lifted me right out of the world."

Ruby lived with the Cohens for two years. "I got very elegant, playing jacks and all. Up until now, we had never played any games that I remember. But while I was with the Cohens, I learned to play marbles and jump rope—it was, as Millie had said, a nicer group of kids in this neighborhood. Sometimes we made up movies and acted them out in the streets. I was really quite content and comfortable. It was all too good to be true."

Toward the end of the second year Ruby noticed that Mrs. Cohen was growing plumper. She wore an apron over the front of the pink and white dress, but there was no mistaking . . . Mrs. Cohen was going to have another baby. Ruby's heart sank. She'd have to move out, she knew that. It was a long time before they told her. She knew they didn't want to hurt her, and they put it off as long as possible. But Mrs. Cohen kept getting fatter and fatter, and the day finally came. "Ruby, dear," Mrs. Cohen said, "I'm terribly sorry, but . . ."

Ruby clammed up again, put up the barricades, and made up her mind that somehow, someway, she was going to have to be a success. Everyone she'd ever known seemed to be a victim of circumstance. Even the Cohens. Much as they liked her, they didn't have the space to keep her. She was determined somehow to earn her own living.

Just before her fourteenth birthday she saw an ad for girls to operate the switchboards at the telephone company. Ruby applied for the job, telling the superintendent that she was sixteen, and got the work. Her salary was fourteen dollars a week, and to a girl who never had had any money of her own, it seemed like all the money in the world. While working at the telephone company, Ruby found that another great source of escape, besides her beloved Pearl White serials, was books. And once she started reading, she read anything and everything she could get her hands on.

She recalls those days and those books with more than a tinge of sarcasm. "I read nothing good, but I read an awful lot. Here was escape! I read lurid stuff about ladies who smelled sweet and looked like flowers and were betrayed. I read about gardens and ballrooms and moonlight trysts and murders. I felt a sense of doors opening. And I began to be conscious of myself, the way I looked, the clothes I wore. I bought awful things at first, pink shirtwaists, artificial flowers, tripe."

At the end of seven months Ruby left the telephone company and set her sights on a higher position with more money. If the books she read taught her anything, it was that there was a hell of a big world out there and she was determined to be part of it. Although she hadn't abandoned her childhood dreams of stardom on the stage, she was wise enough even at fourteen to know that dancing wouldn't put food in her mouth or pay for her room.

She had already developed a talent for bluffing her way through difficult situations, so it wasn't surprising that she managed to convince the woman in personnel at Condé Nast that she knew "everything there is to know" about selling patterns. With that, Ruby Stevens found herself selling patterns for *Vogue* and working in New York at a salary of eighteen dollars a week!

Although Ruby still wasn't very good at making friends, she did listen to the girls in the Condé Nast offices talking. She wrote down the names of books she heard mentioned and then made a point of reading them. She read *My Life* by Isadora Duncan, and Ruby's love of dancing, fed by the fire of Duncan's life, flared up again. Even so, Ruby didn't last at Condé Nast. In a short time she bollixed up "the pattern of almost every woman who came to her for advice."

Another job was imperative, of course, and Ruby began pounding the well-worn streets of Manhattan again. The Remick Music Company on Forty-eighth Street was advertising for clerical workers, and Ruby answered the ad. She'd never been on Tin Pan Alley before, but as soon as Ruby walked into Remick's office, she felt at home. The atmosphere was noisy, boisterous, and incredibly alive. All the pianos were going at once, and popular songs were being tried out all over the place. This was show business, or at least it was a heck of a lot closer to the world of spotlights and greasepaint than the *Vogue* pattern office.

The brash assurance of youth worked in Ruby's favor, and soon she found herself pounding a typewriter on Forty-eighth Street. She still didn't have much time for small talk and friendships, but before long she did manage to gain the confidence of one of Remick's managers,

Bill Cripp. It was Cripp who had hired the fifteen-year-old, and it was Cripp to whom the usually closemouthed kid confided, "I want to get a job as a dancer."

Cripp was not without contacts in the Broadway circle, and not long after hiring Ruby he heard that there was an opening for a chorus girl around the corner at the Strand Roof. Earl Lindsay, a personal friend of Cripp's, was in charge of the show at the Strand. After a little gentle persuasion on Cripp's part, Lindsay found himself watching one Ruby Stevens cartwheel all over his stage, while managing to fit in a few dance steps every once in a while. Mr. Lindsay's reaction to this somewhat athletic audition has been lost to history, but in a few days the Strand Roof had added Ruby Stevens to its chorus line. The homeless waif from Brooklyn with a will of iron had finally gotten her foot in the show business door.

CHAPTER 4

Earl Lindsay hired Ruby Stevens as a chorus girl at forty dollars per week. It seemed like a fortune after the fourteen dollars she was getting from the telephone company and the eighteen dollars she earned at *Vogue*. The years of self-discipline and desperate dreams had made Ruby an excellent chorus girl. She was quick to pick up the new dance routines and always prompt in arriving at the café.

It was the dawn of America's most flamboyant era—the Roaring Twenties—and New York City was second to none in its single-minded plummet toward the shattering fate still eight years ahead. To many, the hoydenish profession of chorus-line cutie seemed to represent this decadence. Ruby didn't see it that way. She'd never had a real childhood, and now she was like a kid in a candy shop. In her seventeen-year-old mind she was on top of the world, and she intended to fight tooth and nail if she had to for the respect she never had had as an orphan shuffling around Brooklyn from one household to the next.

She learned to joke casually with the "cash customers" who threw remarks at her during the show, but as far as she was concerned, that was all part of the job. After hours she had no time for them. "I found that my hard-boiled manner and way of speaking, my knowledge of how to take care of myself—learned when I was a tough kid battling other tough kids—stood me in good stead. I didn't stand for any nonsense." There was one character who gave her a bit of trouble, though. He used to stand in the wings during the ensemble numbers, and his little pig eyes never left Ruby's graceful, weaving body. He used to say things to her as she slid by him to the dressing room . . . things she tried very hard not to hear. "When he looked at me I felt as if I had nothing on. It was as though he had stripped me of even the flimsy garment I wore, by his very eyes."

One night he didn't let her slide by. He cornered her against the wall. "You big caveman," said the panicky Ruby, giggling. "Aren't you the strong one." She wanted to laugh it off, if she could, and get away from him.

"I'm going to take you home tonight." He didn't ask it. He stated it. Suddenly his thick-lipped mouth was blurred before her eyes, and she forgot to joke. She struck at him. His florid cheeks turned purple. "You little devil," he cried in fury. He held her pressed against the wall with one pudgy hand. With the other he jerked down the bodice of her costume and held the red-hot point of a cigar against her breast until she fainted.

Ruby had become close friends with another girl in the line, Claire Miller, and after a few weeks she went to live with Claire and her family at 135th Street and Riverside Drive. When Claire married not long afterward, Ruby joined forces with a couple of other Strand girls, Mae Clarke and Walda Mansfield, and took an apartment on Forty-sixth Street between Fifth and Sixth avenues. They lived over a laundry where the steam and vapors stinging her eyes reminded Ruby of washtubs and squeaking clotheslines. The Sixth Avenue El roared by their windows, and when they were very tired, it seemed to crash through their walls. It was far from being a glamorous life, but for Ruby, at least, it was the first real home she'd ever had. Even today she remembers those days fondly. "It was a cute apartment, but we never admitted that we lived there. Whenever we went out on dates, we were always dropped off at the Astor or the Knickerbocker. Then we'd run like hell to get home. We were making forty dollars a week in the chorus, but it wasn't enough. We never thought of saving. Every cent of that forty dollars went on our backs. We did our own washing, ironing, and dry cleaning, and we served as each other's beauticians. I'd do Walda's hair; she'd give me a manicure."

Eventually the show at the Strand closed, and the girls found work in another Earl Lindsay show, *Keep Kool*, at the Morosco Theatre. The show opened on May 22, 1924, and starred Hazel Dawn, Charles King, and Johnny Dooley. Not only did Ruby appear as one of the sixteen Keep Kool Cuties, but the show also offered her a chance at a specialty. Along with Johnny Dooley, Ruby did an imitation of Louis Wolheim and Hazel Dawn from *The Hairy Ape* in a skit entitled "A Room Adjoining a Boudoir (Apologies to Avery Hopwood)." The bit was a hit, and the show was well reviewed. As for the Keep Kool Cuties, *Variety* noted:

> The hoofiest chorus seen in ages, the sixteen girls are pips, lookers and dancers. They kick like steers and look like why-men-leave-home in their many costume flashes.

Keep Kool moved to the Globe in early July and closed there at the end of August. The show hadn't gone unnoticed, and the following September portions of it were incorporated into the touring company of the *Ziegfeld Follies*. Luckily for Ruby the Hopwood sketch was part of the material retained from *Keep Kool*, and Ziegfeld offered her $100 a week to join the show. All of a sudden Ruby Stevens was a Ziegfeld Girl.

By the time the Ziegfeld tour began, Ruby had added three more numbers to her roster. Along with the chorus she sang and danced in two numbers and appeared as part of the now legendary "Ziegfeld Shadowgraph," in which she did a striptease behind a white screen and tossed her clothes out into the audience. The Ziegfeld tour lasted until early in 1925, and with this experience behind her Ruby had little trouble finding work. One show was basically like another. All involved new routines drummed into Ruby by perspiring but good-

27

natured stage directors; laughing girls who joked and kidded and fought off stage-door Johnnies; and late suppers at Hanscoms or the Astor. April 1925 found Ruby accepting an offer to appear at Anatole Friedland's Club, next to Texas Guinan's on Fifty-fourth Street. The club did a thriving business for about six months, but then the crowds started to go elsewhere and Friedland dismissed most of his chorus. Both Ruby and Mae Clark were among those he asked to go with him on a tour of the Keith vaudeville circuit.

Following in quick succession were some Shubert shows including *A Night in Venice, Artists and Models*, and, in late 1925, *Gay Paree*. Billy Van, Ruth Gillette, and Winnie Lightner were the stars of this one, and Earl Lindsay staged the dances once again. Ruby Stevens's name was listed as one of the "Ladies of the Ensemble."

Ruby Stevens was gaining a reputation within show business circles as a good, dependable worker, and she was finding it easier and easier to find work, although her salary was seldom as good as the $100 paid by Ziegfeld. It was a common practice then for girls in the chorus to double up, working in one Broadway show or another in the evening and then working later at one of the many speakeasies or after-hours clubs. It was just such an arrangement Ruby and Mae Clarke worked out in January of 1926 when they found jobs at a little dive called the Everglades Café. Each night they would wrap up their duties in *Gay Paree*, and, still dressed in the scantiest of costumes, they'd bundle themselves up in their overcoats and race through Shubert Alley to strut their stuff at the Everglades. The chorus girl later recalled, "We worked like dogs and we were as strong as horses." The ordeal of juggling two jobs didn't last very long; *Gay Paree* closed in late January.

The Tavern was a restaurant on Forty-eighth Street frequented by many of the show business crowd. It was owned by a big-hearted soul by the name of Billy LaHiff. LaHiff thought of the customers who congregated in his place as family, and whenever his regulars were temporarily "between shows," he allowed them to run up tabs for their daily meals. For many it was the only thing that kept them from starving or from throwing their hands up in frustration and forgetting about their dreams of fame and fortune.

It was LaHiff who heard that leading producer, director, and playwright Willard Mack was casting a play entitled *The Noose* and needed some chorus girls for the second act. The girls were to play the part of cabaret girls, and, most importantly, they would all have lines to read! It was just a small part, but when she was selected, Ruby's joy knew no bounds. "This was the big time. Willard Mack was directing, and he directed me right out of a dancing yen and into a dramatic one. I was all Bernhardt from that time forth."

The Noose was about a young man condemned to death and the society girl he loved. Ruby's part was that of a chorus girl who loved him but who goes unnoticed by him. In the original plot there was a heavily dramatic scene in the third act during which the society girl begs for the body of her dead lover. The company left for tryouts in Columbus, Pittsburgh, and Philadelphia in an optimistic frame of mind. For Ruby the whole experience was new and exciting. "The day we left New York to open in Columbus I had a new suitcase. I think I packed and unpacked it fifty times. . . . I sat up all night in the Pullman just to see the towns and counties go by."

At first *The Noose* seemed doomed for disaster, but Willard Mack was a veteran of many shows, and he didn't need to read the bad reviews to know that something wasn't working. Beginning in Columbus and right through Pittsburgh and Philadelphia, Mack put the show through major rewrites. At first these changes didn't concern or involve Ruby, but inevitably even her small role was affected. Mack decided that the pathos would be more effective if, in the third act, it was the chorus girl who pleaded for the body of the hanged man. The scene was written, and Dot, the chorus girl, was given an emotional monologue in which she explains to the Governor that she's taken up a collection to bury Nickie. She admits to the Governor that Nickie didn't love her, he loved another girl instead. Now, however, she hoped that she would be allowed to take him to a little cemetery she knew of and that she could tell his deaf ears all the things she wouldn't dare to say while he was alive. Deeply affected, the Governor tells her that Nickie is not dead. There's been a stay of execution. Dot is almost hysterical with the knowledge that Nickie isn't dead and passionately begs the

Governor that Nickie never be told of her visit. Suddenly a minor role in the show had become a critical part of the play demanding a dramatic actress of some skill. An attempt was made to hire Sylvia Field, but she had a commitment to another show on Broadway. There wasn't much time to search for another actress, so, not without a great deal of trepidation, Mack decided to give Ruby Stevens the chance of a lifetime.

She recalls: "It was Willard Mack who completely disarranged my mental makeup. The process, as are all processes of birth and rebirth, I guess, was pretty damn painful, especially for him. I got very temperamental. The truth of the matter was, the bejesus was scared out of me. I'd storm and yell around that I couldn't act—couldn't and, what's more, wouldn't. I believe I can honestly say that it was my first and last flare-up of temperament. It was speedily and effectively nipped in its nasty little bud. For Mr. Mack, who had flattered me, encouraged me, patted me on the back, wisely reversed his tactics.

"One day, right before the entire company, he screamed back at me that I was right, I was dead right, I was a chorus girl, would always be a chorus girl, would live and die a chorus girl, and be damned to me. I swallowed the bait, sinker and all. I yelled right back that I could act, would act, was not a chorus girl, was Bernhardt, Fiske, all the Booths and Barrymores rolled into one."

After being convinced that Ruby Stevens had the part well in hand, he decided to tackle one last problem with his new Duse: as far as Mack was concerned, Ruby Stevens was not an appropriate name for a dramatic actress. One day prior to the opening Mack took Ruby over to the office of theatrical impresario David Belasco. After having Ruby do a scene for Belasco, the two men hovered in a corner talking while Ruby stood nervously near, trying to pick up whatever snatches she could. Belasco seemed impressed with her talent but agreed with Mack on the subject of Ruby's name. "She can't go on as Ruby Stevens," he said, scowling. "It sounds like a burlesque queen's name." He was absentmindedly leafing through some old programs when a name caught his eye. There, on the cover of a book over thirty years old, was a title page reading, "Jane Stanwyck in *Barbara Frietchie.*" Belasco and Mack pondered the names for a few moments. Jane Frietchie wouldn't work, they decided. There was already one famous Jane on Broadway, Jane Cowl. Then they looked at each other and almost in unison came up with a name that would become one of the most well-known names in show business. Exit Ruby Stevens. Enter Barbara Stanwyck.

CHAPTER 5

When *The Noose* opened on Broadway on October 20, 1926, its stars were Rex Cherryman, Ann Shoemaker, and Barbara Stanwyck. Playgoers and critics alike gave it a warm reception, and the show went on to become one of the biggest hits of the season. As for the newly born Barbara Stanwyck, her performance earned her rave reviews of the type young actresses only dream of.

"Barbara Stanwyck," wrote the *N.J. Telegraph*, "as the night club dancer who loves but is not loved, has her chance in the third act and brings the handkerchiefs forth with expediency." *The New York Times* headline read, "The Noose Greeted with Warm Approval." The review went on to note, rather lamely, that "there is . . . further good work by Dorothy Stanwyck."

The *Times*'s faux pas was more than made up for by this review from the *New York Telegram:*

There is an uncommonly fine performance by Barbara Stanwyck, who not only does the Charleston steps of a dance hall girl gracefully, but knows how to act, a feature which somehow with her comely looks, seems kind of superfluous. After this girl breaks down and sobs out her unrequited love for the young bootlegger in that genuinely moving scene in the last act, of course, there was nothing for the Governor to do but reprieve the boy. If he hadn't, the weeping audience would probably have yelled at him till he did.

Even after the opening of *The Noose*, Willard Mack continued to work with his new star. "Enjoy your applause," he told her on opening night, "but don't let it go to your head. Don't forget how much chance means in every success. Enjoy your success. Welcome it—by going on to earn it. Report for rehearsal at ten o'clock tomorrow morning." The show ran for nine months, and throughout the run Mack gave Stanwyck a new play to study each week. In turn, she was grateful for Mack's efforts and studied each play diligently, often reviewing the scenes and her interpretation of them with Mack three or four times a week.

It was during the run of *The Noose* that Barbara Stanwyck found herself entangled in her first serious romance. Rex Cherryman, the star of the play, was a handsome young actor who had made it on Broadway in a play called *Downstream*. The play hadn't been very successful, but Cherryman's matinee-idol good looks combined with formidable acting skills had won him enough of a following to make him a star. The *Newark Telegraph* had noted in its review of *The Noose*: "Rex Cherryman, as the condemned murderer, runs away with every part of the play that he appears in despite the sentimental treatment he must give his lines."

Although the script for *The Noose* called for Stanwyck's love for Cherryman to go unrequited, their personal lives were not bound by any such boundaries. It had taken Rex Cherryman only two years to tire of the coy, empty-headed flappers who threw themselves at his feet. Working with Stanwyck, he found himself disarmed by her brash, streetwise charm and the vulnerable innocence that she had beneath it. Barbara was flattered by Cherryman's attentions and more than a little surprised. She had never considered herself a femme fatale.

Romantically, she had been involved for a while with a young man by the name of Edward Kennedy, and although they had considered marriage at one point, she eventually talked him out of the idea, realizing that they were too young and that her career was still too important to her. Nevertheless, they remained close friends and still dated frequently. Rex Cherryman changed all that. Later, Barbara was to speak of her romance with Cherryman: "It was my first chance at dramatic acting and everything enchanted me. Rex was handsome and young and had great talent and good humor. Ed Kennedy hadn't quite given me up. He was jealous of Willard Mack, but he was wrong there. If he had to be jealous of anyone, he should have focused on Rex. I adored him. Everything about him was so vivid, or perhaps it was because he was an actor and knew how to project."

Stanwyck was still involved with *The Noose* when she was summoned by producer Bob Kane to make a screen test at the old Cosmopolitan Studios on 125th Street and Second Avenue. The young actress's feelings about Hollywood and the motion picture industry were ambiguous at the time, and her experiences making this test didn't do much to sway her favors in the direction of the silver screen. Certainly in her childhood dreams she had seen herself as another Pearl White, but she had only recently begun to gain some assurance on stage, and screen acting seemed like another world.

Upon her arrival at Cosmopolitan, Barbara was greeted by a leering cameraman on the make who did not take kindly to her somewhat more than subtle refusal of his affections. To make matters worse, the director in charge was far from sophisticated, even for 1926. Stanwyck's scene called for her to cry, and the director insisted on using such primitive inducements as a raw onion and a whining violin.

Into this celluloid circus came actress Ruth Chatterton, followed closely by her black maid. Chatterton was then one of the reigning queens of the dramatic theater. As far as Chatterton was concerned, she was belittling her position by even agreeing to a screen test. Nevertheless, to Chatterton and many of her friends, the idea of visiting a motion picture studio or making a screen test held a fascination similar to that they felt for the black clubs in Harlem which had become all the rage. They were, in fact, slumming. So it was with a sense of haughty indifference that Ruth watched Stanwyck's efforts in front of the camera. Although Stanwyck was an actress of limited experience, her instincts were natural, and the cinema trappings she'd encountered so far had rendered her somewhat helpless. Somehow she just couldn't come up with the necessary tears. Chatterton was nothing if not amused at Barbara's efforts. "I wonder," she asked, turning to her maid at her side, "if all cinema actresses have to resort to onions and violins to cry." Stanwyck overheard the remark from her position on stage and hissed for the woman to shut up.

Meanwhile, Wilbur Morse, press agent for Bob Kane, was on the set and found Chatterton's attitude infuriating. Morse bolstered his own courage and walked over to Chatterton. Then, looking her straight in the eye, he told her, "You are probably so busy with your own show that you may not know this girl is Barbara Stanwyck whose crying scene in *The Noose* is bringing the critics back night after night just to have a good cry." Miss Chatterton was not heard from again until her own turn in front of the cameras had come.

As for Stanwyck, she managed to complete her test convincingly and was rewarded by Kane with a secondary role in his next film, *Broadway Nights*, a silent film starring Lois Wilson and Sam Hardy as a nightclub singer and her gambling lover. Barbara Stanwyck had fifth billing as the chorine girlfriend of a producer. Stanwyck's role was a small one, and although the film was well reviewed, for years she did her best to ignore its existence. (The film is of note, however, for the film debut of another actress who would eventually become one of the most well known in the business, Sylvia Sidney.)

The Noose closed in June of 1927, and a few weeks later Barbara was called to audition for a new play being prepared for Broadway by producer-director-playwright Arthur Hopkins. The play, *Burlesque,* had been written by George Manker Watters. Watters and Hopkins felt that the leads called for an actor and actress of exceptional versatility. By the time he had called Stanwyck, vaudevillian Hal Skelly had already been cast. Later he recalled his casting of Barbara Stanwyck in the other role: "After some search for the girl I interviewed a nightclub dancer who had just scored in a small emotional part in a play that did not run. She seemed to have the quality I wanted, a sort of rough poignancy. I engaged her. She at once displayed more sensitive, easily expressed emotion than I had encountered since Pauline Lord."

Stanwyck's role in *Burlesque* was that of Bonny Johnson. Bonny was the wife and vaudeville partner of Skid. Through his wife's efforts, Skid gains considerable fame on Broadway. Eventually, he takes to the bottle and their marriage founders. The marriage is saved in the end when Bonny has a change of heart and helps Skid get back on his feet. It was a great role, and Stanwyck drew on every ounce of ability she had to mold the character of Bonny into someone the audience could identify and sympathize with.

Just as Mack had in the preparation of *The Noose*, Arthur Hopkins worked closely with Barbara during rehearsals of *Burlesque*. The help was greatly appreciated by her, and she was quick to give Hopkins the credit she felt he deserved: "I did feel quite lost until I began to rehearse under Mr. Hopkins' direction. The fact that I was engaged by him gave me some confidence, but it was the way he took hold of me and began to rehearse me that gave me faith in myself. I cannot quite explain it all, but Mr. Hopkins has a way about him.

"I felt from the first that anything he told me to do was right, but it seemed that he carefully refrained from telling me too much. Now that I think of it I remember that I asked him on several occasions about things and instead of giving me a direct reply he would tell me a story, get me to imagine I was in a situation similar to that in the play, suggest that if I was I would do so and so—and then I found myself unconsciously doing just what he wanted. "That is the kind of stage direction that I could understand and take—I think that anyone with any ability would be able to make the most out of it under Mr. Hopkins' direction. He never says 'do it like this' or 'do it like that.' He just explains how a person would naturally do it and leaves it to you."

Burlesque opened at the Plymouth Theatre on September 1, 1927, and was an overwhelming success. No less severe critic than Alexander Woollcott reported in *The World*, "I thought Miss Stanwyck's performance was touching and true and she brought much to those aching silences."

E. W. Ashorn was equally impressed and wrote, "Barbara Stanwyck and Hal Skelly have come out of vaudeville and musical comedy to reveal unexpected powers in legitimate acting. They dance perfectly, but they shine as truly in sympathetic portrayals of the funny hoofer and his proudly faithful wife."

The play did indeed contain many touching scenes, and these were noted by Gilbert Gabriel in his review for the *New York Sun:* "The reconciliation of the hoofers is exquisitely playful. You are watching the actual burlesque show. The two young ones—nimble, funny, shabby, creatures of loose ankles and chapped souls—are dancing dutifully on. And while they dance—in broken, breathless asides— they patch their cheap little quarrel up. A last crazy twirl, like powerless marionettes—and that's all of their amen."

Indeed, Barbara's characterization of Bonny drew a great deal of attention in the press. When Colgate Baker asked her to explain the character for the *New York Review*, she did, at length!

> How can you explain love anyway—you can't. It is one of those things that you can recognize—you know it exists, but seek the reason for and you are up a tree. They say that pity is akin to love and I suppose that has a great deal to do with Bonny's feelings towards Skid. It must have been so in the beginning when she fell in love with him. He needed someone badly to look after him— and it certainly is so in the end and I guess that Bonny felt that she had been elected for the job of loving this poor clown, who has his good qualities along with his bad ones, of course.
>
> Anyway, there are lots of women just like Bonny in the theatrical profession; everyone knows that. She is rather the rule than the exception.
>
> I have often thought of what the finish would be for these two people—what old age would bring to them. They are so human and understandable—in fact every character in the play simply reeks of life. The manner in which Mr. Hopkins has brought out the human appeal of each of these characters is wonderful. He seems to have picked out the salient features of each, according to their comedy values and put them on the stage with such uncanny skill we feel that we are seeing an actual page from life instead of a play.

That to my mind is the acme in stage artistry. It is the thing that the public instantly appreciates and acclaims. People are the most interesting things in life. Ordinarily we do not appreciate this fact, but when we go to see such a play as this we do and we wonder why we have not thought about it before. We come away with the feeling that we have been rather unobservant of the world around us and life holds a great deal more for us all than we thought.

While Stanwyck was busy at the Plymouth in *Burlesque*, Rex Cherryman was appearing elsewhere on the Great White Way in *The Trial of Mary Dugan*. Their romance had flourished, and they were considered Broadway's golden couple. During the summer of 1928, however, Cherryman became ill and doctors recommended he rest. Reluctantly he withdrew from the cast of *Mary Dugan*. He and Barbara bid a tearful farewell as he sailed for a European vacation. Plans called for her to follow as soon as her run in *Burlesque* was over, but just a few days after his departure, terrible news was wired back to the States. Rex Cherryman had taken a turn for the worse en route and was taken off the boat at Cherbourg. He died in a hospital at Le Havre on August 10. He was thirty years old, and Barbara Stanwyck was, again, very much alone.

CHAPTER 6

Early in the run of *Burlesque* Barbara became friendly with the young actor who played the piano player, a peculiar sort of a guy known as Oscar Levant. Levant began to pal around with Stanwyck in the wings and during their time off. One day, near Christmas of 1928, Levant invited Stanwyck to accompany him to the Palace Theatre where a friend of his was appearing. "I want you to meet a friend of mine," he told her as they walked down Broadway. "You'll get a lot of laughs out of him. He's a great guy."

"What's his name?" asked Barbara.

"Frank Fay" was Levant's response.

In 1928 Frank Fay was one of the top stars in vaudeville, along with Sophie Tucker and Eddie Cantor. In many ways Fay typified the vaudeville stars of the day. He was a fast talker and could be found wisecracking on the corner of Forty-seventh Street and Broadway as commonly as he could be found on the Palace stage. He was an impish man with a shock of red hair and the look of a leprechaun. One of

Broadway's best-known ladies' men, he'd already been married and divorced twice and was reputed to work his way through each Broadway chorus line systematically. Added to all of this was a trigger-sensitive Irish temper, making Frank Fay one of the most volatile personalities in show business. What Stanwyck's friend Oscar Levant didn't know, however, was that she had seen him once before. She and Mae Clarke had caught his act a year before in Lynbrook, Long Island, when he was trying out some new material, and Stanwyck was unimpressed by Fay's irreverent personality. "I can't stand that guy," she'd remarked to her friend.

Nevertheless, not wanting to hurt the notoriously thin-skinned Levant, Stanwyck agreed to meet Frank Fay. She and Levant watched Fay's show from the wings, and afterward Fay came over to chat. It was the usual wisecracking banter centering around the great love of Frank Fay's life—Frank Fay. Barbara remained quiet through most of the conversation, silently thinking of a cutting response to each of Fay's remarks. When Levant asked her what she thought of Fay, she put her cards on the table. "I've met conceited men before," she told him, "but I've never met one as conceited as that hombre. I'd like to hoof as good as he thinks he is."

Levant couldn't resist passing Stanwyck's opinion of Fay on to the gentleman himself. Fay was not pleased. "Tell her," he snapped back, "I don't think she's so hot either." Over the next few months Stanwyck and Fay would inadvertently run into each other at various clubs in the area, and when they did, they would only continue to fire their already shaky acquaintance with snappy patter and sarcastic retorts. Fay, meanwhile, began to sense a somewhat illogical attraction in himself for the actress. Perhaps it was because she was the only woman he knew who could dish it out as well as he could. She didn't respond to Frank Fay the vaudeville star. She responded to Frank Fay the boozing leprechaun with the chip on his shoulder.

Stanwyck, of course, throughout this period was very heavily involved with the building of her career. Her time was spent polishing her performance as Bonny and studying as many other contemporary dramas as she could get her hands on. Through years of emotional deprivation, she'd come to subconsciously subliminate her emotional needs. Her affair with Rex Cherryman more than adequately filled the bill in this respect. Romantically, Rex Cherryman was everything little Ruby Stevens had ever dreamed of and, when, as Barbara Stanwyck, she did slip and allow herself to build castles in the air, Rex was there as her Prince Charming.

Then, on August 10, Cherryman died and left Barbara Stanwyck alone again. It was only with Cherryman's death that Barbara realized just how much she needed his presence and the warmth it provided. She'd come to rely on his affections, and now that he was gone she felt like an empty shell. It was as if she was a little girl again and everyone had left her alone. Later, speaking of Rex Cherryman, she admitted, "I nearly died getting over the loss of him." Only this devastation on Stanwyck's part could explain her activity over the next few weeks.

When news of Cherryman's death reached Broadway, Frank Fay went immediately to Barbara Stanwyck's side. She needed comforting, and he gave it to her. She needed companionship, and he was there. She sought someone who could belong exclusively to her, and Frank Fay was willing to be that someone. Frank Fay had a contract to appear at the Missouri Theatre in St. Louis and left to do so in mid-August. Almost simultaneously, *Burlesque* closed on Broadway and went on a short hiatus prior to starting a national tour.

On August 25, 1928, Barbara Stanwyck boarded a train for St. Louis. She arrived at her destination the next day at 1:00 P.M. and went directly to the home of William L. Tamme, the St. Louis Recorder of Deeds. There, in a simple ceremony, witnessed by Spyros Skouras and Mrs. Harry Niemeyer and performed by Justice of the Peace Harry Pfiefer, Barbara Stanwyck became Mrs. Frank Fay. At 5:00 P.M. she boarded another train bound for Newark, New Jersey, where *Burlesque* would open its national tour the next day.

CHAPTER 7

When it became apparent to Louis B. Mayer, Jack Warner, and Samuel Goldwyn, among others, that talkies were here to stay, they were faced with another, equally devastating discovery. Many of their most appealing silent film stars couldn't talk. The motion picture industry went into shock as one career after another withered and died at the sound of a shrill or incoherent voice. The studios were forced to turn to the greatest source of vocal dramatic acting available, the Broadway stage. Offers began going out to the stars of the Great White Way on a daily basis. Many were accepted, but just as many were not.

Stanwyck's first experience in motion picture-making, in *Broadway Nights*, had been an embarrassment to her and had left her unsure of her own future on the silver screen. She had wanted desperately to re-create the role of Bonny in Paramount's remake of *Burlesque*, *The Dance of Life*. The director, John Cromwell, had wanted Stanwyck for the part and had depended on Paramount to sign her. Unfortunately, at the time, Barbara Stanwyck was bound by a run-of-the-play contract with Arthur Hopkins. She had no choice but to turn down Paramount's offer. Over the next few months, while Barbara continued to wow critics and public alike onstage nightly in *Burlesque*, Hollywood continued to take notice, and numerous offers followed Paramount's. But Stanwyck was grateful to Hopkins for his help and would not listen to any suggestions that she break her contract and head for Hollywood. Each offer was firmly refused.

Stanwyck's contract with Hopkins ended in August just prior to her marriage to Frank Fay, and the possibility of a move to California was something she and Fay took very seriously. Burlesque was already doing the dance of death, and Fay's own future was, therefore, in jeopardy. As for Stanwyck, she had no reason to believe that the offers would stop and was enjoying the prospect of being in a position to choose the best.

Marriage to Fay complicated things somewhat, however. His ego was of legendary proportions, and he would never allow it to be said that he and his wife were moving to California because she was going to make pictures. When Stanwyck returned to the East Coast as Mrs. Frank Fay, she did so with Fay's orders not to accept any offers from the West Coast until after he had. The move, he made it perfectly clear, was contingent upon his own career, certainly not hers. Luckily, it wasn't long before Warner Brothers had signed Fay to appear on screen, as the host of their forthcoming musical extravaganza, *Show of Shows*.

Joseph Schenck, head of United Artists, was in New York in August of 1929 and approached Barbara Stanwyck about starring in the film version of Channing Pollock's play *The Sign on the Door*. The film was to star Rod La Rocque and William Boyd, and Schenck promised a top-drawer production.

When Mr. and Mrs. Frank Fay traveled to Hollywood in the fall of 1929, it was in Joe Schenck's private railroad car. It was a trip full of surprises. Barbara didn't expect folks in Hollywood to know much about her theater work in New York. Fay, on the other hand, expected the entire film world to be waiting for him on bended knee. His delusions were shattered early in their trip when a well-known producer approached him on the train and asked, "Mr. Fay, what did you do on the stage?"

Fay tried to hide his fury with a quick-witted retort. "I'm a juggler," he replied.

"Do you think juggling will go over in pictures?" the producer asked.

"I'm a dramatic juggler," Fay explained.

Norma Talmadge, Mary Pickford, Douglas Fairbanks, and Irving Thalberg were among those welcoming Schenck's train when it arrived in Hollywoodland. Stanwyck figured the producer had been gone for some time, but when one of the greats asked him if he had enjoyed his trip, Schenck replied, "Three weeks is too short a time to enjoy New York." Ruby Stevens looked on in amazement and wondered just what she was getting herself into. This Hollywood looked like a crazy town!

The Locked Door did nothing to change her mind. Norma Talmadge had starred in a silent film version in 1921 under its stage title, *The Sign on the Door*. By 1929, when Stanwyck was getting her shot at the story, it was already a tired cliché. The film called for Stanwyck to play a secretary who marries her boss (played by William Boyd). After her marriage a rather unsavory character from her past (Rod La Rocque) comes back to taunt her. All of this results in a confrontation between her husband and the creep from her past. Boyd shoots La Rocque, but Stanwyck is then inadvertently locked in with the dying man and accused of the murder. La Rocque clears matters up, however, before his death by telling police that Boyd pulled the trigger but that it was an accident.

George Fitzmaurice had directed his share of silent-screen classics, such as *Son of the Sheik, Lilac Time,* and *The Cheat,* but he was as new to the talkies as Barbara Stanwyck. Perhaps later in their careers the two could have collaborated on some film work of value, but at this point, it was a case of "the blind leading the blind."

Barbara Stanwyck was a natural stage actress, and like all good stage actresses she had learned to project theatrically. This technique didn't work well on a sound stage where microphones were hidden at all times. Fitzmaurice seems to have been very little help, and the film was a disaster. Reviewers panned the film more often than not, but still seemed to recognize the sincerity of Stanwyck's performance. The *New York Herald Tribune* wrote:

> Miss Barbara Stanwyck gives an honest and moving picture as the distraught wife. . . . It is in every way an excellent piece of work. William Boyd is just about right as the husband, and Rod La Rocque plays the villain as well as could be expected. . . . But you always feel that they should be playing *The Locked Door* in powdered wigs and crinoline.

Barbara Stanwyck felt differently, to say the least. Later in her career she recalled the film with a great deal of distaste. "No stench bomb ever made people walk out of a theater as fast as that picture did. It was incredibly awful. Sometimes a picture can be bad, and a player in it can be good. But I was even worse than the picture. They never should've unlocked the damned thing."

After *The Locked Door*, things went from bad to worse. Barbara Stanwyck, Brooklyn accent and all, was cast as a Mexican temptress in *Mexicali Rose*. In the film Stanwyck plays Rose, a woman of low morals, married to Sam Hardy. When Hardy finds out that she's been cheating on him, he throws her out. Spitefully, Rose returns married to Hardy's younger brother. Eventually her sluttishness catches up with her, and she is murdered.

Stanwyck's youthful vulnerability worked against her in her portrayal, and her pairing with the brutish Sam Hardy did little to heighten the film's credibility. Her director, Erle C. Kenton, had been of no more help to her than Fitzmaurice had been earlier, and it was obvious that, although the young actress had a great deal of potential, she desperately needed guidance. Stanwyck was no more pleased with *Mexicali Rose* than she had been with *The Locked Door*. She referred to the film as "an abortion" and commented that she "didn't even know how to make an entrance and exit. I was the vulture of Mexico. I was supposed to be more vampire than Theda Bara had ever thought of being. I even had to entice the actor who played the comedy relief. Beyond any question of doubt, it was the worst picture ever made. The all-time low."

If ever there was a period when Barbara Stanwyck questioned her own future in Hollywood, this was it. In New York she had worked hard at her craft and had had the assistance and guidance of some of the top impresarios of the Broadway stage. Now, here she was in Hollywood trapped in a career that was going nowhere. United Artists had begged her to come West, offering her promises of stardom and wealth. She'd agreed, expecting the same sort of guidance she had received in New York, but it wasn't there. After all the hoopla surrounding her arrival in Hollywood, she had found herself floundering on a sound stage surrounded by dozens of technicians and the most intimidating apparatus and no one to lend her a helping hand. She found herself in a situation in which she knew nothing about what was expected of her and yet she knew as much as anyone else did. There was no doubt in Barbara Stanwyck's mind, if things didn't get better soon, she was in a lot of trouble.

CHAPTER 8

Legend would have us believe that *The Jazz Singer* was the first motion picture with sound, the first talkie. Not so. On August 6, 1926, Warner Brothers released the first feature film to use the Vitaphone sound on disc system, *Don Juan*, starring John Barrymore. The film was a success and was then followed by Warner Brothers' film *The Jazz Singer*, which premiered on October 8, 1927.

The incredible success of *The Jazz Singer* is, of course, the stuff legends are made of, and it is that film that history has immortalized. Every studio watched carefully as the grosses for *The Jazz Singer* flew through the roof. No one studied the success more carefully than Warner Brothers, which shrewdly realized that the singing was just as much a part of the film's popularity as the talking. It was just a matter of months before studios were proclaiming, "All Talking, All Singing, All Dancing!" In 1929 two MGM film musicals, *The Broadway Melody* and *The Hollywood Revue*, were nominated as Best Picture, and *The Broadway Melody* won. Musicals were obviously here to stay, and although Metro would eventually become the unchallenged champion of the genre, in those early days, Warner Brothers did its best to give MGM a run for its money.

In 1929, Warners' big musical was *The Show of Shows*, a potpourri that included such diverse entertainments as a rotund Winnie Lightner warbling "Singing in a Bathtub," Loretta Young and Sally Blane inviting us lyrically to "Meet My Sister," and John Barrymore emoting in a scene from Shakespeare's *Henry VI, Part Three*. Through all this, Frank Fay acted as master of ceremonies in a self-serving performance that was later to be described as "self-congratulatory and not very funny." Nevertheless, the film was a success, and for a few years Fay managed to double-talk the Hollywood press as well as the general public into believing he had something to do with the film's success.

In 1930 Barbara Stanwyck was twenty-three years old and, as far as she was concerned, a cinematic failure. In addition to appearing in *The Locked Door* and *Mexicali Rose*, she had spent the last few months going from one studio to another testing for dozens of roles. It was a practice she found infinitely more degrading than that of an ordinary audition, but it was a fact of life in the picture business. It was enough to shatter the confidence of even the toughest of characters, and Stanwyck began to lose all hope. With more than a trace of bitterness she would later recall, "No one in Hollywood wanted any part of me. My confidence had almost been destroyed."

Barbara busied herself as Mrs. Frank Fay. She'd had no home life to speak of as a child and was determined that those days were to be put in the past. Happily she turned their home in Brentwood Heights into a haven where her man could escape the pressures of the outside world and be king of the manse. It was to this home that Fay returned each night while working on such films as *Under a Texas Moon* and *The Matrimonial Bed*. He, at least, was on top of the world. His career was moderately successful, and his wife was waiting at home like a good little girl. Fay could not have been unaware of his opportunity to hold Stanwyck through emotional blackmail. Stanwyck was desperate for affection and a sense of belonging. Her marriage to Fay had, in itself, been a desperate measure. She had a strong need to be possessed and to possess in the most childlike manner. She relished the opportunity to think of and refer to Fay as *my* husband and to acknowledge her position as *his* wife.

So, if Fay stayed out a little too long with the boys, or came home a little too drunk, she closed her eyes. And when he made his feelings known that she stay home and forget about acting, she was willing at least to consider it. Knowing that her husband was happy to be the only star in the house, Barbara tried to convince herself that she could be happy in the role of Mrs. Frank Fay. Of course, the studios' disinterest in her made Fay's wishes even easier to fulfill.

Self-delusion was an area Barbara Stanwyck couldn't master. She wasn't happy, and there were no two ways about it. Each time a test came up she ran, building up her hopes that she would get the role, whatever it might be; and each time she lost out, a little more of the light within her went dim. Finally, Fay could no longer ignore his wife's unhappiness. Something had to be done to give her the shot in the arm she needed. Using his influence at Warner Brothers, Fay arranged for still another test to be done—this one in color. Ray Rennahan was shooting an early Technicolor picture on the Warners' lot at the time and was assigned as director of photography. As director, Warners' sent over a gentleman who had come to the States from Germany a few years before, Alexander Korda. Since coming to Hollywood, Korda had directed a series of singularly unsuccessful pictures and had already accepted his failure and inevitable return to Europe.

When Stanwyck arrived on the set where the test was to be shot, she found no makeup man and no script. It was obvious to her that the studio was only halfhearted in its interest. Korda came over and introduced himself, telling her, "I've been asked to direct this test. Can you suggest something?" Stanwyck was later to comment on the cruel realization that she was "being given the brush-off" by the studio, but for now she was determined to make the best of the opportunity at hand.

She suggested to Korda that she do the final scene from *The Noose* (in which she pleads with the Governor for the life of the man she loves) since she knew it by heart. Korda agreed, and after setting the lights and giving Barbara a minimum of direction, he instructed her to begin.

At once Stanwyck was back in character as Dot, the chorus girl, a character she knew as well as her own. The scene lasted only three minutes, but when Barbara was through Korda stood there with tears in his eyes. Still struggling with his own composure, he told Stanwyck, "I want to apologize to you for the way this studio has treated you tonight. It doesn't mean anything coming from me. I'm leaving Hollywood a failure. But I wanted you to know it has been a privilege to make this test with a real actress—a privilege I won't forget."

Korda's praise bolstered Stanwyck's hopes high enough that she began to believe that the test might lead to some work, but Warner Brothers still wasn't interested, and when Rennahan inquired a few days later about the studio executives' reaction to the test, he was told, "neither the director nor the girl have anything to offer to motion pictures." Stanwyck's morale dropped even further, and when Columbia, to which she was still under option, asked her to see one of its directors for yet another interview, she did so only halfheartedly.

Frank Capra was preparing *Ladies of Leisure* for Columbia, and he already had an actress in mind for the lead when Harry Cohn asked him to consider Barbara Stanwyck for the role. Cohn was not a man one said no to unnecessarily, and Capra agreed at least to speak to Stanwyck. When she appeared at Capra's office, Barbara was an emotional wreck. Her attitude was sullen, and she made no attempt to hide the chip on her shoulder. She was dressed drably and had not even bothered much with her makeup. Obviously, at this point, she couldn't have cared what type of impression she made, since she felt that there was no chance she would work in pictures again. As far as Frank Capra was concerned, she seemed bored with the whole ordeal. Capra began with the usual questions, such as "What plays have you been in?" and "Are you willing to make a test?" After a few of these Stanwyck lashed out at him, "Oh, hell, you don't want any part of me!" With that, she ran out of Capra's office in tears.

Capra was furious and called Harry Cohn to fill him in. "Forget Stanwyck," he stormed. "She's not an actress. She's a porcupine." As far as Capra was concerned, the subject was closed, and he could now return to his original plans for casting.

About a half hour later he took a call from Frank Fay. "Hey, fella," snapped Fay, "what the hell did you do to my wife?"

Capra was dumbstruck. "Do to her?" he asked, his exasperation getting the best of him. "I couldn't even talk to her!"

Fay continued to rant at the frustrated director. "She came home crying and upset, and nobody can do that to my wife," he shouted.

Capra had no intention of taking any lip from a two-bit comic. "Listen, funny man, I don't want any part of your wife or you. She came in here with a chip on her shoulder, and went out with an ax on it."

Capra's own fury seemed to cool Fay off. The comedian was suddenly conciliatory. "Listen, Frank," he soothed, "she's young and shy, and she's been kicked around here. Let me show you a test she made at Warners'." Fay didn't give Capra a chance to refuse. "I'm coming down with it right now," he promised and then hung up.

Capra viewed the test reluctantly, later admitting that "nothing in the world was going to make me like it." Thirty seconds into the film he was hooked. "I got a lump in my throat as big as an egg. Never had I seen or heard such emotional sincerity. When it was over I had tears in my eyes. I was stunned." Capra told Fay to wait in his office as he rushed over to Harry Cohn. Bursting into Cohn's office he yelled, "Harry, Harry, we've got to sign Stanwyck for that part."

Looking up at the director, Cohn wondered if he had just lost his mind. "What're you, nuts? Half an hour ago you told me she was a kook."

"Yeah, yeah," Capra agreed, "but I just saw a test of her. She'll be terrific. Frank Fay's in my office. Sign her up. Don't let her get away!"

CHAPTER 9

Ladies of Leisure began what may well have been the single most successful collaboration between an actress and director. Capra made films about the people who went to see films. He dealt with breadlines and governmental despotism and girls from the wrong side of the tracks. But he did so with a warmth and optimism that reminded his viewers that there was good in this country, in its people—and that they could be a part of it. They, in fact, were the reason for it.

Barbara was ideally suited for such films. She wasn't beautiful in the conventional Hollywood manner epitomized then by Clara Bow and Greta Garbo, but in a more common manner. She could play a working girl or a girl of ill repute or even a farm girl and look the part. Hers was a natural beauty that women could identify with. It was this quality that Capra would draw upon in his work with Barbara Stanwyck.

Ladies of Leisure was a film adaptation of the 1924 play Ladies of the Evening. Scripted by Jo Swerling, the film is about a party girl, played by Stanwyck, who is hired by an artist, played by Ralph Graves, to pose. She is a girl who covers up her own vulnerability with a wisecracking exterior until she falls in love with Graves and all her pretensions crumble. Unfortunately Graves's father has no intention of welcoming the girl into his family, and Stanwyck's character eventually realizes the futility of the relationship and runs off on a pleasure cruise to drown herself. Graves discovers her intentions and manages to contact the ship in the nick of time, thus allowing for their reunion before the picture's end. The script could easily have developed into a maudlin, soapy piece of business, but Capra's own vision of it as "human, witty and poignant" saved it from such a common fate.

Stanwyck couldn't have been more ideally suited for the role. Her characterization of the party girl, Kay Arnold, is at once tough and vulnerable. The audience is keenly aware of both sides of Kay's personality at all times, and when her tough shell begins to crack, the little girl beneath it is one they can understand and identify with all too well. Even while she is delivering her acid retorts, Stanwyck's eyes and body language reveal the very soul of the woman inside. Capra, of course, gave as good as he got. His direction was intelligent and sensitive. Love scenes have always been a nemesis of sorts for Capra, but his handling of them in *Ladies of Leisure* was flawless.

In Capra, Stanwyck had found a director who was as serious about his work as she. Like Willard Mack and Arthur Hopkins before him, Capra was willing to work with Barbara in whatever manner was necessary to get a successful performance from her. Their first few days of working together were full of discovery and, in many ways, set each of them in awe of the other.

Joseph Walker had been assigned as cinematographer on the film, and prior to the start of the production Harry Cohn had directed him to let Stanwyck appear as glamorous as possible. Walker and Capra used Barbara's first scenes to be filmed as a chance for experimentation. They spent a great deal of time lighting her just so and shooting much of the scene in close-up. Viewing these scenes the next day in rushes, the two men agreed that Barbara looked gorgeous, but as far as Capra was concerned, something didn't work. He explained to Walker, "I feel we are losing something. I think she is potentially a great actress, a unique personality, but we are not getting it on the screen. I want to shoot the sequence over with no makeup, no glamorous portraits—just show her as she really is and I think she will be great."

It was Stanwyck's natural, believable beauty that Capra was after and that he and Walker eventually caught on the screen. All was not smooth sailing, however. Two weeks into shooting, Barbara viewed the dailies for the first time. In her usual self-critical manner, she tore her appearance to shreds. As far as she was concerned, "my hands looked awkward, my gestures seemed abrupt, and I pulled my mouth to one side when I talked fast." The next day she changed her approach, throwing her hands around in elaborate gestures and enunciating her lines very carefully. Capra didn't comment but invited her the next day to view the rushes again.

Stanwyck watched, this time embarrassed by what she saw. When the lights went up, Capra admonished her, "See what you're doing? You're trying to look beautiful. And in doing that you're losing the wonderful thing you had—complete naturalness. If you lose that, you're sunk. I want you to promise me not to look at the rushes again." Stanwyck agreed.

Capra found another area that presented some difficulty. Stanwyck always gave her best performance the first time she did a scene. Rehearsals and retakes only succeeded in taking the fire out of her work. Capra realized that. "Stanwyck doesn't act a scene. She lives it. Her emotions are so genuine that they must be captured in their first expression. Her best work is the result—not of timing and rehearsing and study—but of pure feminine reaction. She gives everything she has, and its great sincerity and strength must be caught at fever heat." Even Capra's thorough understanding of the actress and her problem didn't make the situation less difficult. Years later he explained his solution in his autobiography, *The Name Above the Title*:

I had to rehearse the cast without her; work out the physical movements without her. The actors grumbled. Who ever heard of an actress not rehearsing? I had to take the "heart" of the scene—the vital close-ups of Barbara—first, and with multiple cameras so she would only have to do the scene once. Multiple cameras aggravate the difficulties of lighting and recording in geometrical progression, i.e., four times as complex with two cameras, eight times with three cameras.

On the set I would never let Stanwyck utter one word of the scene until the cameras were rolling. Before that I talked to her in her dressing room, told her the meaning of the scene, the points of emphasis, the pauses. Her hairdresser Helen had become her confidante. I let Helen give her the cues from the other actors. I talked softly, not wishing to fan the smoldering fires that lurked beneath that somber silence. She remembered every word I said—and she never blew a line. My parting admonition was usually this: "Remember, Barbara. No matter what the other actors do, whether they stop or blow their lines—you continue your scene right to the end. Understand? Good girl."

The film was a triumph for all with reviewers falling over themselves in raving about Barbara Stanwyck. The *New York Review* said that the film "gives Barbara Stanwyck an excellent opportunity to show that she is as good an actress in the talkies as she is on the stage," and under the headline STANWYCK TRIUMPHS, Mordunt Hall in *The New York Times* spoke of "the restrained performance of nearly all the players and the general lightness of handling that commends the direction of Frank Capra." As for Stanwyck, he exclaimed that she "shows a most gratifying ability for comprehending the requirements of her role." *Photoplay* magazine threw all the bouquets Stanwyck's way, claiming: "It is a really fine picture because of the astonishing performance of a little tap-dancing beauty who has in her the spirit of a great artist. Her name is Barbara Stanwyck. Go and be amazed by this Barbara girl."

After the release of *Ladies of Leisure*, Columbia pleaded with Stanwyck to sign an exclusive contract, but she refused. "This Barbara girl" was much too independent, even in this early period of her career, to be tied down to any one studio. Instead she accepted nonexclusive contracts with both Warner Brothers and Columbia. It was a shrewd move on Stanwyck's part. Not only was she now in a position to have parts offered by both studios, but both studios began major publicity buildups.

Stanwyck's next film was *Illicit*, a sophisticated love story done for Warner Brothers. In those days before the Hays office and its stringent moral codes, story lines were far more risqué than they would be five years hence. *Illicit* finds Barbara cast as Anne Vincent, a young woman involved in an affair with James Rennie. All seems to be going well until they finally marry. Soon Rennie is involved with an ex-lady-friend, and Stanwyck is ready to throw in the towel. Luckily they realize their love for each other in time for a final embrace.

Stanwyck's director on *Illicit* was Archie Mayo, and they worked well together, although Mayo tended to allow Stanwyck to work out her own characterization. This resulted in a natural and gentle portrayal on Barbara's part, and although the film wasn't the critical and popular success *Ladies of Leisure* had been, it was well accepted. The film was remade two years later as *Ex-Lady*, starring Bette Davis, and of course the plot would be rehashed countless times over the next fifty years.

During the promotion of *Illicit*, Warner Brothers started a tradition that would be continued throughout Barbara's career. All publicity referred to her as Miss Barbara Stanwyck. It was an honor bestowed upon only three other performers in motion pictures, Mr. John Barrymore, Mr. George Arliss, and Miss Ruth Chatterton.

Little Ruby Stevens from Brooklyn had come a long way.

CHAPTER 10

"A star is only as good as her last picture," Stanwyck told Rodie
Harris late in 1930. "When *Ladies of Leisure* played at one of the local
theaters here, I drove by one evening and parked my car across the
street. There on the marquee, for all the world to see, my name
gleamed high in electric. It was my dream come true. I thought I was
thrilled, but deep down in my heart, I knew I wasn't. Instead, I kept
thinking of that line in *The Royal Family!* 'If your name is in electric light
and the fuse blows, where are you?' I kept thinking of its significance.
It kept me from being thrilled."

Wise words from one so young, but they were the words of a
woman torn between two worlds. In the years ahead Barbara Stanwyck's attitude toward film stardom would remain unchanged, and,
ironically, it would be this same attitude that would be partially
responsible for the durability of her career. In 1930, however, this
attitude was being used against her by none other than Frank Fay.
Although Fay's outward image was that of a wisecracking, devil-may-

care man-about-town, he was actually incredibly insecure. And like many insecure married men, he was also jealous to the extreme. Whenever possible, Mrs. Frank Fay was right there by her husband's side where he could keep his eye on her.

In the summer of 1930, not long after his wife had completed *Illicit,* Frank had to leave for New York to fulfill a two-week engagement at the Palace Theatre. Naturally, he assumed that Barbara would be accompanying him, but when she informed the main office at Columbia that she would be going out of town, they forbade it. In two weeks she was scheduled to begin another film for them, *Roseland,* and they didn't want to take any chances that Stanwyck wouldn't return in time. Fay was outraged, and Stanwyck was heartbroken. He would be away for their second wedding anniversary, and she had had her heart set on their spending it together. Nevertheless, Stanwyck would have found the situation easier to bear if Fay hadn't made things more difficult. He stormed through the house in a Black Irish rage and insisted that Barbara follow him anyway. "You're my wife first and an actress second," he told her, "and unless you remember that, this marriage will be a thing of the past, fast!" Stanwyck tried a compromise with Columbia, begging them to at least let her go to New York for Fay's opening. "Just one day," she implored, "and I'll come right back." But even that was out of the question. Finally, Fay stormed off to New York, leaving a shaken wife in his wake.

It was obvious to Barbara that there were priorities to be weighed and decisions to be made. All was well as long as she could keep both her man and her studio happy at once, but now she was being torn in opposite directions and something had to give. She had every intention of fulfilling her contract with Columbia, but she wouldn't sacrifice her marriage at the altar of Harry Cohn or anyone else. So it was that she explained to Rodie Harris, "It's because of such things that when my present contract expires, I will retire. I won't allow anything to interfere with my happiness. No career is worth it. Love is the only important thing in the world to any woman." Early in September filming began as scheduled on *Roseland,* which had been retitled *Ten Cents a Dance.* The film co-starred Ricardo Cortez and Monroe Owsley and was directed by Lionel Barrymore. It was, in fact, the last film to be directed by the distinguished actor, who had been nominated for an Academy Award for his direction of *Madame X* just two years before. By this time he was ailing and not at his best. Crippling arthritis confined him to a wheelchair, and his medication caused him to fall asleep, even while directing.

Although Ricardo Cortez recalls Barrymore's direction being nonexistent, Stanwyck is somewhat kinder when she says, "He tried his best. As a performer you just had to try harder." Whatever the problems on the set, *Ten Cents a Dance* was a good little film. Stanwyck's portrayal as the dime-a-dance girl whose hell of a husband forces her to compromise herself to save him from prison was all Barrymore could have asked for. The film was successful, and Stanwyck's following increased. Barbara Stanwyck's professionalism, well known now, was apparent even then. During production of the film, while backing away from Monroe Owsley during an argument scene, her heel caught on something and she fell backward, injuring herself badly and then fainting. She was rushed to the Osteopathic Hospital where it was apparent that she was partially paralyzed and doctors feared that she had fractured her pelvis. Her recovery was quick, though, and she returned to work the next day. Cortez recalls her attitude on the film as "no nonsense. She came to the studio to work. I admired her for her dignity and professionalism. She was a perfect lady at all times."

Immediately after completing work on *Ten Cents a Dance*, Stanwyck went to Warners to make the first film of her new contract, *Night Nurse*. This time she was joined by Joan Blondell and a young newcomer on the threshold of breaking through, Clark Gable. The film found Barbara as a nurse assigned to care for some children whose own mother is too deeply involved with her chauffeur (Gable) and bootleg booze to care whether her kids live or die. It was the first of Stanwyck's characters to exhibit the tough demeanor she would become well known for. Her performance was sure, and again she scored well with critics and public alike. In fact, she was more well received than the film itself. Reviews of the film seem to be summed up by this one from the *Hollywood Reporter*: "The best things about *Night Nurse* are its title and cast names plus the Misses Stanwyck and Blondell stripping two or three times during the picture."

Night Nurse might have been delegated to the lower half of a double bill if Metro hadn't just released *A Free Soul* starring Norma Shearer and Gable. Suddenly Clark Gable was all the rage and everyone wanted to see *Night Nurse.* Warners emphasized Gable in all the advertising, which was fine with Stanwyck who shrewdly realized that the more who came to see Gable, the more would see her.

As Barbara Stanwyck's career grew more and more successful, her husband's career seemed to run itself into the ground. His latest films for Warners, *Bright Lights* and *God's Gift to Women,* were critical and public disasters, and Warners seemed hesitant about following up with another. Fay began to drink more heavily, and rumors of discord in the Stanwyck–Fay marriage became more and more common. What the Hollywood gossips hadn't counted on, though, was Ruby Stevens and her indomitable spirit. She was not about to give up without a fight, and in March of 1931 she was still telling the press where they could go with their rumors. When one reporter called her at home and asked her to comment on the state of affairs in the Fay household, she told him, "I'm making a pot of tea and a bit of shortbread for him this moment. Does that sound like we're separated? Would any wife do that much for a husband she was mad at?"

In the spring of 1931, Barbara Stanwyck and Frank Capra were reunited in their second collaboration, a film called *The Miracle Woman.* The film was based on the play *Bless You, Sister* by John Meehan and Robert Riskin. It was the story of an Aimee Semple McPherson-type evangelist who is in the business only to milk her believers for all she can get. Somehow her sermons give courage to a blind ex-aviator, played by David Manners, who is considering suicide. They fall in love and in the end she abandons her phony "calling," but not before her temple is set on fire. She remains on stage, valiantly forcing the crowd to sing "Onward Christian Soldiers" as they calmly march out to safety. Then, surrounded by flames, she is saved by David Manners.

The Miracle Woman was a powerful film, and Stanwyck's performance as Florence Fallon was her best to date. David Manners recalls Stanwyck's intense concentration during the film and remembers her "sitting alone in a studio chair—almost in meditation." Although *The Miracle Woman* was banned in the British Empire because of charges of irreverence, critics in America were more impressed. *Silver Screen* magazine called it "a brilliantly directed study of modern evangelism."

Early in June, Warner Brothers announced that they were canceling their contract with Frank Fay ahead of time. The official announcement was that Darryl Zanuck and Fay couldn't agree on stories and were terminating the contract by mutual agreement, but the truth wasn't hard to figure. Frank Fay had flopped in films. His talents were ideally suited to the hokum of Broadway and burlesque. Film called for a subtler kind of comedy than Fay could offer. Talking pictures were killing burlesque, and soon burlesque would no longer exist.

Meanwhile, Warners announced that in September they would star Barbara Stanwyck in a new film, *Safe in Hell*, written by Houston Branch. The fact that this announcement followed so closely behind that of the Fay–Warners break only emphasized what seemed obvious at the time: Frank Fay's career might be going downhill fast, but his wife's success had only just begun. Again rumors of trouble in the Fay marriage ran rampant, and Barbara Stanwyck felt it necessary to come to her husband's defense.

"I am Mrs. Frank Fay first, and Barbara Stanwyck second," she told reporters. "But this is Hollywood. Frank asked to leave Warners because he felt they had unsuitable stories and that greater opportunities lay elsewhere. He worked very hard for his release and I am glad that he got it. He already has had offers from two major companies and will sign with one or the other." Then, as if to make it clear that she was certainly no bigger a star than Fay, she added, "I am a star today, but give me one or two bad pictures and Hollywood will consider me a flop again." Nevertheless, the pressure Stanwyck was under to stroke Fay's ego in public while presenting a picture of domestic harmony was never more apparent than in her final comment. "He's old-fashioned. He thinks a woman's place is in the home but he wants me to be happy."

Meanwhile, even as Barbara denied the discord, her marriage was again in a turmoil. Shortly after the break with Warners, Frank Fay began to plan a return to New York and stage work. And again Stanwyck was torn. She was to start another Capra film, *Forbidden*, in a couple of days. She wanted to do it. She enjoyed working with Capra, and it was a good script, but Fay wanted her in New York. The situation was made even more complex by the subtleties involved in any announcement made to the public. Whereas Fay may have been demanding that Barbara accompany him, public image was that of the inveterate pro—the vaudeville trouper—and it was against everything he stood for to have anyone believe that he would insist his wife walk out on a contract. Barbara Stanwyck, on the other hand, was a proud and strong-minded woman, a serious professional. She wouldn't walk out on a contract without good reason, and the power brokers in Hollywood knew this. Her only recourse, she decided, was to base any move on the two principles most people would understand: love and money.

On July 17, 1931, Barbara Stanwyck telephoned Harry Cohn at Columbia to inform him that she would not be reporting for the start of work on *Forbidden* two days later. Instead, she explained, she would be traveling to New York to be with her husband. Then, almost as a diversionary tactic, she informed Cohn that if he really wanted her back on the film, he would increase her salary from $30,000 to $50,000. Cohn's response was typically Cohn. "You've gone off your nut!" he bellowed. "I'll sue you!" Cohn was as good as his word. Within days the lawsuit was the hottest subject of conversation throughout the movie colony. Naturally, the press had a field day. Movie magazines painted Stanwyck as "the girl who finds no sacrifice too great for love." Columnists, on the other hand, chastised Stanwyck for what they considered irresponsible behavior, but Stanwyck stuck to her guns.

Columnist Harrison Carroll interviewed the Fays at home. Ironically, Carroll summed the entire situation precisely in his lead: "Independent as they make them is Barbara Stanwyck—independent of everybody except Frank Fay."

"Fay is the man of the house," Carroll reported. Stanwyck did all she could to show her agreement. "There really isn't any reason I should work at all," she explained. "Just this week Frank got a stunning offer to go back East. I can go with him."

Then the man of the house chimed in, "I never did want Barbara to go into pictures." It didn't take Fay long to get around to his favorite subject, Frank Fay. "A lot of people are calmly reading me out of the picture business because I settled my contract with Warners. But if I want, I'll be in pictures long after these mugs have disappeared."

Surprisingly enough, the columnists were not fooled. Slowly they all seemed to back Barbara. Perhaps Louella Parsons was responsible for their change in attitude when she went public with a suspicion they all seemed to agree on. "I do not mean to imply that Frank Fay is selfish and self-centered," Parsons hedged, "but from all I can gather it is Barbara who is making all of the sacrifices. I am inclined to believe that her demand for $50,000 is her own little act of trying to disguise the real reason."

Throughout the summer Stanwyck's lawyers battled Cohn and Columbia, but each side seemed as hardheaded as the other. The situation became even more complex as Stanwyck's September start date for *Safe in Hell* at Warners came even closer. "No Columbia pictures, no Warner Brothers pictures," Harry Cohn stated emphatically, and Darryl Zanuck at Warners seemed to agree.

Zanuck announced that *Safe in Hell* would be postponed until after Stanwyck had settled her differences with Columbia and *Forbidden* was in the can. "She's a great bet," Zanuck admitted, "but how do we know that she won't do the same thing to us that she has done to Columbia?" On September 11, Columbia Pictures obtained an injunction preventing Barbara Stanwyck from working for any other studio until her contract with them had been honored. Perhaps it was at this point that Stanwyck finally believed that Columbia would not back down, or possibly her lawyer, Charles Cradick, felt he had exhausted every possible argument. Whatever the case, on September 15 Stanwyck and Columbia agreed that she would return to work on September 30.

To his credit, Harry Cohn did not gloat unreasonably over his victory. He was pleased to have Stanwyck back and promised her a first-rate production in *Forbidden*. Leslie Howard was cabled in London and asked to return immediately to play opposite Barbara and Adolphe Menjou in the film but was unavailable, and Ralph Bellamy was summoned in his place. Cohn met with Stanwyck privately and told her how happy he was that they were working together again. He realized that the lawsuit and concurrent press attention had cost Barbara her own sense of integrity, and more than likely he understood her motivation. His final gesture certainly showed no hard feelings: He raised her salary to $50,000 a picture.

CHAPTER 11

Frank Capra admits that Jo Swerling's screenplay for *Forbidden* was based loosely on the Fannie Hurst tearjerker *Back Street*. Stanwyck falls in love with a politician played by Adolph Menjou, but they can't marry because he won't leave his invalid wife. They continue their affair, and Stanwyck gives birth to Menjou's child. Eventually, realizing the futility of the romance, Stanwyck enters into a marriage of convenience with Ralph Bellamy. When Bellamy threatens to ruin Menjou's career with the truth about his affair with Stanwyck, she kills him and is sent to prison. Menjou is elected governor, pardons Stanwyck, and is then taken seriously ill. He dies with her at his bedside but not before handing her a will that admits their affair and leaves her half his estate. The film ends as Stanwyck destroys the will and returns home. *Forbidden* was the type of film audiences of the thirties loved and studios turned out by the dozens. Stanwyck certainly made her share of them, as did Bette Davis and Joan Crawford. But

Capra's sensitive, intelligent direction set this one above most of the competition.

Production of the film went smoothly for the most part except for one incident on the beach during filming in Malibu. Barbara and Adolphe Menjou were supposed to be riding horses by the ocean's edge. This was before Stanwyck's proclivity toward horses, and a stunt woman was used for most of the shots. While Barbara was sitting on top of a horse for close-ups, however, the horse was frightened by the lights and threw her to the sand, where she remained unconscious for fifteen minutes. Incredibly, as she came to, she told Capra, "Hurry, we'll have to finish this scene now. My legs are stiffening." Action was called quickly. Stanwyck and Menjou walked into the surf, swam fifty yards offshore, and returned. Only then was Barbara rushed to the hospital where X rays showed that both legs had been sprained. She returned to work two days later.

Two weeks later misfortune struck the Fays. They were attending a party in Hollywood when they received a call from Frank Fay's father, who was living with them. The elder Fay was calling from Malibu where the couple's beach house had just been totally destroyed by fire. The blaze had started two doors away. Fanned by a stiff inshore breeze, it had then spread quickly through the home of their neighbor, director Joseph Santley, and on to the Fay residence.

In March, after completing work on *Forbidden*, Barbara took a short sabbatical from film and returned to New York where she and Frank appeared at the Palace Theatre for two weeks. Their portion of the bill included the comedy monologues Fay was so well known for, a few comedy routines involving both Frank and Barbara, and then Barbara re-creating her most powerful scenes from *Ladies of Leisure*, *The Miracle Woman*, and *Forbidden*. The performances were very successful, and many of the New York critics took note of Miss Stanwyck's star quality. Their run at the Palace might have gone on indefinitely had it not been for Stanwyck's film commitments in Hollywood.

Behind the scenes, however, everything was not entirely rosy. The Fays were arguing more often than not. Usually their quarrels were instigated by Frank's compulsive jealousy. Never was this more apparent than during their stay in New York. Fay kept a persistently watchful eye on her, and during his solo turns onstage, he insisted that she remain in the wings where he could see her at all times. Shocked onlookers wondered just how much longer this marriage would last.

Returning to Hollywood, Barbara went almost immediately into production of *Shopworn* with Regis Toomey. The film remains one of Stanwyck's least memorable pictures and one of her least favorites. Regis Toomey recalls that during production she seemed somewhat "aloof and very unhappy." Nevertheless, Stanwyck had earned the respect of most critics by now, and her efforts seldom went unnoticed. This attitude was apparent in *The Times* (London) review, which called the film "a dull and characterless study" but noted that Barbara "does what she can with a thankless part." Stateside, the *New York Herald Tribune's* review said:

> There is something about the simple, straightforward sincerity of Miss Stanwyck which makes almost everything she does upon either stage or screen seem credible and rather poignant. I fear, however, that *Shopworn* is a trifle too much for her. It happens, you see, that the film is not *Shopworn* in name only. That unfortunate, but descriptive, title provides, among other things, a pretty good critical estimate of the work.

Luckily, Barbara Stanwyck's next film had a good deal more to offer. Edna Ferber's novel *So Big* had been one of the most popular books of its day and had won for Miss Ferber the Pulitzer Prize. The part of Selina Peake, as written by Ferber and as translated in the screenplay by J. Alexander and Robert Lord, is a woman of courage, dignity, and love. Stanwyck never let Ferber down. Her Selina is a magical creature as warm and as giving as one would imagine. For her performance in the role, Barbara earned some of her finest notices to date, including this one from William Boehnel of the *New York World-Telegram*:

> By her performance in *So Big* Barbara Stanwyck definitely establishes herself with this writer as being a brilliant emotional actress. No matter what one may think about the picture, the final conviction of anyone who sees Miss Stanwyck's Selina Peake will be that she herself contributes a fine and stirring performance,

making of it a characterization which is direct and eloquent all the way.

Barbara's next film, *The Purchase Price*, was far less successful and not nearly as memorable. Stanwyck had begged Warners to buy Arthur Stringer's story "The Mud Lark" for her, and *The Purchase Price* was the result. The film, which was known as *The Night Flower* throughout production, cast Barbara as a hard, bitter Manhattan torch singer who runs to North Dakota and a mail-order marriage (to George Brent) to escape her gangster lover. *The Purchase Price* is an enjoyable and somewhat unusual film, but it wasn't up to the quality of *So Big* or the Stanwyck–Capra collaborations. Again, reviewers did their best to ignore the film while praising Stanwyck's performance.

Ever since their return from New York in March, Barbara and Frank Fay had been working even harder at trying to solve their differences. There were still periodic rumors of separation, most of which were not commented on by either of the Fays. Frank's film career was almost nonexistent at this point, and his drinking was becoming a far more serious problem than it had been before. The year before he had been arrested on charges of drunk driving and hit-and-run when his car crashed into another on Beverly Boulevard. Mysteriously, the charges were dropped a few days later when the district attorney explained that "the only witnesses in the case did not care to be involved in a criminal prosecution and have left for their homes in San Francisco."

Early in the summer of 1932, Barbara and Frank became foster parents to an infant. The child, John Charles Greene, had been born to one Vivien Greene on February 5, 1932, and had been put up for adoption almost immediately. Legal proceedings for that adoption were begun in late November, and on December 5, 1932, Barbara and Frank became legal parents to the ten-month-old baby boy. Soon afterward he was rechristened Dion Anthony Fay. Barbara's first gift to her new son was a beautiful bracelet engraved with a quotation from Hugh Walpole, "It isn't life, it's the courage you put into it."

At last Ruby Stevens' family was complete, and there was no doubt to anyone around her that no matter how hard the struggle, she would do whatever she could to keep it that way.

CHAPTER 12

Throughout the early thirties Barbara Stanwyck's career and popularity had grown steadily. Although she was not yet considered the equal of such stalwarts as Joan Crawford, Norma Shearer, and Greta Garbo, Stanwyck had joined with some of her contemporaries such as Katharine Hepburn, Bette Davis, Sylvia Sidney, and Kay Francis to form some very powerful competition. If anything, Stanwyck was in the strongest position of any of these ladies. As an independent she could be somewhat choosier about the roles she accepted and was open to offers from all of the studios. Nevertheless, Warners and Columbia did their best to monopolize her time and were always announcing that she had been signed for one role or another. Many of these never materialized; for instance, in 1932 Warners announced that Stanwyck would star in *The Story of East Lynne*, but the film was never produced.

She was originally offered the lead in *British Agent* but turned it down, explaining later, "Then they wanted me to do *British Agent* with Leslie

Howard. I'd read the book twice, because I found it so absorbing, but it's a man's story. Howard was made to order for the part, but I turned it down because I saw no reason why I should play second fiddle to anyone. I've worked too hard to get to the top to give up top billing for no good reason. I don't mean the actual billing, because that's unimportant. I mean the top spot in the picture. In a few years, I suppose, I'll have to resign myself to leads and supporting parts—we all come to that eventually—but I don't feel I've reached that point yet." She was replaced by Kay Francis. Francis replaced her again in *The Jewel Robbery*, and Carole Lombard took over her role in *Brief Moment* when Stanwyck decided to play the Palace in New York instead.

Even so, Barbara probably worked harder during this period of her career than ever before and ever since. In many ways she was still learning her craft. Her normally inquisitive nature made the motion picture a wonderland for her to wander through. Beginning in these early years she spent as much time learning what went on behind the camera as she did learning what to do in front of it. She gave as much respect to the photographers and lighting engineers as she did to the screen legends she came in contact with. As far as she was concerned, she was serving an apprenticeship, and it was during this time that she developed an understanding of and respect for the craft of filmmaking that would serve her well for the next fifty years.

After completing *The Purchase Price*, Barbara accepted a role in yet another Frank Capra production—a somewhat offbeat story for that time, entitled *The Bitter Tea of General Yen*. In it Stanwyck played an American missionary, Megan Davis, who travels to China to marry another missionary. Before the ceremony, however, she is kidnapped by the evil General Yen (Nils Asther) and taken to his luxurious palace. At first she abhors General Yen and everything he stands for. They clash repeatedly over his unscrupulous methods until she begins to realize that, for Yen, it is simply a means of survival. Soon her hatred turns to empathy and then respect. After his mistress brings about Yen's downfall, Megan confesses her own love for him. When she tells him that she has decided to stay with him, he realizes the pain this will cause her, and, determined to have an honorable death, he drinks a cup of tea he has poisoned.

The Bitter Tea of General Yen is a strange, beautiful, and powerful film that was far ahead of its time and yet couldn't have been made under the more prohibitive moral codes that were soon to rule the movie industry. Interracial love and marriage were subjects seldom treated then and somewhat sensational even now, but as usual Frank Capra handled the story with honesty and good taste.

Stanwyck has never been more beautifully photographed. This was the fifth time she had worked with cinematographer Joseph Walker, and although they would work again some years later, it would remain Walker's favorite experience in working with Barbara. The motion picture camera either loves you or hates you, and the love affair between Barbara and the camera was apparent throughout *Bitter Tea*. Walker even invented a special four-inch close-up lens to use on Barbara that seemed to surround her with a halo of light.

Columbia pulled out all the stops in publicizing the film. "Drawn together by fate," read their ads, "a man of the East . . . a woman of the West . . . their forbidden love wrecked an empire." *The Bitter Tea of General Yen* was the first film to play at Radio City Music Hall, and it was met by an extraordinary amount of public controversy. Although the film was successful in the States, Stanwyck's fans did not take kindly to her "falling in love with a Chinaman." Only the fact that General Yen was portrayed by the incredibly handsome Swedish actor Nils Asther made the situation at all acceptable to the somewhat horrified moviegoers. Many critics were also puzzled by the film, and reviews were mixed. In the end the film lost money and was even banned by the British for condoning miscegenation. Stanwyck, as usual, made it through the experience unscathed, and today the film is appreciated for the work of art that it is.

Barbara's next two films were decent thirties programmers that did nothing more for her than to keep her name on the screen and in the public eye. The first of these was *Ladies They Talk About*, and the title tells the whole story. Stanwyck's co-star was Preston Foster, and the best thing to be said about the film is that it was only sixty-nine minutes long. This one was followed by *Baby Face*, a film made to meet the requests of Stanwyck's fans that she get to do something "glamorous." "Everyone else has glamour but me," Stanwyck explained to the press. "So I played in *Baby Face*." Glamorous she was, dolled up in a series of wigs and a wardrobe designed by Orry-Kelly.

Critic William Boehnel adroitly summed up the film when he headlined, *"Baby Face is rescued by its star."* Demanding that Stanwyck be given roles worthy of her, Boehnel wrote, "I can only repeat that she is ammunition for larger and more powerful guns than this, but she never ceases to be the magnificent and intelligent trouper she is."

Ever in My Heart, the film waiting for Barbara, was another "little" film, but it was a good little film. Then, as now, a film that appealed almost entirely to women was rather condescendingly called "a soap opera," and many of the films Barbara had made up to this time fell within this category. *Ever in My Heart* was saved from such a fate by an intelligent script, gentle direction of a shattering love story, and genuinely warm performances by Stanwyck and her co-star, Otto Kruger.

The film is about a German professor (Kruger) and his American wife (Stanwyck). Upon their marriage in 1909 they settle in the United States, where he becomes a devoted father and well-respected member of the community. World War I, however, surrounds him with ethnic prejudice. He and his wife are ostracized, and after their child dies, he sends his wife back to her family. "They won't let me be an American," he tells her sadly and then returns to his native Germany. Later, during the war and after their divorce, she is working for the Red Cross in France, where she meets her husband, who she finds out is working as a spy for Germany. She is still far too deeply in love with him to turn him in, although she knows his information could kill thousands of men. When Kruger visits her apartment, she slips some poison into their wine, then begs him to remain until morning. As he dies in her arms, she sings to him, and then finally, as she settles into her own death, she sings the last line of the song that has meant so much to them throughout their marriage, "You will never know how much I love you."

It is perhaps one of the most magnificent moments of Stanwyck's film career, and yet it is a film that is almost forgotten today. Even then the reaction was mixed, but the reviews were, for the most part, glowing. The *New York World-Telegram* wrote that, "Barbara Stanwyck demonstrates that she is one of the first—the very first—actresses

72

among the more exalted leading ladies in Hollywood. She gives a fine, dignified performance. I think it is one of the most searching and authentic characterizations she has yet offered."

The critic at the *New York Mirror* exclaimed, "Miss Stanwyck has never made another picture like it, nor has any other star. The story is bitterly real." Most ironic, though, was the review from *The New York Times*, which praised the "warm and intelligent acting" but commented that "the tragedy is meaningless to this new generation." World War II was just seven years away.

Ever in My Heart was Barbara Stanwyck's fourth film in a row in less than a year with no rest in between. During this period, as she became more sought after with each film, her husband's career had stagnated, almost to the point of total oblivion. Vaudeville's decline was almost complete by this time, and although entertainers such as Sophie Tucker, Eddie Cantor, and Frank Fay could still draw audiences, there weren't many theaters left. The Depression and the motion picture industry had put most of them out of business, and in just two years the Palace Theatre, mecca for all of vaudeville, would turn into just another movie theater.

With the backing for live vaudeville shows disappearing fast, and with Frank Fay badly in need of work, he and Barbara decided to produce their own revue. Whether Fay had any cash to put up himself is doubtful; although he was usually very highly paid for his work, he enjoyed living well above his means. Stanwyck, on the other hand, had earned a great deal of cash in the past year alone, and although she was certainly not living a frugal existence, years of poverty had given her a healthy respect for every dollar she earned. In a desperate gesture to help Frank's career and possibly save her marriage at the same time, Barbara put over $125,000 behind the revue, entitled *Tattle Tales*. As a final measure of her support Stanwyck agreed to star opposite Fay in the show.

Tattle Tales went on tour in April 1933, working its way through the larger cities on the way to New York. Reviews were mixed, but box office receipts were not disappointing. Barbara Stanwyck had developed quite a following throughout the country, and many of these fans went to see her in *Tattle Tales*. Nevertheless, Fay was a seasoned veteran and knew that New York audiences were cut of a different cloth. For two months Barbara, Frank, and their troupe of traveling players worked at getting the show into shape for New York.

When *Tattle Tales* opened at the Broadhurst Theater on June 11, 1933, the New York theater crowd turned out in droves. Stanwyck and Fay went through their well-rehearsed paces, and the reaction in the theater seemed promising. The critics, for the most part, approved, and although Burns Mantle of the New York *Daily News* found the show to be of inferior quality, he admitted that Barbara and Frank were "still a little bit of Class A." As far as Stanwyck was concerned, Mantle wrote that she was "blessed with that certain subtle something that distinguishes the real from the imitation, a sort of unconscious self-consciousness that we classify as poise."

Tattle Tales might have managed to run at the Broadhurst for a few months if it hadn't opened during the hottest summer on record in New York. The heat kept audiences home, and *Tattle Tales* closed after twenty-eight days. Barbara Stanwyck was somewhat poorer, and her marriage was no better than it had been. As for Frank Fay, he was drinking more than ever.

CHAPTER 13

Hollywood had taken possession of Barbara Stanwyck by now. She fought the movie town's types every step of the way, insulted them at every opportunity, and denounced any affection she might have for them, but still they claimed her as their own. When she took a short sabbatical from film to tour with her husband in *Tattle Tales*, Hollywood was outraged. Not surprisingly, all the blame was laid at Frank Fay's feet. He had not endeared himself to the Hollywood press over the last few years, and the columnists and reporters were more than willing to sacrifice him for Stanwyck. In an article plaintively captioned GIVE US BACK BARBARA, columnist Jim Tully wrote, "Fay . . . returned to the stage and took his genius wife with him. But surely now he will encourage her to return to the films. They are sadly in need of her. There is a niche which she alone can fill."

As usual, the Fays did everything they could to hide the turmoil within their household. "It looks sometimes as though Hollywood doesn't want people to be happy," Barbara complained to the press. "I'd like to 'sock' people who don't leave us alone. We're going to be happy in spite of everybody—or anybody." Hollywood gossips, in particular, were a thorn in Barbara's side, and she gave them their share of her anger. "They seem to be determined that nobody shall have any private life that is immune from chatter or scandal. You feel that people are watching you all the time, looking for the slightest word or moment that will give them material to talk about. And if they don't see anything to gossip about, they make it up just the same. That is why Frank and I never go out except to visit a few close friends. All we ask is to be allowed to live our own lives in peace. But some people resent that. Well, they'll just have to go on resenting!"

Stanwyck's public support of her husband remained unchanged. She insisted on signing all autographs as Barbara Stanwyck Fay, sometimes to the dismay of her fans. When one cried, "This autograph won't be right in a year or two, when you're divorced," Barbara tore the piece of paper out of the girl's hand and snapped, "Prophets of your sort are without honor in Hollywood."

As for young Dion Anthony Fay, he was kept behind closed doors. The Lindbergh kidnapping had put a scare into parents all over the country but most particularly into those of celebrity status. The Fays refused to allow photographers into their home, and on those few occasions when Dion was taken out, it was with the firm understanding that there be no photos.

The press corps need not have feared that Stanwyck was bowing out of films. She had no such intention. After the failure of *Tattle Tales*, Barbara embarked on another spell of back-to-back film production. The first of these films, *Gambling Lady*, cast Stanwyck opposite Joel McCrea for the first time. The two found a comfortable chemistry on the screen, and the film was a solid success.

Stanwyck's next film, *A Lost Lady*, had a great deal more potential, but unfortunately it remained unfulfilled. The film had little resemblance to Willa Cather's classic novel and was made even less believable by the casting of Frank Morgan as Stanwyck's husband. Eileen Creelman of the New York *Sun* found the film a "heavy and somewhat dismal drama" but gave Stanwyck her usual due in noting that "Barbara

Stanwyck, as usual, almost saves the day by giving one of her earnestly honest performances."

The Secret Bride is probably the most boring film Stanwyck has ever appeared in and has been almost forgotten. Even director William Dieterle admits, "of all the films I have directed, this is the picture I don't like to think about anymore."

The Woman in Red was Barbara's next film and the last in her contract with Warner Brothers. The film was based on Wallace Irwin's novel *North Shore* and was known by that title throughout production. Stanwyck appeared in the film as a professional horsewoman married to socialite Gene Raymond. Any plot the film could be credited with centered around the couple's problems dealing with his highbrow family and their obvious disdain for Stanwyck. *Variety* called the film "better than average entertainment" and said that Barbara enacted her role "with that straightforward sincerity which stamps her best portrayals."

After completion of her commitments to Warner Brothers, Barbara decided to take some well-deserved time off. The demands of continuing a successful career and fulfilling all the obligations that it entailed, while still struggling with a difficult situation at home, were exhausting. The fact that Barbara Stanwyck was a perfectionist both at home and in her work didn't make her life any easier. With each day it seemed that she and Frank fought more and grew further apart.

Fay's happiness was out of Barbara's hands. The story, a common one in Hollywood, was told over and over again on film but perhaps most poignantly just two years later when Janet Gaynor starred in *A Star Is Born*. In order to save himself, Fay needed work fast. Without it there was no tearing him away from the bottle. Only booze made it possible for him to live with his worst fear, that of becoming Mr. Barbara Stanwyck. It would have been a fate far too cruel for a performer who was once among the top in his profession.

While Barbara stayed home with her family, she put her career entirely in the hands of her agent and close friend Zeppo Marx. Marx was, of course, one of the famed Marx Brothers as well as one of the most successful agents in the business. As soon as the word spread that

Miss Barbara Stanwyck was accepting contract offers, Marx's office was deluged with calls from every studio in Hollywood. Eventually, serious negotiations were begun with Universal Pictures, but when these didn't work out the way Barbara hoped, Marx strongly advised her to free-lance rather than pursue any of the other offers.

Barbara agreed and accepted an offer from United Artists to star in *Red Salute*. It is obvious to anyone watching the film today that it had no pretensions toward anything but romantic comedy. Nevertheless, at the time of the film's release, it was greeted by more than a modicum of controversy. In the film Barbara appeared as a college girl whose interest in a young radical has turned her toward Communism. Robert Young is a young American soldier, patriotic to the extreme, who crosses paths with Stanwyck the radical, and tries to show her the error of her ideals during a cross-country trip in a stolen house trailer.

Red Salute was Stanwyck's first comedy, and she handled herself commendably, especially during the scenes of banter and bickering with Robert Young. For his part, Young was impressed with Stanwyck during the film's production. He remembers, in particular, her incredible punctuality. Each morning Young would show up a few minutes early and was amazed that no matter how early he arrived, Barbara was already there, on the set, reading her script. After a while he made a game of it, coming in a little earlier each day, hoping to beat Stanwyck at least once. Barbara kept a watchful eye on her co-star's increasingly earlier arrivals, unaware of his motives. When Young finally expressed total exasperation, Barbara thought the situation hysterically funny.

For the most part *Red Salute* was not a success. It was banned in several cities and protested in many others. Considering the fact that Stanwyck is brought back to Americanism before the film's climax, these reactions were somewhat surprising. Critic Richard Watts summed up his opinion of the film adroitly: "It should be enough to say of *Red Salute* that it is amiably played by Miss Barbara Stanwyck and Robert Young, that it is a dim carbon copy of the mood of *It Happened One Night* and that it was made in Hollywood."

"I'll never divorce Frank Fay and Hollywood can't make me do it," Barbara angrily told one columnist early in 1935. "They can jabber as much as they please, say whatever comes into their heads, gossip from now 'til Doomsday. If I can't stay married and stay in pictures, I'll get out of pictures."

The denials were made in vain. There was nothing unusual about the problems haunting the Stanwyck–Fay marriage. More than half the marriages in Hollywood probably faced the same troubles at one time or another, and many of them hadn't lasted nearly as long as the Fays'. What helped the Fays' marriage last as long as it did was Stanwyck's indomitable fighting spirit and her inordinate need for the security of a family and home life.

What finally destroyed the Fay marriage was not Barbara's film career. It was Fay's failure at a film career; the decreasing need for his vaudeville talents; his extraordinary ego; a severe drinking problem; and, probably more than anything else, his violent temper. Not that

Stanwyck was a slouch in the temper department. She could and would give as good as she got, but her priorities were clear, and Fay and their marriage were always on the top of the list. Priorities aside, Barbara Stanwyck had a great deal of pride in her own character to contend with. She was no quitter and couldn't bear the thought of anyone selling her as one. She had been the downtrodden Ruby Stevens long enough, and she had fought hard to put herself in a position where she could hold her head up high. She was determined that Ruby Stevens was a thing of the past and would stay that way. She was fighting for her own survival as well as Frank Fay's and that of their marriage.

During the summer of 1935, however, the marriage reached its crisis point. Fay's drinking problem was becoming increasingly worse and over the past few months had often caused embarrassing headlines. The press coverage of his arrest for drunken driving and hit-and-run, earlier in the year, had been damaging enough, but since then there had been more than a few comments about Fay's drunken sprees and alcohol-induced public arguments. The worst of these came on November 9 when Fay and Eddie Mannix, general studio manager of MGM, almost came to blows at the famed Brown Derby restaurant.

At home he was just as unpredictable and just as much out of control. At times he could be the perfect family man, solicitous of Barbara's needs and extremely proud of her success. When out in public, Fay made it perfectly clear that he was "the star" in the family and Stanwyck merely "his wife" whom he "allowed" to work. The tight rein he kept on the little woman was visible at all times. When drunk, he was capable of abhorrent behavior with no aversion to brutality. At one point, when drunk and arguing with Stanwyck, Fay scooped young Dion up in his arms and threw him into the swimming pool.

Privately, Barbara had threatened divorce many times, but Fay had just laughed, knowing how desperately she wanted to avoid such a move. Eventually, though, she could stand it no longer. Pride and public face aside, it just wasn't worth it anymore. The arguments, the beatings, the public humiliation all became intolerable, and in August of 1935, Barbara and Dion moved out of the house she and Fay had built in Brentwood Heights.

Almost immediately, she filed papers for a divorce, and by November the Fays had reached an agreement on a property settlement. Although lawyers for Barbara promised that there would be no specific incidents cited, they did explain to the press that Barbara's petition was based on mental cruelty. The Fays signed a predivorce settlement on December 31, 1935. Among other terms, Barbara was given full custody of Dion, although it was specified that Frank could visit twice a week. Fay relinquished all claims to the couple's home in Brentwood Heights, and Barbara and Dion moved back in.

While Stanwyck's lawyers haggled over the terms of her divorce, her agent diligently lined up enough work to keep her busy and keep her mind off the failure of her marriage. Her talents were eagerly sought after by all of the studios, and within the next eighteen months she would make films for RKO, Twentieth Century–Fox, Metro, Paramount, and United Artists. If Crawford was the queen of Metro, Davis the future queen of Warners, and Claudette Colbert the queen of Paramount, Stanwyck was without a doubt the queen of the independents.

RKO had announced in the spring of 1935 that Barbara would soon star for them in a film entitled *Shooting Star*, based on the life of the legendary woman sharpshooter Annie Oakley. Soon after filing for divorce and moving back into her Brentwood home, she threw herself into the part.

Annie Oakley was as straight a talker as she was a shooter, and her indomitable spirit made the role exceptionally well suited to Stanwyck's own personality. Director George Stevens came to the film directly from his success in guiding Katharine Hepburn through *Alice Adams*, and he managed to bring the same touches of poignancy and humor to this picture as he had to *Alice Adams*. Annie Oakley was Stanwyck's first Western, and she handled the shooting and riding admirably. Although she and Preston Foster didn't exactly burn up the screen with their chemistry, they did work well together and the film was extremely successful. Critics, as usual, were impressed with Barbara's work. The *New York World-Telegram* wrote that, "The talented and attractive Barbara Stanwyck gives by far the best screen performance of her career. Miss Stanwyck plays the role with such commendable restraint and with such feeling for the character that she almost becomes Annie Oakley." Critic Richard Watts praised the entire film and said that "Miss Stanwyck has never been more real and touching than she is in the title role."

A Message to Garcia, Barbara's next film, was something of a letdown. The film was made for Twentieth Century–Fox, and, for the first time in quite a few years, Barbara took second billing, to John Boles and Wallace Beery. Why Stanwyck ever accepted a role in this film or agreed to the lesser billing will never be understood. Even with her extraordinary acting skills, she was straining credibility as a Cuban girl of Spanish descent. For the most part, critics ignored the film and the public stayed away.

Such was not the case with *The Bride Walks Out*, a romantic comedy in which Stanwyck shared top honors with Robert Young and Gene Raymond. Stanwyck had a great deal of fun making the film, and it was apparent in the finished product. The director, Leigh Jason, remembers working with Stanwyck as "a delight" and adds that she was "a real craftsman. She was the only one I ever worked with who would dig to the bitter end for what you really wanted—and then gave it to you." The film opened at Radio City Music Hall during the summer of 1936 and was reasonably successful at the box office.

Paramount Pictures had signed Barbara to a one-picture deal, and during this period they were rumored to be preparing one of two roles for her. The most promising seemed to be a lead opposite Gary Cooper in *Invitation to Happiness*. If that didn't meet her approval, they wanted her for the lead in Ferenc Molnár's story *The Pastry Baker's Wife*. Neither of these films was made, for reasons unknown. At the same time Metro was considering her to play opposite Cary Grant in *Holiday*. The role went to Katharine Hepburn, however, and Grant and Stanwyck, two of film's most respected actors, never again had the opportunity to work together.

Naturally, Barbara's life was undergoing many changes during the days following her divorce. She sold the house in Brentwood to Jack Oakie for over $80,000 and then, with the help of Zeppo Marx, found a beautiful 140-acre ranch in the San Fernando Valley. She and Marx went into business together breeding horses at the ranch, called Marwyck. Meanwhile she and Dion took up residence there, far from the ever-watchful eyes of the Hollywood gossips. She socialized only with her closest friends, Zeppo and Marion Marx, Jack and Mary Benny, Joan Crawford, and Joel McCrea. Buck Mack, who had been a beau of her sister Mildred Stevens's twenty years earlier and had known Barbara as a funny little redhead with pigtails, moved into Marwyck and ran the ranch for her while she worked in films. When she needed an escort, she accepted dates from George Brent, or else she set tongues wagging by appearing on the arm of an unknown but dashingly handsome gentleman, her brother, Malcolm, now working in Hollywood as an extra using his middle name, Byron.

CHAPTER 16

At Marwyck, Barbara found a peace and contentment that she had never known before. Situated more than thirty miles from Hollywood in the town of Northridge, Barbara's home was a long, rambling Irish farmhouse built of rough gray stone and topped with a thatched roof. Inside, the decor was cheerful with a yellow carpeted living room dominated by an enormous brown marble fireplace. Next to the living room was the "playroom," decorated in redwood trim with a hand-braided light gray rug and furniture made of chromium and scarlet leather. On one side of the house was a long covered porch with a red flagstone floor. The porch looked over a wide terrace and a large swimming pool to the valley below where, in a rectangular pattern, were set the whitewashed stables, paddocks, foaling and brood-mare barns. Circling the beautiful groomed lawn was a silken half-mile track.

Even with all these creature comforts, though, it was the Santa Susanna hills nearby and the rolling valleys that Barbara came to love.

She'd been a city girl all her life, but she loved nothing more than "to dress in breeches and sneakers all day long." More importantly, she felt this was the best of all possible worlds for Dion. "He can have his own pony and a dozen pancakes for breakfast," she said enthusiastically.

Shortly after settling in at the ranch, Barbara invited writer Dixie Willson to visit her there. It was an unusual move for Stanwyck to make. Although she had always been cautious and cooperative with the press when it concerned her career, her private life had been taboo. The only time she spoke of it publicly was when she felt it necessary to respond to the various rumors surrounding her marriage to Fay. It's possible that her interview with Willson was meant to make it clear that Barbara Stanwyck was alive and well and surviving very nicely without Frank Fay, thank you. It was possibly one of the most revealing interviews of Barbara's career.

She spoke frankly with Dixie Willson on a number of subjects. When asked what she liked best . . . and least about life in Hollywood, she replied, "Best . . . that it gives me a place to call home. Least . . . the fanfare and hullabaloo that seem to be a part of pictures. I really don't know why there should be fanfare, for people who play in pictures are not incredible human beings. And I never quite know why the foremost impression of Hollywood should be glamour, because glamour actually has nothing to do with making pictures at all."

When asked if her elaborate spread at Marwyck didn't represent the type of glamour associated with Hollywood, Barbara quietly disagreed. "Everyone in the world has a home. And everyone's home, whatever and wherever it is, means to them exactly what my home means to me. . . . A place where, if you demand, there can be peace."

Before parting, Barbara and Dixie discussed Stanwyck's new beginning and what she would change about her past. She was adamant. "I wouldn't change anything. There are things I wish I could forget, but I wouldn't change them. You see, I really have very little to regret . . . and I have what I wanted . . . home and the baby." In response to Dixie's final question, Barbara laughed poignantly. "Is there anything more I wish for? No . . . nothing more. I've stopped wishing."

Marion and Zeppo Marx were Barbara's closest friends, and often the three of them would hit one Hollywood nightspot or another. One evening on the way to the Trocadero, Zeppo told Barbara they had a special friend they wanted her to meet that evening. He kept calling this friend "R.T.," which Barbara misunderstood to be Artique. That evening the Marxes were even more solicitous than usual and seemed obsessed with the whereabouts of Mr. Artique, "whoever the hell he was."

Finally a handsome young man approached their table. The Marxes greeted him effusively and introduced him to Barbara. It was the mysterious Mr. Artique, Robert Taylor. Taylor joined them at their table, and the four of them spent an enjoyable evening together during which Barbara and Bob danced together quite often. Barbara was impressed the next morning when she received a box of long-stem red roses from Taylor, thanking her for "a thoroughly delightful evening." She was thrilled a little while later when he called and asked if she'd go dancing with him at the Beverly Wilshire. Barbara agreed, and in a few short days she and Taylor became close friends. They went to Ocean Park together and rode the roller coaster, often taking Dion along.

Before long, friends saw a difference in Barbara. She seemed to glow from within as she never had before. Whether riding a couple of thoroughbreds together or dancing cheek to cheek at a Hollywood nightspot, Barbara Stanwyck and Robert Taylor had the look of a couple very much in love. Although it would be quite some time before Barbara or Bob would confirm the seriousness of their relationship, she knew soon after meeting the magnetic Mr. Taylor that he was most definitely the man for her.

Taylor had been born Spangler Arlington Brugh on August 5, 1911, in Filley, Nebraska. Young Taylor had drifted into dramatics at Pomona College, where he appeared in such productions as *Camille* and *The Importance of Being Earnest*. While there he was offered an MGM contract, but he turned it down, telling talent scout Ben Piazza that he wanted to finish college first. Taylor graduated in June 1933 and began studying at the Neely Dixon Dramatic School. Meanwhile, his father became ill and died in October 1933. His mother then moved to Los Angeles to be near her son, and for the next three years Ruth Brugh ruled every aspect of Bob's life. She objected to his dates, his clothes, his habits, and anything else that might conflict with her own rigid and oppressive standards.

In February 1934, Taylor was signed to a seven-year contract at Metro-Goldwyn-Mayer. Metro changed his name to Robert Taylor, paid him thirty-five dollars a week and turned him over to drama coach Oliver Tinsdell. Although Taylor photographed handsomely, Metro executives did not yet hold his dramatic talents in much regard, and their first move was to loan him to Twentieth Century–Fox for a role in *Handy Andy*. Following this, Taylor was loaned to Universal for two small roles before finally being given a bit part in Metro's *A Wicked Woman*. More bit parts followed before he was cast opposite Chester Morris and Virginia Bruce in *Society Doctor*. He and Miss Bruce worked well together, and at last Metro began getting fan mail about their new contract player. Metro quickly paired him again with Miss Bruce in *Times Square Lady*. John Gilbert and Virginia Bruce were in the process of divorcing, and soon Taylor and Bruce became a hot item. As their romance became more serious, Taylor grew more independent of his mother and soon moved into his own apartment. Miss Bruce and Taylor broke up before long, and Taylor began a relationship with actress Irene Hervey. Metro, however, would not allow any talk of marriage. As far as Metro executives were concerned, women preferred their matinee idols unmarried.

By now, Taylor's career was doing nicely, and the seriousness with which he approached his work was gaining him a great deal of respect. One of his co-stars from this period, Loretta Young, recalls Taylor as "a surprisingly normal person, neither fussy nor conceited. He was simply doing his work and letting matters take their own course."

By the time Taylor approached Barbara Stanwyck's table that night in the Trocadero, he had already parted company with Irene Hervey, and he had already been told by Metro that they had just cast him opposite Miss Stanwyck in *His Brother's Wife*. Taylor and Stanwyck enjoyed working together during the production of *His Brother's Wife*. Although the script left a great deal to be desired, their own romance lent more than the usual credibility to their love scenes. Director W. S. Van Dyke liked to shoot everything in one take and was particularly pleased to see how well both Barbara and Bob worked under such conditions. Although reviews of the film were mixed, the Stanwyck–Taylor romance brought the public out en masse. The columns were full of the town's favorite lovers, Barbara and Bob. The couple was followed everywhere. Photographers snapped their pictures dancing, smoking, talking, even standing in front of Taylor's car. The romance had captured the imagination of the public as well as the press.

Stanwyck's straightforward manner of speaking to the press, combined with her distinctive Brooklyn accent and the number of tough-girl roles she had played in her films, gave her a somewhat unwarranted reputation as a woman of experience. She had, of course, intentionally hidden her own vulnerability behind this facade. In years to come she would appear in a great many different types of roles, but for the most part it would be her portrayals of tough, hardened women that would be remembered and make her Hollywood's favorite bitch.

In reality, she was a sensitive, kindhearted, hardworking woman who simply had no tolerance for laziness, dishonesty, or double-talk. At the time of her romance with Taylor she was a divorced woman, twenty-nine years of age, with a three-year-old son and a desperate need for affection. Nevertheless, it was with her usual facade firmly in place that she remarked, regarding Taylor, "The boy's got a lot to learn and I've got a lot to teach."

Their friends nodded knowingly as Bob tried to sum up his fascination for the woman he loved. "Barbara," he admitted, "is not the sort of woman I'd have met in Nebraska."

CHAPTER 17

Barbara's distinctive manner of speaking and easily recognizable voice made her ideal for radio work, and throughout the thirties she was one of the actresses most sought after by that medium. During the thirties and forties, abridged versions of current film hits were a staple of radio broadcasting, and such shows as *Lux Radio Theatre* and *Screen Guild Playhouse* were among the most popular shows on the air.

As part of their initial publicity campaign for *His Brother's Wife*, Metro had arranged for Taylor and Stanwyck to appear in a radio adaptation of the film on WABC. Although this wasn't Barbara's first performance on radio, it was one of her earliest, and it was her first radio drama. After that she began appearing on radio more often, and on August 3, 1936, made what would turn out to be the first of many appearances on Cecil B. DeMille's *Lux Radio Theatre*. DeMille used Stanwyck more than any other actress, sixteen times between 1936 and 1943. Many of these shows were, of course, adaptations of her own films, but more importantly, *Lux Radio Theatre* gave Barbara the opportunity to appear in many roles she wouldn't otherwise have had the chance to do. These included *Main Street, These Three, Dark Victory, Morning Glory, Only Yesterday, Smilin' Through, Penny Serenade, This Above All,* and *Wuthering Heights.* Her performance in this last show was particularly moving.

Meanwhile, of course, Stanwyck still had quite a few film commitments lined up. The first of these was *The Plough and the Stars.* The story was filmed in the summer of 1936 for RKO. Although Stanwyck had top billing and her role was an important one, the film didn't give her much to do. Preston Foster played Stanwyck's husband in this film about the 1916 Easter rebellion in Dublin, and they made an extremely attractive couple. Although Sean O'Casey's drama originally dealt with the effects of the rebellion on a cross section of the populace, Dudley Nichols' screenplay centered on the married life of Jack and Nora Clitheroe (Foster and Stanwyck). Director John Ford brought a special grace and bittersweet quality to much of the film although his integration of actual newsreel footage was somewhat disquieting.

After completing the film Ford went to Hawaii for a brief vacation, and while he was gone, executives at RKO screened the film. Deciding that Stanwyck and Preston would be more interesting if they were unmarried lovers, RKO assigned an assistant director and recalled the cast for additional filming. It was a disastrous move. Barbara was extremely unhappy with the revised storyline, and during the filming of the additional footage she gave a lackluster performance. The film, as completed, was uneven and sometimes confusing. Although Ford was furious at RKO's tampering, the studio had the final say, and it was RKO's version of the film that was shown to American audiences, to mixed reviews at best. Ford's film, on the other hand, was shown in Ireland and England, where it was well received. It is Ford's version that survives and is shown on television today.

From RKO, Stanwyck moved to Twentieth Century–Fox, where she and Joel McCrea appeared in a somewhat inconsequential but entertaining film entitled *Banjo on My Knee.* The film was based on a folk novel by Harry Hamilton concerning a couple of young newlyweds prevented from consummating their marriage when he runs into trouble with the law and has to flee. While Barbara awaits his return she becomes an entertainer, and during this segment of the film

Barbara sings both in solo and in duet (with Buddy Ebsen and Tony Martin). This was the first time Barbara was called on to sing in one of her films, and although she didn't prove to have any major vocal skills, her singing was pleasant enough for *Variety* to note that "her voice is good enough to have her singing in plenty of pictures to come."

Stanwyck and McCrea went directly from Twentieth Century–Fox to Paramount, where they worked together again in *Internes Can't Take Money*, the first of the films about Dr. Jim Kildare. Director Alfred Santell enjoyed working with Barbara and was impressed to find that not only had she memorized all of her own lines by the start of the film but everyone else's as well.

The romance of Barbara Stanwyck and Robert Taylor had continued to provide reams of copy for the fan magazines. Twentieth Century–Fox decided to make the most of it, realizing that a film starring the lovers would mean big box office. The film at hand was known during initial production as *Private Enemy*, but the title was changed midstream to *This Is My Affair* for obvious reasons.

The film was a costume drama set during the turn of the century. Barbara played Lil Duryea, a music hall entertainer in love with a U.S. Navy officer (Taylor, of course) who is working undercover as a bank robber for President McKinley. When McKinley is assassinated and Taylor's cover gets into trouble, there is no one to vouch for his innocence. It is left to Stanwyck to plead his case to President Roosevelt. Barbara looked particularly lovely in the period costumes and, again, had the opportunity to sing in the film.

She and Taylor were delighted to be working together, and director William Seiter felt that, if anything, their romance made production easier and, of course, added a great deal of fire to their love scenes. The sincere affection between Taylor and Stanwyck was apparent throughout pre-production and filming and contributed to a relaxed atmosphere on the set. Each remained on the set during the other's work, and shooting schedules were arranged so that they had the same days off. During the pre-recording of Barbara's song from the film, "I Hum a Waltz," Taylor watched intently from a chair within the orchestra. The entire orchestra broke up into good-natured laughter when Stanwyck threw her hands up in frustration and shouted at

Taylor, "If you don't stop looking at me like a mooing cow, I'm going to walk right out of here. Come out of that orchestra so I don't see you while I'm trying to sing!"

Earlier in the year, while working with Joel McCrea in *Banjo on My Knee*, Barbara had heard that Samuel Goldwyn had decided to produce a film based on Olive Higgins Prouty's extremely successful novel *Stella Dallas*. The story had been filmed earlier—a 1925 silent starring Belle Bennett—and it was recognized as one of the greatest stories of mother's love ever told. Stanwyck wanted the part and wanted it desperately, but Goldwyn seemed to have other ideas. He offered the role first to Ruth Chatterton, who turned it down, feeling it was "too unpleasant."

Meanwhile, Stanwyck's interest in the role came to the attention of Joel McCrea who appealed to Goldwyn on her behalf. Still Goldwyn held out. He admitted to Barbara that he didn't believe she could handle the role and felt that she was too young. On the other hand, King Vidor, the director, was entirely in Barbara's corner. He and McCrea both put pressure on Goldwyn, who finally agreed to let Barbara test for the part.

At first Stanwyck was infuriated at the suggestion that she needed to test for anything. She was a well-respected actress with hundreds of glowing reviews to attest to her talents, and she hated tests. Nevertheless, Goldwyn was adamant, and once McCrea had convinced her it was the only way she would get the role, Barbara agreed to test in a scene from the film.

Anne Shirley had been cast as the daughter, and she, Stanwyck, and Vidor spent an entire day working on the five-minute scene chosen for the test. The scene chosen was the birthday party segment when Stella and her daughter realize that no one is going to show up, and Stanwyck and Shirley worked together beautifully. Once Samuel Goldwyn saw the test, he knew that Barbara would be perfect for the role.

Goldwyn surrounded Barbara with an excellent cast including John Boles, Barbara O'Neil, Alan Hale, Marjorie Main, and Anne Shirley. King Vidor, of course, was a top director, having already been involved in almost forty films including the recent hit about a down-and-out fighter and his son, *The Champ*.

The story of Stella Dallas is, of course, well known by now. Stella was a cheap young woman who coveted wealth and a position in society. She marries well but just doesn't fit into her husband's world, and after the birth of their daughter they separate. Stella is a devoted and sacrificing mother to the girl. When her daughter reaches her teens, Stella realizes that the best thing would be for the girl to live with her well-to-do father and his wife. It means giving up her daughter once and for all, and she does so. Later, having secretly watched her daughter's wedding, she walks away, bravely holding her head up high.

The film is full of incredibly touching moments, all beautifully handled by the cast. Nevertheless, it is Stanwyck's film from beginning to end. Her characterization of Stella is complete. She turned herself over willingly to designer Omar Kiam, who rebuilt her completely, padding everything down to and including her legs. Rather than rely on wigs most of the time, she had her own hair styled in the frizzled, blowzy look necessary and even allowed cotton to be stuffed into her cheeks when necessary. All of this helped her turn in an incredibly believable performance.

Anne Shirley mirrored the feelings of most of those who had worked with Barbara before:

> The whole word is pro. Miss Stanwyck was hired and paid to perform a service. She presented herself for work before time. She was prepared to the very top of her ability. Dialogue learned perfectly. Hair, clothes, energy ready. There was no "I am not feeling well today" or "I have a personal problem" and then a request to be excused for the day, as happens with so many actresses. I believe she clearly felt she was in a business. By a business, I mean that it was not something in which you indulged yourself. You gave a day's work for a day's pay. Barbara Stanwyck did not think of it as a super art form, but rather as a business. And this is rare.

Barbara received the most glowing reviews of her career for her work in *Stella Dallas*. *The New York Times* wrote:

> Miss Stanwyck's portrayal is as courageous as it is fine. Ignoring the flattery of make-up man and camera, she plays Stella as Mrs. Prouty drew her—coarse, cheap, common, given to sleazy dresses, to undulations in her walk, to (with the aid of pads and extra layers of this and that) fatty degeneration of the profile. And yet magnificent as a mother.

Other reviews followed suit, such as this one from the *New York Herald Tribune*:

> Miss Stanwyck's Stella is more restrained and credible than Belle Bennett's in the silent version. She gives an underlying strength to a weak, fatuous woman that makes the portrayal vividly sympathetic and lends needed motivation to the tale. It is her best acting in years.

The Academy of Motion Picture Arts and Sciences seemed to agree because when the nominations for 1937 were announced, Barbara's name was among them, along with Irene Dunne for *The Awful Truth*, Greta Garbo for *Camille*, Janet Gaynor for *A Star Is Born*, and Luise Rainer for *The Good Earth*. Further admiration for the film was shown by the Academy's nomination of Anne Shirley in the supporting actress category.

Although the competition was tough, Stanwyck was optimistic about her chances to win and attended the ceremonies at the Biltmore Hotel on March 10, 1938, with Robert Taylor. Disappointment came early in the evening when Anne Shirley lost to Alice Brady (for *In Old Chicago*). This was followed by Luise Rainer's triumph for *The Good Earth*. Rainer had won the year before for *The Great Ziegfeld* and was so sure she wouldn't win again that she hadn't even shown up for the ceremony. Stanwyck was heartbroken and regretted the loss for years, commenting, "My life's blood was in that picture. I should have won."

CHAPTER 18

It was the same old story. Bette Davis had triumphed in *Of Human Bondage,* in 1934, and followed it with a "nothing" called *Housewife.* She followed her Academy Award–winning performance in *Dangerous* with a forgettable film called *The Golden Arrow.* Barbara Stanwyck had a great success in *Forbidden,* and then did the ill-conceived *Shopworn,* and now with critics singing her praises for *Stella Dallas,* Stanwyck was caught without a suitable follow-up film waiting.

Breakfast for Two was a sophisticated comedy of the sort popular in the thirties. Stanwyck's role in the film, opposite Herbert Marshall, was not a very demanding one. As a matter of fact, she had come to consider her work in comedy films as a form of relaxation and explained to the press:

> I couldn't possibly have followed *Stella* with another emotional role. It had run the gamut. So I had to let down and give the boys a chance. I do very little in *Breakfast for Two.* It's practically Herbert Marshall's picture.

I feel more comfortable in drama. It's more my field—but comedy has become relaxation. It's awfully easy—for me any-way—to do movie comedy. It's really like a vacation. I was playing—not working.

Barbara worked well with Alfred Santell, and he later commented that she was "all things a performer should be." Critics again were pleased and the *New York Herald Tribune* reported:

With excellent acting from a thoughtfully picked cast, cunning direction by Alfred Santell, and a steady flow of clever dialogue, this comedy is good entertainment.

Barbara Stanwyck shows intelligent understanding of [her] role. With commendable skill, she is both cocky and demure, assured and sorrowfully frustrated.

Once *Stella Dallas* was released, Barbara realized that she would have to be more selective about which roles she accepted if she was to continue the momentum that seemed to be building. Limited, nonex-clusive contracts had been signed with RKO and Twentieth Century–Fox, and both studios sent her a constant stream of scripts. Ordinarily, Barbara would have had no trouble selecting one script or another; those submitted were certainly no worse than some she had appeared in. Now, however, she was looking for a better-caliber film than the programmers she was offered, and none seemed to suit her require-ments. Script after script was returned to the studios as unacceptable. Eventually, both studios became intolerant of what they considered an unreasonable dissatisfaction on Stanwyck's part, and Stanwyck was put on suspension.

Barbara took her contracts seriously and would never have consid-ered defaulting on an agreement without reason. As far as she was concerned, the scripts offered were just not worth doing, and she felt it was the studios' responsibility to find properties worthy of an actress of her talent and reputation. She was certainly not so independently wealthy that she could thumb her nose at the industry and had no intention of doing so. She was proud of her reputation in the industry for her professionalism; nevertheless, she felt that a little pressure on the studios for better scripts couldn't hurt.

During this period of suspension Barbara filled her time with work on her ranch and whatever radio appearances she was offered. When one of her two horses won at the Santa Anita race track, she quipped, "I'm glad someone in the family is working." This period of comparable inactivity was a disconcerting one for Barbara. Her work in films had become the centerpiece of her life, and without it she felt at odds. Sometime after the suspensions were resolved, Barbara talked about the motivations for her strong stand against the studios.

> If you feel a thing strongly enough, you should have the courage of your convictions to carry it through. That's my philosophy, and it's gotten me into plenty of hot water. The reason I argue is because I know myself. There are things I know I can do, and other things I can't do.
>
> A lot of times, a studio knows better than a star whether or not a picture will be a success. But I have to go on my instincts. Sometimes I've been wrong, but more often I've been right. Last year I was suspended for seven months because I wouldn't do two pictures at two different studios. They were rabid about these "great" pictures. But neither one has yet been made. That's vindication right there, I think.
>
> I have to keep working to keep happy. They could work me every day and I'd love it. Those seven months away from the studio I didn't know what to do with myself. But if the same argument came up tomorrow, I'd probably go on another suspension. That's how I am.

Stanwyck grew weary waiting for RKO and Twentieth to come up with appealing film work and began looking around herself. One film she wanted desperately to star in was *Jezebel*. She pleaded with Jack Warner to give her the role, but it went to Warners' reigning queen, Bette Davis.

The role was to win Davis her second Academy Award. Barbara was an inveterate movie fan, and after seeing *Jezebel*, she was so impressed by Davis' performance that she called to tell her so. "I'm sorry, but Miss Davis is asleep," she was told by Davis' maid. Barbara called the next day. Davis was asleep again. The third day, the same story. Finally,

98

after calling a fourth time, and receiving the same response, Barbara left a message—"When Snow White wakes up, tell her I thought she was marvelous in *Jezebel!*"

Twentieth Century—Fox couldn't offer Stanwyck anything to compete with *Jezebel*, but she did finally agree to wrap up her contract with them by appearing in a remake of *Gallant Lady*. The film was retitled *Always Goodbye* and co-starred Herbert Marshall, Ian Hunter, and Lynn Bari. It was another story of mother love and sacrifice, but only a poor man's version of *Stella Dallas*. *Variety* was generally unimpressed with the film but gave Barbara her usual pat on the back: "Both Miss Stanwyck and Marshall turn in fine performances in the face of the material they have to work with. Miss Stanwyck does a highly sympathetic role and Marshall also has the audience with him throughout, yet it all doesn't jell for the touching sock."

Having fulfilled her responsibilities at Fox, Barbara next set out to do the same at RKO. Happily, the film at hand was a somewhat more appealing property. *The Mad Miss Manton* was the first of three films Barbara would make with Henry Fonda, but their friendship wouldn't really hit its stride until their second film, three years later. Nevertheless, *The Mad Miss Manton* was a delightful screwball comedy in which Barbara portrayed a madcap heiress who, together with a group of her debutante friends, solves a double murder. The direction, by Leigh Jason, had a light touch and Barbara again proved that she was as comfortable with comedy as she was with drama. Nevertheless, the production was not without its problems. The film was shot during the summer of 1938, and some of the outdoor scenes had to be done at the Warner ranch in 100-degree temperatures—with Stanwyck and the debs wrapped in furs. As for Henry Fonda, he was totally disinterested in the character he was asked to play and went through production feeling rather sullen and unreceptive. Thankfully, his resentment toward the picture didn't prevent him from giving his usual professional performance.

Critics this time were impressed, and it was immediately obvious that the Stanwyck—Fonda pairing was one well worth repeating. "The romance in the hands of Henry Fonda and Barbara Stanwyck," wrote Frank Nugent in *The New York Times*, "is refreshingly natural, considering the unnatural background it moves against. The Wilson Collison–Philip Epstein script is dredged with bright lines and cheerfully absurd situations."

Cecil B. DeMille continued to use Stanwyck on the *Lux Radio Theatre* throughout this period but had somehow never had her perform in a film. Then, in late 1938, he began production on *Union Pacific* with a million-dollar budget and Barbara Stanwyck, Robert Preston, and Joel McCrea as his stars.

Barbara's role in *Union Pacific* was a plum. She was cast as Mollie Monahan, the Irish postmistress of the portable town that followed the building of the Union Pacific Railroad across the country. Stanwyck's portrayal of the strong-willed but well-loved woman was one of her best, encompassing many moods and giving her a chance, for the first time, to get involved in some rough-and-ready action. She worked closely with her stunt woman in the film and did many of her stunts herself. This was a facet of filmmaking she particularly enjoyed and would quickly become expert at.

Regis Toomey was also in the cast, in a small role that called for him to die and for Barbara to comfort him in that scene. He recalls "the compassion that seemed to comfort me as she bent over me—not playacting compassion—real compassion."

Cecil B. DeMille was notorious for his own professionalism and demands for perfection. He was a director who was very hard to please and seldom satisfied. Nevertheless, when he wrote his autobiography some years later, it was Barbara Stanwyck he singled out as his favorite actress:

> I would have to say that I have never worked with an actress
> who was more cooperative, less temperamental, and a better
> workman, to use my term of highest compliment, than Barbara
> Stanwyck. I have directed, and enjoyed working with many fine
> actresses, some of whom are also good workmen; but when I
> count over those of whom my memories are unmarred by any
> unpleasant recollection of friction on the set or unwillingness to
> do whatever the role required or squalls of temperament or
> temper, Barbara's name is the first that comes to mind, as one on

whom a director can always count to do her work with all her heart.

The premiere of *Union Pacific* was launched with a fine day-trip on the Union Pacific train from Los Angeles to Omaha, Nebraska. On board were Cecil B. DeMille, Barbara Stanwyck, and a hoard of studio and railroad executives. The film's reviews were consistently favorable, and *Union Pacific* was one of the biggest hits of 1938.

The next year, 1939, was an incredible year in film history. Never before or since have there been so many classic films or films of such high quality released in one year. *Gone With the Wind, The Wizard of Oz, Mr. Smith Goes to Washington, Dark Victory,* and *Wuthering Heights* were all released during that year, and Barbara was to have her own classic. Clifford Odets' play, *Golden Boy,* starring John Garfield and Frances Farmer, had been one of Broadway's biggest hits in 1937. Frances Farmer had turned her back on Hollywood to work with Odets and The Actors Guild and although her own success in New York had equaled the play's, filmland was unforgiving. She wasn't even considered for the film version of *Golden Boy.* Instead, Columbia signed Barbara Stanwyck to appear as Lorna Moon, a dame from Newark.

Harry Cohn wanted to use John Garfield in the film to re-create his characterization of Joe, the young man torn between his violin and the boxing ring. The director, Rouben Mamoulian, however, had seen a test done for Paramount by a twenty-one-year-old newcomer, William Holden. Mamoulian felt Holden had the qualities he was looking for and fought to have him cast in the film. Cohn eventually agreed, and Stanwyck, Holden, and Mamoulian went to work along with Lee J. Cobb and Adolphe Menjou.

Prior to *Golden Boy,* William Holden had only done bit parts in two or three films, and his acting experience was minimal. The part of Joe was an enormous challenge for him, and throughout the early stages of production there was some question whether he was up to it. Holden's inexperience made him difficult to direct, and Mamoulian found the experience frustrating. To make matters worse, Holden would sometimes try to tell the director how to direct. Mamoulian was not amused, and when he and Cohn viewed the rushes, they did so in an uneasy silence. Cohn began to pressure Mamoulian to dismiss Holden, but the director was hesitant to do so; somehow he still felt the actor could fill the bill.

Tensions on the set grew, and as they did, the pressures on Bill Holden worsened. He was working a seventeen-hour day: working on the set, training in a gym for the scenes in the boxing ring, and studying the violin so that he could finger the strings expertly in close-ups. Before long he seemed to be taking the express route toward a nervous breakdown.

It was at this point that Barbara stepped in and took the situation in hand. She began by confronting Harry Cohn. Through the years Cohn had intimidated many people, but Stanwyck had never been one of them. She urged Cohn to give Holden a chance. "My God, he's only had a week," she yelled. "Leave him alone and he'll find himself. I don't know of any actor who could do it better. If you want youth, he's got it. If you want a fairly good boxer, he's it. He can't be champion, because that's not the story. He's a very sensitive, intelligent young man. I don't know what other qualities you want. None of us can walk on water." With Cohn convinced that Holden deserved a better chance, Barbara began working closely with the young actor on every facet of his performance. *Golden Boy* was Stanwyck's thirty-fifth film, and she had a great deal to offer Holden in the way of professional guidance. After each day's filming the two retired to Barbara's dressing room to work on the next day's scenes. Barbara coached him on everything from nuances of speech to proper movement in front of the cameras. These evening sessions continued throughout the production. And with Stanwyck's assistance, Holden grew more assured and comfortable in front of the cameras.

During filming, Barbara even went so far as to let takes get printed that did not show her performance to the best advantage, if these takes happened to be more flattering to Bill Holden. In the end Stanwyck and Holden both succeeded in giving sterling performances. Mamoulian was more than satisfied with Holden's work and later commented, "chemistry, looks, that mysterious quality, and iron determination, carried him through. Also the will to work and Barbara Stanwyck."

Barbara's sensitive performance as Lorna Moon ranks with the best work she has done. As usual, she mesmerized both the fans and the film critics. *Variety's* review was representative: "Miss Stanwyck is standout as the girl first in love with Menjou, but later the guiding influence setting Holden on the right path. Her performance does much to add a sincere ring to the picture."

As for William Holden, *Golden Boy* launched his career in style. He and Barbara became close friends, and throughout his forty-year career he always credited her with his success. To Holden she was "Queen," and each year, until his untimely death in 1981, he never failed to show his appreciation to Barbara Stanwyck by sending two dozen red roses and a white gardenia on April 1, the anniversary of the film's starting date.

CHAPTER 19

The romance between Robert Taylor and Barbara Stanwyck had continued unabated, and by early 1939 they were as much as living together. In 1937 Taylor had purchased the acreage adjoining Barbara's ranch in the San Fernando Valley, and shortly thereafter he began building his own home there. While still involved in building the house, Taylor was sent to England to film *A Yank at Oxford* with Maureen O'Sullivan, and during his absence Barbara took over supervision of the construction and decorating of Taylor's new home.

Before leaving for England, Bob Taylor had begged Barbara to marry him, but she was determined not to throw caution to the wind. She had her son's happiness to consider, as well as her own, and although Dion seemed to like Bob Taylor well enough, Barbara didn't want to make another mistake.

The months while Bob was in England were devastating for both Barbara and Bob. Cables flew back and forth, and telephone bills mounted. Later, Taylor would admit that in a desperate moment of loneliness he went to a London movie house to see *Stella Dallas* and cried throughout the film. When he returned to the States, his arms were full of gifts for Barbara and her son.

Upon his return Taylor found that work on his ranch had been completed, and he and Barbara settled into a comfortable domestic routine only slightly hampered by their separate residences. Barbara, Bob, and Dion represented a tight family unit, and Frank Fay was evidently nonplussed by the situation and brought suit against Barbara again, this time claiming that she was intentionally preventing Dion from spending time with him so that he would grow more accustomed to Taylor.

Barbara denied the accusations and demanded that the court order a psychiatric examination of Fay. She claimed that Fay had become obsessed with religion and was not fit to spend time with their son. As the battle grew more bitter, Barbara's attorneys submitted affidavits from the couple's friends, including Bill Frawley and Buck Mack, testifying to Fay's unsound mind. Frawley and Mack claimed that Fay would mutter a prayer over every cigarette he smoked and that once, at the Brown Derby, Fay had abased himself before "the Great God Nicotine." Furthermore, they stated that whenever driving past a church, Fay would remove his hands from the wheel and pray, thereby endangering the lives of others. Barbara further testified that Fay had once knocked her down "with a wallop to the jaw" at the Trocadero nightclub.

"I want my son to be happy," Barbara asserted to the press. "Above everything else, I want him to have that sure sense of security in his home, that sense of peace and stability that I missed so much in my own childhood. I can't let him be a little emotional foothold tossed about this way and that. I want to try to give him the courage and confidence to face life and make a good job of it. I know it takes hard knocks to develop! But he'll get those soon enough. I don't want him one of those so-called movie children. The spoiled and pampered variety. That's why I'm sending Dion to military school soon."

In the end the court left the child's custody in Barbara's hands. Soon afterward Fay ceased seeking time with young Dion, and eventually he bowed out of the child's life altogether.

By 1939 Hollywood was firmly entrenched in a never-ending war with its reputation as a modern-day Sodom and Gomorrah. Studio publicists and the Chamber of Commerce worked together to portray the people of Hollywood as hardworking, patriotic individuals. Fan magazines, such as *Photoplay, Modern Screen,* and *Screenland,* were then at their peak. The power of these magazines was incredible, and the studios eagerly sought the cooperation of these publications in spreading the word that the wages of sin were not tolerated in Hollywood or the film industry. The magazines, on the other hand, had to rely on the studios for a great deal of their materials, and so one hand washed the other. Nevertheless, every once in a while, members of the Hollywood press ignored the urging of the studios and wrote what they wanted. More often than not, this took the form of a written tirade from either Louella Parsons or Hedda Hopper, Hollywood's most powerful reporters, but once in a while, the trouble came from unexpected sources.

One of the more devastating of these surprises came in January 1939, when *Photoplay* published an article by Kirtley Baskette entitled "Hollywood's Unmarried Husbands & Wives." In one fell swoop, Baskette revealed the truth about the supposedly platonic relationships between Charles Chaplin and Paulette Goddard, Clark Gable and Carole Lombard, George Raft and Virginia Pine, and, of course, Robert Taylor and Barbara Stanwyck.

" 'Just friends' to the world at large," Baskette proclaimed, "yet nowhere has domesticity taken on so unique a character as in this unconventional fold." Baskette's exposé made it clear that these men and women, some of them the most well known and respected in the industry, were living together although legally unmarried. Some, Baskette revealed, such as Clark Gable and Constance Bennett, were still married to others.

Its secrets laid bare, Hollywood was horrified. Through the industry orders went out to the studios' contract players: "If you're living with someone—marry them!" Louis B. Mayer was one of the most domineering of studio moguls. More than any other studio, MGM was identified with family films and a reverence for a happy home life. Mayer looked at Metro's contract players as an extension of his own family. He delighted in telling Joan Crawford or Judy Garland, "This is your home. Think of me as your father. I only want what is good for you." Once, in the mid-thirties, Robert Taylor grew discontented with his salary at Metro and approached Mayer for a raise. As he came out of Mayer's office, his agent asked if he'd gotten the raise. "No," Taylor replied, "but I got a father!"

Although Louis B. Mayer was willing to tolerate Gable's relationship with Lombard and Taylor's with Stanwyck as long as the public was ignorant of the truth, Baskette's article had changed everything. The two men were given the same ultimatum. Gable was the first to comply, and on March 29, 1939, he and Lombard were married.

On Saturday, May 13, 1939, Barbara Stanwyck and Robert Taylor drove to the San Diego home of a friend, Thomas Whale. They were accompanied by Marion and Zeppo Marx, Buck Mack, and Louis B. Mayer's secretary, Ida Koverman. Hoping to evade the jinx of marrying on the thirteenth, the couple waited until after midnight to wed. Then, at 12:30 A.M. on May 14, Bob Taylor and Barbara Stanwyck were married by Justice of the Peace Phillip Smith. Barbara was dressed in a navy blue silk crepe dress and Bob in a brown business suit. Marion Marx served as Barbara's maid of honor, and Buck Mack was best man.

After breakfast the wedding party returned to Beverly Hills, where at two o'clock that afternoon Mr. and Mrs. Robert Taylor announced that they had been married. They explained that since Barbara was needed at Columbia Pictures, where she was still working on *Golden Boy*, their honeymoon would be delayed. During the conference Barbara wore her slender gold wedding band encircled with rubies and Bob's wedding gift to her of a gold St. Christopher medal engraved on the back GOD PROTECT HER BECAUSE I LOVE HER.

CHAPTER 20

After her marriage to Robert Taylor and the completion of *Golden Boy*, Barbara went to work again at Paramount in Mitchell Leisen's production of *Remember the Night*. Barbara's co-star in the film was Fred MacMurray, and the cast was rounded out by Beulah Bondi, Elizabeth Patterson, and Sterling Holloway. The script, by Preston Sturges, was warm and witty, and *Remember the Night* became another star in Stanwyck's crown. It remains, to this day, one of her most enduring films.

Meanwhile, Barbara's reputation for professionalism continued to grow. Chico Day, assistant director on *Remember the Night*, remembers one incident typical of those that endeared Barbara to the crews on every one of her pictures. One afternoon Leisen dismissed Barbara after she finished a scene. When Chico heard Stanwyck had been dismissed, he was confused. She had another scene scheduled for that afternoon. He immediately called her dressing room and reminded her of the scene yet to be done. He needn't have worried. "I know, dear,"

Barbara told him, "don't worry about me, ever. I always remain in the studio until the company wraps—ready, made up, hair dressed and wardrobed."

It was the same story on every film. Immediately upon reporting for work on a new picture, Barbara went around to each crew member and either introduced herself or renewed a previous acquaintance. The fact that Barbara remembered each of their names and the names of their wives and their children's birthdays left the crews in awe and totally in love with the woman they all called "Missy." Cameramen, electricians, script girls—all of them grew intensely protective of their Missy and she of them. When news reached her that one of them was in trouble, she simply took out her checkbook and took care of the financial end of the problem. It didn't matter what it was; too many doctor bills or too little work, Stanwyck was there to help. As often as not, the help came anonymously, but still the legend of Missy's kindness grew. Chico Day sums up the feelings of Hollywood's technical crews when he says unhesitatingly, "Miss Stanwyck is the greatest lady I ever worked with."

Stanwyck's reputation as a favorite of directors and her lack of allegiance to any one studio put her in an enviable position. Dozens of scripts were sent over for her perusal, and she chose only the best. After completing *Remember the Night*, Barbara was reunited with Frank Capra for her first starring role opposite Gary Cooper in *Meet John Doe*. Barbara loved working with Capra and accepted the part before even reading the script. Once production began Barbara wasn't disappointed. As she explained to a reporter at the time, "You make other pictures to live, but you live to make a Capra picture."

She and Cooper had a great deal in common and worked beautifully together. Cooper had made a successful career out of portraying ordinary, common men in an incredibly natural style. He was a man other men could identify with and yet not feel threatened by. Barbara Stanwyck was Cooper's female counterpart. More often than not, her characters were real women showing honest emotion and coping with problems in a way everyone could identify with. Her performances were so natural that they seemed almost effortless.

Production of the film took two months and for the most part was uneventful. The ending, however, presented a problem. The film was a blatant attack on fascism and called for a strong ending, but Capra and his screenwriter, Robert Riskin, couldn't come up with one they considered powerful enough. Riskin wrote four endings, and all of them were filmed. The set was built in an abandoned icehouse and, to help re-create the necessary snowstorm, the temperature was set at 10 degrees. It was under these conditions that the ending was shot, but even after filming was completed, Capra couldn't decide which version to use. The film was released in various cities with three different endings. None of the endings pleased him. Then, from nowhere, an anonymous suggestion signed "John Doe" came to Capra's attention. Capra called his crew back to the icehouse and reshot the ending. The new ending was still a little weak, but it was this ending that was used on all subsequent prints of the film.

Barbara's performance in *Meet John Doe* was one of her best. The film was enormously popular, and most critics considered it Capra's finest work. Naturally, Barbara's performance received the usual praise. William Brehnel wrote in the *New York World-Telegram:* "Mr. Capra's direction is brilliant . . . Gary Cooper has never been better . . . and Barbara Stanwyck is supremely good as the columnist, lovely and talented. They don't come better than this one."

By this time, Paulette Goddard and Charlie Chaplin had reacted to Baskette's article by marrying, and Goddard dropped out of her next scheduled film. The film was *The Lady Eve*, and Barbara stepped in to take Goddard's place opposite Henry Fonda in the delightful Preston Sturges comedy. Stanwyck and Fonda had worked together previously, of course, in *The Mad Miss Manton*, but Fonda's displeasure at that time had hindered the development of any friendship between the two professionals. Such was not the case with *The Lady Eve*. The two enormously enjoyed working together on the film, and forever after Henry Fonda would state unequivocally that Barbara Stanwyck was his favorite leading lady. Years later, in his autobiography, *My Life*, he wrote, "I've loved Barbara Stanwyck since I met her. She's a delightful woman. We've never had an affair. She's never encouraged me but, dammit, my wife will verify it, my daughter and son will confirm it and now you can all testify to the truth. Stanwyck can act the hell out of any part, and she can turn a chore into a challenge. She's fun and I'm glad I had the chance to make three movies with her. *The Lady Eve* was the best." Barbara responded to Fonda's confession, "Yes, *The Lady Eve* was a good picture, but about the rest of Fonda's talk, he was single when I was single and where was he?"

Besides allowing Stanwyck and Fonda to develop more fully their partnership's potential, *The Lady Eve* helped to develop another area of Barbara's screen personality. Until *Eve*, Barbara was well dressed on the screen but had never demanded or received much attention in this area. Of course, this was partially because Barbara's films stood on their own without the crutch of a fabulous wardrobe to redeem them. Some of Joan Crawford's films at Metro, for instance, relied on Crawford's spectacular clothes. Barbara's own manner of dress had always been rather simple. She favored tailored or unpretentious suits and dresses, and when on her ranch, she usually dressed in slacks and shirt. She seldom wore much jewelry except for various gifts from Bob Taylor and a diamond horseshoe-shaped ring to which she was partial.

On *The Lady Eve*, however, one of motion pictures' most renowned designers, Edith Head, was assigned to create Barbara's wardrobe She found Barbara's slim build and perfect posture a pleasure to work with. The clothes she designed for her, with a somewhat South American flair to them, were a sensation and launched a major trend all over the country. Stanwyck was thrilled with Head's work and the public reaction to it and arranged for Edith Head to design the wardrobe for her next sixteen films. All in all, twenty-three of Barbara's films would feature Edith Head fashions.

Career-wise Barbara was on a roll, and her portrayal of Jean Harrington in *The Lady Eve* belongs in any gallery of her best. Film critics were as complimentary as usual, and many noted Barbara's remarkable appeal. Years later, critic James Harvey discussed her work in *The Lady Eve* and, in doing so, defined the qualities that endeared Barbara to her public and made her performances so memorable:

> Her effects were so plain and undecorated, so forthright and down to earth. Stanwyck's communication with camera and

audience was peculiarly direct and unmeditated. And yet, just because of this, she illustrates Norman Mailer's insight into the star's personality better, more simply and clearly at least, than anyone: the sense the star gives us of having other things on his mind. Stanwyck always seemed both very sensible, and rather sad. And in *The Lady Eve*, all her energy and activity—her flights of comic enthusiasm, her self-delighted feats of impersonation and deception—seem superimposed on an essential reserve, something final and deep held back. Her voice is both flat and eloquent, oddly both nasal and husky, and most at home perhaps in assured declarative statements. But its huskiness suggests not so much whiskey or disillusion or sexual provocation, as it does the quite unsentimental sound of tears—which have been firmly and sensibly surmounted, but somehow, somewhere, fully wept.

The third Fonda–Stanwyck film that Henry Fonda referred to in his autobiography was also Barbara's next film, *You Belong to Me*. Although the film was not quite up to the caliber of *The Lady Eve*, it was a delightful comedy and enjoyed some success.

Immediately afterward Barbara went back to work for Samuel Goldwyn in *Ball of Fire*, another comedy written by Billy Wilder and Charles Brackett. Stanwyck played Sugarpuss O'Shea, a burlesque entertainer recruited by reclusive professors to help in the writing of a dictionary of slang. Gary Cooper played opposite as the youngest of the seven professors, the egghead who falls in love with Stanwyck, the stripper. It was an outrageous role and Barbara reveled in it. Whether she was dancing joyfully during her boisterous rendition of "Drum Boogie" (with Gene Krupa), leading the professors in an impromptu boogie, or shamelessly teasing Cooper by telling him in mock innocence, "Oh, you know once I watched my big brother shave," Barbara was obviously having a hell of a lot of fun.

The film was so much fun, in fact, that even those involved in it were surprised that the Academy of Motion Picture Arts and Sciences had the insight to recognize the true depth of Barbara's performance. Nevertheless, Stanwyck's performance did catch their eye, and in 1941 she was nominated again for the Best Actress award. She was in good company. Also nominated that year were Bette Davis for *The Little Foxes*, Joan Fontaine for *Suspicion*, Greer Garson for *Blossoms in the Dust*, and Olivia DeHavilland for *Hold Back the Dawn*. The award went to Joan Fontaine.

CHAPTER 21

The year 1941 had been busy for both adult members of the Taylor residence. Barbara had appeared in four films, three of which would remain among the most popular. For his part, Bob Taylor had completed three: *Billy the Kid, When Ladies Meet,* and *Johnny Eager,* one of the best of his career. Meanwhile, they were working very hard at their marriage. Soon after they wed, Bob sold his own ranch and moved into Marwyck while they shopped around for a house in Beverly Hills.

Since they worked as much as they did, there was little time for socializing. What time they did have was spent with their few very close friends: Barbara's public relations woman, Helen Ferguson; Jack and Mary Benny; Marion and Zeppo Marx; and Gary Cooper. When not too exhausted, they attended the necessary industry events. They had few hobbies. Barbara tried golf but gave up after a while claiming, "After months on the links, I've finally got my score down to 212 for the first nine holes!" Taylor had a passion for flying, indulging it whenever he had the chance.

As a mother, Barbara was extremely cautious and protective. Few photos were allowed of Dion, and she took every precaution to see that he wasn't spoiled. At birthdays and Christmas she asked friends to keep gifts at a minimum, and when such precautions weren't heeded, she and Dion selected a few choice gifts and sent the rest to charity. As often as possible, Fridays were reserved for her and Dion to spend together until the time came when Dion was sent away to a military academy. Stanwyck told the press that the decision to send Dion away to school was made to protect him from the possibility of pampering and to provide the companionship of boys his own age, but in retrospect the decision remains a bewildering one. Throughout her childhood Barbara had been denied the love and compassion that comes with a normal family life. She adopted a son to fulfill her own need for a family and claimed to be enormously attached to the boy. Then, in a move that would seem to contradict everything in her character, she sent him away. It's possible that Barbara simply wanted to protect her son from her own compulsive feelings for him or that, even at this early date, Barbara and her son were already in the first throes of the alienation that would eventually destroy their relationship.

Throughout the early years of their marriage, reams of copy were written about Barbara and Bob. A great deal of this was devoted to stories of Barbara's tutoring her young husband in the ways of filmland. Bob didn't hesitate to admit his wife's influence to the press. At one point he explained, "Barbara has been wonderful in helping to keep my balance. People praise and compliment me to my face all day long. It might be so easy to start taking myself seriously if it weren't for Barbara. She's on the level in everything she says and I know she is the only person I can depend on."

At home, Barbara was definitely Queen of the Manor, but she made a habit of staying out of the kitchen. Traditional domesticity was not for her. "No knitting, no petit point, and no darning," she claimed, "and furthermore, I don't intend to try anything like that ever!" She did, however, enjoy rearranging the furniture and redecorating the house. "I have a passion for moving furniture from one place to another. Bob says he'd never sit down in any room in the dark because he'd be sure

115

to land on the floor. I love to change colors in furniture, too. If I could afford it, I'd redecorate my house every month. When Bob sees me eyeing the davenport, he knows it will be changed from gray to lipstick red next week!"

In the usual up-front Stanwyck manner, Barbara admitted that overwork was not the only reason the Taylors stayed at home most nights. It seems that buried beneath her tough-talking exterior, there were still buried a few remnants of little Ruby Stevens. In some respects Barbara was still the poor girl who didn't fit in, looking through the window at the actors and actresses she used to dream about. "I don't believe I'll ever get over the fear of going into a group of strangers," she admitted. "If I'm to visit Ty Power and Annabella and know that the Millands or the Bennys are to be there, I'm all right. But if I think I won't know anyone, I suffer horrors. I'll go to Ciro's or the Trocadero with Bob some evening. I'll be wearing a lovely gown, and my hair all doozied up. No sooner do I get there when I think, gee, I look awful. I see Claudette, and she looks divine, or I see Dietrich looking like something out of this world, and I imagine I look like some dowdy little shopgirl."

If there were any problems in the Taylor–Stanwyck marriage, it centered around Barbara's somewhat domineering attitude as well as her possessive dependency on Bob as a source of affection. Taylor found himself in a vulnerable position. Each day, when he reported to work at Metro, he found himself involved in celluloid romances with some of the most beautiful women of the day. The first few years of marriage found Bob involved on film with such beauties as Hedy Lamarr, Vivien Leigh, Joan Crawford, Greer Garson, and, in *Johnny Eager*, Lana Turner.

This last pairing was perhaps the most dangerous situation as far as his marriage was concerned. Although only twenty years old at the time, the irrepressible Lana was probably at the height of her beauty and was an outrageous flirt. Taylor suddenly found himself in over his head. He and Barbara had been married for two years, and he was beginning to wonder whether he had taken a wife or a second mother. His own mother had dominated his every move until his affair with Barbara, and now it seemed that Barbara was willing to pick up where

116

Mrs. Brugh had left off. Now, with Lana Turner in his arms, he felt in control. Soon, Taylor began to believe that, just maybe, what he felt for Stanwyck was simply respect and admiration and that he was in love with Lana. He and Turner began to fall into a relationship. Years later Lana would admit with wide-eyed innocence, "I flirted with him, but for me it was no more than that. Certainly our mutual distraction didn't hurt our love scenes. Oh, we'd exchange kisses, romantic, passionate kisses, but we'd never been to bed together. Our eyes had, but not our bodies."

Nevertheless, it is possible that Bob thought about a divorce. According to Lana Turner, Bob told her that he was going to speak to Barbara about the situation and she "strongly discouraged him." Lana told him, "I care for you, but don't make me the solution to your marital problems. Don't tell Barbara anything about us. As far as I'm concerned, there's nothing to tell." Unfortunately, Bob didn't heed Lana's warning. He told Barbara what was going on, and she was devastated. The way Lana remembers it, Barbara fled from Taylor and stayed at the home of her maid, Harriett Coray, for four days. Soon afterward Barbara and Bob reconciled, and the entire incident was kept under cover.

Then, on October 7, 1941, Barbara was rushed to Cedars of Lebanon Hospital with deep gashes on her arm and wrist. Taylor explained that Barbara had been trying to open a window in their Beverly Hills home and found that the window was painted closed. Barbara tried hitting the window with the heel of her hand and accidentally put her hand and arm through the glass, cutting the arteries in her arm. The injuries were taken care of, and Barbara was sent right home. Some Hollywood gossips were skeptical and spoke among themselves of a suicide attempt on Barbara's part, but she had no time for denials. "This is one of those times," she told a friend, "when I think of an old Irish proverb: The more you kick something that's dead, the worse it smells."

CHAPTER 22

Though the road to a happy marriage may have been rocky at times, there was nothing rocky about Barbara's film career. *The Great Man's Lady*, another William Wellman film, followed *Ball of Fire*. Barbara's role in the film, which was known as *Pioneer Woman*, was the kind of part many actresses would die for. *The Great Man's Lady* was sort of a Western *Back Street*, with Joel McCrea appearing as Barbara's lifelong love interest. The two worked together well, and Barbara gave an incredible performance, full of well-thought-out subtleties of emotion, as well as various changes in her physical presence. It was another success in Barbara's increasingly long list and is one of Barbara's personal favorites.

The Gay Sisters, with George Brent and Geraldine Fitzgerald, came next and was extremely successful although not of any particular importance. *Variety* called Barbara's performance "vibrantly believable." Next came *Flesh and Fantasy* with Charles Boyer and more good reviews.

Since *Stella Dallas* in 1937, Barbara had appeared in twelve films, each of them very successful and better than the average film fare. In a thirteen-year film career, Barbara had had surprisingly few embarrassing cinematic moments. Her next film, *Lady of Burlesque*, was one of the few. Based on Gypsy Rose Lee's novel, *The G-String Murders*, *Lady of Burlesque* was an "A picture" that had "B picture" written all over it. It was Barbara's second shot at portraying a burlesque queen, this time one Dixie Daisy. Her best moment in the film was her throaty rendition of the risqué ditty "Take It off the E-String, Play It on the G-String." This and a couple of agile dance routines proved to the critic of *The New York Times* that "she hasn't forgotten her early chorus training on Broadway." Stanwyck's presence in the film helped it draw well enough at the box office, but once its initial run was completed, she made it perfectly clear that she hadn't much regard for the film and, as a matter of fact, considered it her least favorite.

Stanwyck was a veteran of forty-four films by now and was often asked for advice by aspiring actresses. It was a subject she was more than qualified to discuss and was more than willing to expound on:

> The tragic thing about kids who want to get into pictures is that they don't have any great driving urge to learn their trade. The only thing they have an urge for is glory. They don't get any particular enjoyment out of work. Their thoughts are on the fanfare, the luxuries they have never had, the limousines, the pretty clothes. That's all very nice. But it's one thing to like it, and another to appreciate it. You can't appreciate it without earning it. And you can't hang on to it, either, without earning it.
>
> I can think back to four or five years ago, to pretty girls and handsome boys who came up from nowhere to be hailed as "great finds." You never hear of them now. The public lost interest in them. They were monotonously the same in role after role. No one ever found out how much talent those boys and girls had— because they, themselves, never dug under to find out.
>
> Don't get me wrong. I'm not lumping all of today's new stars in one heap. I'm not saying that there isn't one of them who knows what acting is all about. Though, by implication, their publicity is

saying exactly that. Even the girls who have earned their stardom, worked hard for it, are called Cinderellas just like the rest— keeping alive the fatal legend that, with luck, any girl can become an actress.

What would I tell a young girl with movie ambitions? The most important thing I could tell her would be: Don't let anyone sell you the idea of trying to start at the top. And don't envy the girls who do start there. Give yourself something those girls don't have. A thorough understanding of the business of acting. Start at the bottom and build up. Put your ambition on a solid foundation. Don't be afraid to work. Expect to work. And don't be impatient at the time it takes to learn acting. Remember that what Flaubert told de Maupassant about writing is just as true of acting: Talent is long patience.

Every time you take a step forward in your career, somebody will always tell you: "Well, you've arrived." That's particularly true in Hollywood. And it's particularly fatal to believe it. You've never arrived. If you try, you can always take another step forward. And you had better try, because, if you don't, someone else will. You never can believe for one moment that you are the best this or the best that. Because just around the corner, there may be another fellow who is fifty times better.

Barbara had developed a reputation as a tough, no-nonsense girl from Brooklyn who would neither dish out nor allow any bull. She had no tolerance for laziness or a lack of professionalism, and gossip, as far as she was concerned, was just so much garbage.

Privately, she could let loose with a tirade of profanity when pushed too far. At one of the few Hollywood parties she attended while Bob was away, she found herself being cased by an ambitious young actor who apparently thought it might help his career if Barbara took an interest in him. Every time she moved, the obnoxious character followed. She went from the living room to the dining room to the den and back to the living room, and still the unwanted shadow followed. Finally, she turned on him. "What the hell is this," she demanded, "the mating season?"

Once the Lana Turner incident was a thing of the past, the Stanwyck–Taylor union settled back into a somewhat more peaceful routine. Both Barbara and Bob were kept extremely busy by their separate careers, and they really didn't spend as much time together as they would have liked. By 1943 the ranks of Hollywood's leading men were being depleted by the war, and it was inevitable that Robert Taylor would end up in uniform. He neither wanted to nor tried to dodge his military obligations, and in the spring of 1943 he enlisted in the Naval Air Corps. Taylor was commissioned a lieutenant and asked for combat service as a pilot, but he was thirty-two and considered too old. Instead he wound up a flying instructor and director of seventeen training films.

At home, Barbara sold the Beverly Hills house they had purchased soon after their marriage and moved into another, somewhat smaller house in the same neighborhood. Her spare time was spent at the Hollywood Canteen, where such top stars as Judy Garland and Bette Davis entertained the West Coast–based servicemen. Most of all, though, she worried about Taylor and the amount of time he spent in the air. This resulted in Taylor's wearing a chain full of St. Christopher medals around his neck. "She doesn't trust me for nothing in a plane," he told the press. "But anything she says is good for me, I'll wear."

Barbara visited her husband when he was stationed in Louisiana, and they managed to spend a few days together, but eventually Hollywood called, and Bob had to go back to the waiting planes. Somewhat disconcerted by Taylor's loss of twelve pounds and his Navy crew cut, Barbara quipped to the press, "He's still the handsomest man I've ever laid eyes on, but he looks about eighteen. People will think I'm his mother!"

CHAPTER 23

After rising in the morning, Barbara would drink four glasses of water and then take a hot, then cold, shower. Next, her luxurious hair was brushed for ten minutes. This routine was followed by a large breakfast. As often as not, she would skip lunch altogether. Barbara disliked fancy food. Steak and baked potatoes made up her favorite meal, and she'd tell whoever was cooking that meal just to pass the steak over the flame on its way to the table! She drank too much coffee, smoked incessantly, and seldom drank liquor. The perimeters of her life were bound on one side by her career and on the other side by her marriage. With Bob Taylor in the service, Barbara had nothing else to do but to concentrate on filmmaking. There was no activity she liked better than working at her craft, and her next film really gave her something to work with.

Over the past fifteen years Stanwyck's gallery of film characterizations had included all sorts of women from murderers and sharp-shooters to burlesque queens and señoritas, but more often than not she had played ordinary-but-troubled women. Yet, more than any role, she was still identified with the self-sacrificing mother in *Stella Dallas*. *Double Indemnity* changed all that.

In developing *Double Indemnity*, Billy Wilder and noted crime novelist Raymond Chandler expanded a story that had been written by James M. Cain. The story was based on a New York murder case of 1927 in which a wife and her lover killed her husband to gain his insurance money. Once the script was completed, Wilder set about casting the parts. Approaching Stanwyck first, he explained to her that the role he wanted her for, that of Phyllis Dietrichson, was different from any she had ever done. Phyllis was a tough, sexy, calculating, and ruthless broad and . . . she was a murderer. For the first time Barbara was unsure of herself. She wasn't sure she could carry it off or what the public's reaction would be to her portrayal of an out-and-out bitch. Wilder told her he could get Fred MacMurray if she would do the film. In that case, Barbara said, she would think about it.

Next Wilder approached Fred MacMurray. MacMurray had been portraying easygoing, affable guys throughout his career. His reaction was the same as Barbara's, but before MacMurray could refuse the role, Wilder told him that Barbara would do the film if MacMurray would agree to it. "There being nobody, then or now," MacMurray states, "whom I respect more, not only as an actress but as a person, I said okay." Sneaky guy, Wilder.

Stanwyck fans knew they were in for some surprises as soon as she appeared on the screen. Sporting a shoulder-length light blond wig, complete with bangs, and dressed loosely in a silky robe, Barbara exuded raw, unadulterated (but obviously adulterous) sex. Barbara's presence throughout the film was incredibly sensual. Edith Head's costuming of the coldhearted dame was appropriately confined to very tight skirts and sweaters or alluring garments alluding to silk and sex. The package was even wrapped with a gold ankle bracelet.

The Wilder–Chandler dialogue kept the film moving at a steady pace and did a great deal to define both Stanwyck's and MacMurray's characters. Their scenes together were infused with sexual anxieties almost never before seen on film. In one scene MacMurray's brazen dialogue only verbalizes the thoughts the audience senses are going through Stanwyck's mind. While trying to seduce him, Stanwyck plays the innocent. "I wonder if I know what you mean," she says. "I wonder if you wonder" is the smart retort. The eroticism between these two can almost be touched.

The impact of *Double Indemnity* as *film noir* cannot be overstated. Stanwyck's performance in the film reached legendary status, and years later, in writing about the best films of the forties, Tony Thomas would comment, "She seems a beautiful wraith, cold and bloodless, luring men with a faintly evil smile. Truly a remarkable performance."

Early in 1945, when the Academy Award nominations were announced, *Double Indemnity* had been nominated in seven categories, including Best Picture, Best Direction, Best Writing, and, for a third time, Barbara Stanwyck was nominated as Best Actress. Incredibly, MacMurray's casual, yet chilling performance was ignored completely. Never one to deny the Oscar or its respect, Barbara was nonetheless wary of too much excitement. Already accustomed to losing, she remarked to her agent, "I feel like one of Crosby's horses."

Barbara must have been disappointed anyway, when she lost to Ingrid Bergman for *Gaslight*. Nevertheless, the day after the awards, when a space salesman from *Variety* asked her to take out a page ad congratulating Miss Bergman, Barbara reminded him that she had ordered just such an ad the week before the awards. It was with some degree of sadness that Barbara would tell a reporter, "My doors are not held up by Oscars, and I have never had a chance to get up on a platform and say, 'I am practically unprepared.' "

Double Indemnity was followed by another of Barbara's personal favorites, *My Reputation*, in which she played a young widow battling a domineering mother and a group of hypocritical socialites. The film was shown solely to American soldiers overseas before being released in the States in 1946. Barbara's remarkable string of successful films continued unabated as she wrapped up a brief appearance in Warner Brothers' all-star *Hollywood Canteen* and then appeared with Dennis Morgan in a delightful farce entitled *Christmas in Connecticut*. There had been eighteen films in the nine years since *Stella Dallas*, and every one had made money and increased Barbara Stanwyck's fame. There is probably no other actor or actress with such a record. All of this was brought even more clearly into focus when the U.S. Treasury announced that Barbara Stanwyck had been the highest-paid woman in the United States in 1943, earning $323,333.

Finally, on November 5, 1945, Lieutenant Robert Taylor, U.S.N.R., was discharged at the Naval Personnel Separation Center in Chavez Ravine. Although he claimed that he was anxious to return to his famous wife and perhaps take her on a vacation, Taylor told the press, "Sure, it's good to be home, but it's rather tough to leave the gang you've been with for so long. You get that lumpy feeling about where you tie your tie."

CHAPTER 24

Robert Taylor's return to civilian life did little to take his wife away from Hollywood's sound stages. Whether Barbara's obsession with work was a part of her basic nature or a reaction to her personal life, as yet unfulfilled, is unknown. Nevertheless, more of Barbara's time seemed to be devoted to her career than to anything, or anyone, else.

In short order she made three more successful films: *The Two Mrs. Carrolls* with Humphrey Bogart, *The Bride Wore Boots* with Robert Cummings, and *The Strange Love of Martha Ivers* with Van Heflin and Kirk Douglas. There seemed to be very little chemistry between Bogart and Stanwyck in *The Two Mrs. Carrolls*. Bogart was miscast as the psychopathic artist, and the film in general was very strange.

Barbara and Bob Cummings got along beautifully during the filming of *The Bride Wore Boots*. Cummings admits that he was madly in love with her and calls her "one of the most honest, forthright and compelling people I've ever known." Although Barbara usually got along very well with her directors and was not known for giving ultimatums, an incident occurred while making *The Bride Wore Boots* that did cause her to put her foot down.

During a very hot July afternoon the cast was gathered at the Midwick Country Club near Los Angeles, where some very tricky and strenuous steeplechase scenes were to be shot. The most difficult riding scenes involved Cummings but not Barbara. Portable dressing rooms were nearby, and Barbara waited in the air-conditioned comfort of her own dressing room while director Irving Pichel put Cummings and the race horses through their paces. Pichel ordered that the race, which was run down the entire length of the country club, be shot in its entirety for each take. During the race Cummings was to ride in some precarious positions, and the actor found it quite a hair-raising experience. Nevertheless, Pichel thoughtlessly ordered take after take. It was a brutal ordeal, and Stanwyck kept an eye on the situation from her dressing room window. After the thirteenth take, cast and crew alike held their breath, hoping against hope that Pichel was satisfied. Then, the director slowly raised his megaphone to his mouth and said, "Once more, it's not good enough yet!"

Reluctantly everyone began preparing for another take until, almost in unison, everyone became still, their eyes focused on Barbara Stanwyck walking toward Irving Pichel with all the calm, cool self-assurance expected of her. Once she was a few feet away from the director, she looked him straight in the eyes, with a smile on her face but fire in her eyes and said coolly, "Mr. Pichel, if Mr. Cummings rides that goddamned race one more time, you'll never work in films again." With that, she turned on her heel and, with enormous poise, strode the two thousand or so feet back to her trailer as Irving Pichel, biting his lip, said, "Print takes one, four, and thirteen. That's it for today!" It was a very rare show of temper by Barbara.

Barbara was no slouch when it came to bits of eye-catching business. While working in *Martha Ivers* with Van Heflin and Kirk Douglas, she showed how well she could protect her own screen time. Van Heflin had come up with a bit of business meant to establish his character as a professional gambler. The trick involved Heflin's absentmindedly rolling a coin end over end over his knuckles while concentrating on his dialogue. It was a gimmick that was sure to keep audiences' eyes riveted on Van during his scenes.

Barbara watched Van's trick quietly throughout rehearsals. Then before filming she told him, "Van, that's a wonderful piece of business, but if you do that during my important lines, I have a piece of business that will draw attention away from yours. Any time you start rolling that coin while I'm talking, I'm going to show them a trick a hell of a lot more interesting than yours. I'll be fixing my garter. So be sure you don't do that when I have important lines to speak." Heflin never questioned Barbara's threat and used the trick only briefly during Barbara's scenes.

Around this time Barbara convinced Warner Brothers to buy the rights to Ayn Rand's best-selling novel *The Fountainhead*. The part of Dominique was one of the first that Barbara had actively sought in some time, and she encouraged Warner Brothers to cast Humphrey Bogart opposite. Somehow it didn't work out, and the film was shelved for a little while. When Warners started production in late 1947, King Vidor was assigned as director, and Vidor refused to cast Barbara as Dominique, claiming that she had no sex appeal. Barbara was very disappointed when the film was finally made starring Gary Cooper and Patricia Neal.

Barbara's disappointment didn't slow her down. Four more movies were made in quick succession. The first, *California*, was a Western teaming her with Ray Milland. It was also Barbara's first Technicolor film. Next came *The Other Love*, based on a short story by Erich Maria Remarque and co-starring David Niven, Richard Conte, and Gilbert Roland. The third film, *Cry Wolf*, gave Barbara an opportunity to work opposite one of the most important male stars of the thirties and forties, Errol Flynn. Finally, Barbara went to Metro to appear opposite Van Heflin and Charles Coburn in *B.F.'s Daughter*. She and Van Heflin worked beautifully together, and the company on *B.F.'s Daughter* was a particularly happy one, full of practical jokes and good fun. This film and the three previous ones were again well received by the press and the public.

In *Double Indemnity* Barbara's appearance had undergone a radical change through the use of a blond wig and tight-fitting clothes. In *B.F.'s*

Young Ruby Stevens with older brother, Malcolm Byron
Stevens, in front of the house on Classon Avenue,
Brooklyn. Circa 1909. (Author's Collection)

An early portrait, taken while Barbara was appearing in
Burlesque. 1927. (Author's Collection)

With Ralph Graves in *Ladies of Leisure*. 1930, Columbia Pictures. (Author's Collection)

Barbara and Frank Fay relaxing in their Malibu beach house shortly before the fire that destroyed it in 1931. (Author's Collection)

Barbara with roommates Mae Clarke (left) and Walda Mansfield (center) in *Burlesque*. 1927. (Author's Collection)

With William Boyd and Betty Bronson (center) in *The Locked Door*. Barbara's comment: "They should never have unlocked the damned door!" 1930. United Artists. (Author's Collection)

As Annie Oakley in the film of the same name. 1935. RKO. (Author's Collection)

With Fay out of the picture, Barbara
was often escorted by her brother,
Byron. The two at a premiere
in February 1936. (Pictorial Parade)

Barbara and Anne Shirley as mother and daughter in
Stanwyck's most famous film, *Stella Dallas*. 1937. United
Artists. (Author's Collection)

As Mollie Monahan with Joel McCrea (center) and Robert Preston in *Union Pacific*. 1939. Paramount Pictures. (Courtesy of the Doug McClelland Collection)

Horses were one of Barbara's great loves. Agent Zeppo Marx, Barbara and Bruce Cabot (right) at the race track in June 1938. (Pictorial Parade)

With Adolphe Menjou and William Holden (right) in *Golden Boy*. 1939. Columbia Pictures. (Author's Collection)

Barbara and Henry Fonda in *The Lady Eve*.
1941. Paramount Pictures.
(Author's Collection)

Barbara with Robert Taylor and son,
Dion, at the race track. (Author's
Collection)

One of Hollywood's favorite
couples, Robert Taylor and
wife, Barbara, traveled to the studio
by motorcycle during gas rationing.
Circa 1940. (Author's Collection)

As Sugarpuss O'Shea in *Ball of Fire* with Gary Cooper. 1942. RKO. (Author's Collection)

A rare cheesecake photo. Circa 1943. (Author's Collection)

Robert Taylor at the height of his career at MGM. 1943. (Author's Collection)

Robert Taylor of the U.S. Naval Air Force with wife, Barbara, just before Taylor left for active duty. 1943. (Author's Collection)

Barbara as the ruthless Phyllis Dietrichson, with Fred MacMurray in *Double Indemnity*. 1944. Paramount Pictures. (Author's Collection)

With Humphrey Bogart in *The Two Mrs. Carrolls.* 1947. Warner Brothers. (Author's Collection)

Barbara received her fourth Academy Award nomination for *Sorry, Wrong Number.* 1948. Paramount Pictures. (Author's Collection)

With Clark Gable in *To Please a Lady*. 1950. MGM. (Author's Collection)

With Ralph Meeker in *Jeopardy*. 1953. MGM. (Author's Collection)

Fredric March, Barbara, William Holden, June Allyson and Paul Douglas in MGM's all-star film *Executive Suite.* 1954. (Author's Collection)

Relaxing on the set of *The Violent Men,* with co-star Glenn Ford. 1955. Columbia Pictures. (Author's Collection)

A publicity still for *The Barbara Stanwyck Show* with her dress designer, Werlé. 1960. (Author's Collection)

As Jo Courtney in *Walk on the Wild Side*. 1962. Columbia Pictures. (Author's Collection)

On the set of *Calhoun*, an unsuccessful TV pilot, with Jackie Cooper. 1964. (Author's Collection)

With Elvis Presley and Joan Freeman in a publicity picture for *Roustabout*. 1964. Paramount Pictures. (Author's Collection)

Barbara chats with Cesar Romero and Gloria Swanson after the premiere of *The Night Walker.* 1965. (Author's Collection)

Peter Breck, Barbara, Linda Evans, Lee Majors, and Richard Long as the Barkley family in *The Big Valley.* 1966. ABC. (Author's Collection)

Barbara and William Holden presenting an
Academy Award together in April 1978.
(Frank Edwards © Fotos International)

In January 1982, Barbara was given a special career award by the Los Angeles
Film Critics. With her is longtime friend Nancy Sinatra. (Frank Edwards
© Fotos International)

Accepting her honorary Academy Award for "superlative
creativity and unique contribution to the art of screen
acting," Barbara's first Oscar, April 1982. (Pictorial Parade)

As Mary Carson in *The Thorn Birds*. 1983.
ABC. (Author's Collection)

Daughter her appearance was changed just as radically, but in another more permanent and personal manner. Since the early forties, Barbara's hair had been graying slowly, steadily, and prematurely. Studio art departments had been kept busy retouching photos and stills; in black-and-white films the gray simply appeared to be blond highlights. For *B.F.'s Daughter* Barbara had her hair cut short and suddenly found that the gray was more obvious than ever. The studio asked that she dye it, but Barbara steadfastly refused, wearing the gray like a badge of honor. "I have no desire to hide my age," the forty-one-year-old star told the press, "and besides, I simply couldn't face sitting there six hours every two weeks with a bottle of dye." As the gray appeared more rapidly over the next few years, Barbara and her hairdressers were pleasantly surprised to find her new look extraordinarily flattering.

On the set Barbara was all business, and although Stanwyck's sets were known for the camaraderie between cast and crew, she seldom gave her professional acquaintances a glimpse into her private life. Even co-stars such as Joel McCrea and Fred MacMurray, those she worked with most often, seem to have been kept at a distance. Nevertheless, most of them have strong protective feelings toward Barbara and single her out as their favorite co-star.

Stanwyck made it clear that her marriage to Bob Taylor left her off limits to any romantic overtures, and her feelings were respected although some, Robert Cummings and the late Henry Fonda among them, admitted to having been madly in love with Barbara.

After Bob Taylor's return from the service, he and Barbara took their place in Hollywood as "one of filmland's happiest marriages." Fan magazines went on and on about their blissfully happy state, and Taylor even wrote an article for one of the magazines on how to keep a wife happy. They seemed the ideal couple, two mature professionals: he the handsome vet, she the beautiful actress, devoted to each other. But all was not what it seemed.

In many ways Barbara and Taylor were incompatible. He was an outdoorsman who loved hunting, fishing, and flying. Barbara hated flying but gave it a go once in a while to satisfy Bob. She'd never been hunting but agreed to give it a try. She and Taylor went on an expedition with two of his friends, Gary Cooper and Ernest

Hemingway, but Barbara was unimpressed. It was her first and last hunting trip.

Barbara's career was of primary importance to her; Taylor couldn't have cared less about his own. As far as he was concerned, it was a job and nothing more. Perhaps this ambivalence was a result of the difficulty he and so many other veterans in the film industry had in picking up the pieces of their movie careers after the war. Bob had a gregarious personality and loved entertaining, but Barbara had little time for it. She was a voracious reader and could stay up late into the evening reading. She'd suffered from insomnia for years. Taylor slept like a log at the drop of a hat and was happy retiring at seven o'clock. As for his wife, "She should belong to the book-of-the-day club," he complained good-naturedly.

Barbara was forty-one now, Taylor was thirty-seven, and once in a while his eye would still wander over the younger women anxious to throw themselves at him. Jealousy is usually a sign of insecurity, and Barbara's past had certainly given her enough cause to feel insecure. Whatever the reason, Barbara was jealous and very possessive, and as a result, her ever-watchful eye began to wear on Bob. He became restless and defensive, and the atmosphere in the Taylor household grew uneasy. It was obvious to Barbara and Bob that something would have to be done soon if their marriage was going to survive.

Even so, Barbara's tremendous love for her husband remained unchanged. It was as steadfast as it had been when they married nine years earlier. She was a one-man woman, and as far as she was concerned Bob was her man.

CHAPTER 25

In the fall of 1947 a new Hollywood Republican Committee had been formed to encourage the motion picture industry in backing the Republicans in 1948's presidential campaign. George Murphy was elected president of the committee, and charter members included Walt Disney, Bing Crosby, Joel McCrea, Fred Astaire, Robert Taylor, and Barbara Stanwyck. The committee's favorite candidate for the presidency was Governor Earl Warren of California. These were the early days of the great Red Scare soon to obsess the country, and Warren helped light a fire under the committee by telling them "for every Communist or fellow traveler in your industry, there are literally thousands of men and women who abhor Communism."

Although patriotic to the extreme, Barbara had always remained uninvolved politically. Robert Taylor, on the other hand, had become increasingly active in politics since his hitch in the Navy, and publicly, at least, Barbara supported his causes. These causes came to public attention for the first time in May 1937, when Robert Taylor testified to the House Un-American Activities Committee that he had been "forced" by an aide of the late President Roosevelt to make a film he felt "favored Russian ideologies, institutions and ways of life over the same things in our country." The film in question was *Song of Russia*, which Taylor had made in 1943, before enlisting in the Navy.

Taylor explained that he had objected to appearing in the film, but that he was then summoned to Louis B. Mayer's office where he was confronted by Lowell Mellett, assistant to President Roosevelt. Mellett made it clear that Taylor would find it impossible to get a commission in the Navy unless he appeared in *Song of Russia*. Louis B. Mayer explained further that the Office of War Information wanted the film made to improve the American public's image of Soviet Russia at a time when that nation was our ally in World War II. Taylor admitted that many elements he had considered pro-Communist were taken out of the script and did not appear in the final film.

After his testimony Taylor told the press in his best down-home dialect, "If there is anyone against Communism, it's me. I'm agin' 'em. I think its influence is serious enough that more actors should become aware of it. I always try to make my position in the matter emphatically clear and I always welcome any opportunity that I have to do anything I can against Communism." Barbara hadn't been asked to testify, Bob explained, "But if she had, she would be tickled to death to come down and she would come a-running."

A few months later Bob Taylor's political leanings came to the forefront again when newspaper headlines all over the country proclaimed, "Taylor Names Actors Believed Red Tinged." The Red witch-hunt was fully ablaze now, and its destructive fires were tearing the industry apart. Throughout the Hollywood community fingers were being pointed at anyone who even seemed to have Communist leanings. Dozens of careers were ruined as Hollywood's blacklist grew. The list was compiled through many sources, but a great many of the names came from the testimony of others within the industry, including Taylor.

In his own testimony Taylor stated that some of his fellow actors "act an awful lot like Communists," and singled out Howard Da Silva and Karen Morley as followers of Communist Party tactics. When asked if he would appear in a film in which someone he felt was Communist was cast, Bob Taylor replied, "I would have to insist either it was him or me. Life is too short to be around people who bother me as much as they do. If I had my way, the Communists would all be sent back to Russia or some other unpleasant place."

Barbara, meanwhile, continued to keep a low profile when it came to Bob's political activities. She was much more concerned with the somewhat shaky state of their marriage. With her and Taylor working more often than not and the conflicting schedules that usually entailed, they had little time to spend together and mend fences. Consequently, they seemed to grow further apart. It was a situation neither was happy with. Both of them took their marriage seriously and wanted to find a solution to their problems. In an effort to get away from the demands of their careers and spend some time away together, Barbara and Bob planned a European vacation for February of 1947.

After a leisurely cruise from New York the Taylors arrived in Paris on February 20 for what they hoped would be a few weeks of sightseeing and relaxation before moving on to London for the premiere, scheduled for March, of Barbara's film *The Other Love*. But it was not to be. Little is known about what went on between Barbara and Bob, and their vacation seems to have been surrounded by a veil of mystery. It is said that they went directly to the Hotel George V, where they were ensconced in one of the hotel's most luxurious suites. However, on February 24 the press reported that Barbara Stanwyck had been staying at the American Hospital in Neuilly since her arrival in France. Obliquely, it was explained that Barbara found the hotel so cold that she had decided to stay, instead, in the hospital where it was warmer. Then, even more strangely, the press went on to state, "Several times Miss Stanwyck has driven into Paris for dinner with Taylor but went right back to her hospital bed." Suspicions that Stanwyck had been taken ill were denied. "There's nothing the matter with Miss Stanwyck except that she has a cold," reported a nurse.

How could a simple cold have kept Barbara and Bob from spending these weeks together—weeks that were to have been so important to them? How could this period of hopeful renewal have been shattered to the point that Barbara and Bob simply met for dinner "several times"?

Obviously, there was a great deal more to the story than the press had reported. Under ordinary circumstances it would have taken more than a cold to keep Barbara and Bob apart.

Perhaps it had become obvious to them during their ocean crossing that there was nowhere to go with their marriage. Perhaps Barbara considered their relationship so unbearable by then that she sought the refuge and privacy afforded by a hospital stay. Or maybe Barbara had taken ill on board the ship. Perhaps the crossing had been even more tragic than that. Stanwyck's reputation was one of invulnerable strength. The rumors of a suicide attempt six years before had passed quickly without consequence, probably because they worked so completely against the grain of Barbara's public image. She was too proud a woman to cry publicly. It is interesting to note that there seems to be no press coverage of the Taylors' arrival in France: no reporters at the dock, no one to witness their arrival. It seems irrefutable that something happened during their trip that caused Barbara to be taken directly to the hospital in Neuilly. Years later, Barbara would often be asked to write her autobiography. She steadfastly refused, explaining, "Unless I told the whole truth it would be silly to write a book. Since I'm not about to let it all hang out, I'm not going to write a book. Besides, it would be too damn painful for me to go back through so many personal experiences." This trip to France most likely is one of those experiences Barbara doesn't want to relive.

At any rate, she and Bob were reunited before the end of their French sojourn and made the rounds of the obligatory nightclubs, including the Folies Bergére, where Barbara was surprised to see "thousands of girls running around with just a piece of chiffon on." Barbara visited the French designers, too, just for a look but swore by the "buy American" oath. "I think American designers did a terrific job during the war with inferior material, and I think American women who go over there buying French fashions are unfair."

From Paris, the Taylors vacationed for a while in Belgium and Holland and then went on to London. The first part of their stay there seemed quiet enough with little activity reported by the press. Then, on March 27, they attended the premiere of *The Other Love*—their presence caused a riot. Arriving at the Empire Theatre on Leicester

Square, they found 5,000 surging fans awaiting them. Shoving the mounted police guards aside, the fans rushed toward Barbara and Bob. Just then, before the stars could be hurt, seven policemen hoisted them in the air above the heads of the mob and carried them into the theater. Although somewhat disheveled and unnerved by the experience, neither was injured. As Bob Taylor knelt at his wife's feet, rubbing her ankles and wrists, Barbara commented, "It was so overwhelming, I was terrified for a few moments, then I realized that they were good-humored!"

Soon after the premiere Barbara and Bob returned to the States, sailing on the U.S.S. *America*. It was a pleasant and uneventful trip except for a brief incident in the ship's dining room on the last evening. There was a group of foreigners seated at the table next to the Taylors, and they were being very vocal about their dissatisfaction with the service from the American staff. These same characters had been complaining throughout the cruise; now they were really going at it. "This is what you can expect on an American ship," said one of the foreigners loudly. "Anyone who travels on an American ship is insane. The food is poor and the service dreadful."

Barbara could stand his whining no longer. Turning in her chair to face the four foreigners, she snapped, "Is that so? When American troops were going overseas not so long ago, we didn't hear any of you complaining about American service. You were pretty damned happy to see those GI's when they liberated Paris. You were pretty damned happy to get American food and supplies from the American Red Cross!" As she finished her patriotic tirade, the offenders clammed up and buried their heads in their menus.

Frank Fay was then starring on Broadway in the comedy *Harvey*, and it had been the biggest triumph of his career. When Stanwyck arrived in town with Bob, she was asked if she planned on seeing the show. "Not likely," she snapped. "I saw all the rabbits Frank Fay had to offer, a long time ago!"

She and Taylor proceeded to Chicago by train but parted company in the Windy City. Taylor wanted to fly back to the West Coast in his private plane (ready and waiting at a Chicago airport), but Barbara was just as afraid of flying as ever. Stating that she would go aloft "only when I can see my San Fernando ranch from Lake Michigan," Barbara continued on by rail. She was met there by Bob who had arrived sometime earlier. "Europe and its people are wonderful," she told the press waiting to interview her, "but I'm staking my claim right here in Los Angeles."

CHAPTER 26

Good solid film work awaited Barbara when she returned to Hollywood. Paramount Pictures had signed her to appear in *Sorry, Wrong Number*, based on Lucille Fletcher's famous radio play. Agnes Moorehead had starred in the 1943 radio drama, and although her excellent performance had been very well received, she was not considered a big enough star to carry the film.

Barbara tackled the demanding role of Leona Stevenson with all the power and persuasion she had at her command. A great many of her scenes had to be played in bed, as she tried desperately to phone for help. Asked by director Ralph Nelson if it had been difficult for her to build up her terror throughout the picture, Barbara explained: "I was very, very lucky. Anatole Litvak was the director, a very fine director and a marvelous person to work for. I had twelve days of the terror in bed. And he very kindly—which as you know, being a director yourself, is difficult for a director to do—asked me did I want to do those twelve days all at once or spread them in between continuity.

And when I thought it over, I thought it would be better if I could do the twelve days at once so that I myself might have continuity. And he very graciously fixed his schedule as such. And I did twelve days—consistently."

For his part, Litvak found Barbara very easy to work with. "We didn't have a very long schedule and Barbara had to work practically every day from morning to night. There was never a word of complaint—only encouragement and enthusiasm, which certainly influenced and helped not only me in my work but everyone connected with the film."

The affection felt for Barbara by her film crew was obvious to the director throughout the production, but never so clearly as during the shooting of a particularly emotional scene that was to come just before the film's ending. Striving for perfection, Litvak had Barbara do the scene over and over. After quite a few takes, he called for a pause to give Barbara a chance to rest. Litvak left the set for a drink and immediately the crew all complained to Barbara, telling her that Litvak was being unfair to her, her work had been good enough. Barbara wouldn't accept their well-meant sympathy and told them so in no uncertain terms. As far as she was concerned, only the director should judge her performance, no one else. And "good enough" was not good enough.

In the end, Barbara's performance was sensational and became one of those most vividly remembered. The critics, as usual, loved her. *Time* felt that: "It gives Barbara Stanwyck her fattest role since *Double Indemnity*, and she makes the most of the pampered, petulant, terrified leading character."

The entire film was praised. This review from *Cue* magazine seems to sum up the reaction from press and public alike:

> For sheer, unadulterated terror there have been few films in recent years to match the quivering fright of *Sorry, Wrong Number*—and few performances to equal the hysteria-ridden picture of a woman doomed, as portrayed by Barbara Stanwyck. Miss Stanwyck gives one of the finest performances of her career—a carefully calculated, skillfully integrated picture of developing psychological terror that provides a filmic highlight of the year.

138

Barbara was nominated for her fourth Academy Award, this time competing with Jane Wyman in *Johnny Belinda;* Olivia DeHavilland in *The Snake Pit;* Ingrid Bergman in *Joan of Arc;* and Irene Dunne in *I Remember Mama.* By this time the experience frustrated her, and she told columnist Darr Smith, "I absolutely will not win the Academy Award for Best Actress this year! I haven't been nominated enough. Only been nominated four times. It all depends on my work in 1949. If I get nominated next year, they'll have to give me the door prize, won't they? At least the bride should throw me the bouquet."

Barbara was right, and she again walked away from the ceremonies empty-handed. The award went to Jane Wyman, and it was some time before Barbara came close to the honor again.

Meanwhile, there was a great deal more work waiting for her, and Barbara threw herself into it. She was reunited with Robert Preston in *The Lady Gambles,* and her performance as a compulsive gambler was extraordinary. In *East Side, West Side* she worked again with Van Heflin and with a young actress just beginning her career, Nancy Davis. This was only the newcomer's third film, and she was very nervous about working opposite Barbara with whom she had "one big scene." As usual, Barbara did her best to put her at ease and applauded Nancy after the scene was completed in one take. It was during the making of *East Side, West Side* that the director, Mervyn LeRoy, introduced Nancy to an actor from Warner Brothers, Ronald Reagan.

East Side, West Side was followed by *The File on Thelma Jordan* with Wendell Corey and then *No Man of Her Own* with John Lund and Phyllis Thaxter. This latter film, known as *The Lie* throughout production, gave Barbara a chance for some of her beloved stunt work in a scene in which she and Phyllis Thaxter were to be involved in a train wreck. It was Thaxter's last scene, and although she was somewhat hesitant about doing the extremely difficult stunts involved, she found herself going along with them just because of Barbara's willingness to do so. When they were through, Miss Thaxter felt a little the worse for wear but noticed that Barbara was unfazed and ready for the next shot.

Barbara's next film, *The Furies,* found her working opposite Walter Huston and Gilbert Roland. The teaming of Barbara and Walter Huston as father and daughter was a stroke of genius. Both played their roles with extraordinary passion, and Barbara developed a great admiration for Huston. During one scene Huston was to give Barbara a fatherly kiss. She later recalled, "He came into the house and gave me a lusty kiss. The director said, 'You're playing father and daughter you know,' and Walter said, 'Leave me alone. I'm enjoying it. I'll play it my own way!' "

This was the third film Barbara had made with Gilbert Roland, and like so many before him, he found her "the complete actress, sincere, genuine with no display of artistic temperament."

Sadly, *The Furies* was Walter Huston's last film. He died shortly after its completion. Barbara's admiration for the man was well known, and she was asked to dedicate a scholarship in his name at the University of Arizona. Later, when the film premiered, Barbara spoke first to the audience: "You are about to see the Hal Wallis production of *The Furies* in which, unfortunately for our industry, Walter Huston plays his final role. It is Walter's picture. Mr. Wendell Corey, Mr. Gilbert Roland, Miss Judith Anderson, and myself are in the supporting cast. For me, this is the greatest honor I have ever had."

After finishing *The Furies*, Barbara went back to Metro, where she worked again with Clark Gable for the first time since *Night Nurse*, nineteen years earlier. The new film was about a newspaper columnist and a racing driver. Entitled *To Please a Lady*, the picture was very well received by press and public alike, with *Variety* noting: "Miss Stanwyck's assignment sees her as a glib, nationally read columnist. The two stars give it all importance with pleasing performances. Dialogue between the principals is flip and adult and they give it a certain air that pays off with chuckles."

By 1950 Hollywood was not producing as many films as it had before the war. Television was already cutting into the market, and the cost of producing films was soaring. Barbara's career, like many others, was already feeling the brunt of the slowdown. Although she had still managed to make three films in 1950, she wasn't being submitted as many quality scripts, and in 1951 she would only make one film.

Bob Taylor's career had never recovered after his stint in the service. He'd done one film in 1946, one in 1947, none in 1948, one in 1949, and then, like his wife, three in 1950. One of these, *Conspirator*, had been made in England in 1949. Rumors of a fling between Bob and his co-star, Elizabeth Taylor, then almost eighteen, made their way to the States but were soon forgotten when her romance with Glenn Davis became public. Nevertheless, *Conspirator* took four months to make, and that meant four months away from Barbara.

Upon his return in May of 1949, Louella Parsons interviewed Taylor and asked if he had been homesick while he was away. "I was so lonely and homesick," he told her. "Would you think I was a sissy if I told you I almost cried?"

"I would not," fawned Parsons. "I would think you were just what I always thought you were—a nice boy!"

Stanwyck's reaction to Bob's four-month absence and the rumors pairing him with Elizabeth Taylor remains unrecorded. Still the dutiful, faithful wife, she was just happy to have him home, and for the next year they would continue to spend as much time together as possible. As far as Barbara was concerned, if there was something bothering Bob, it was nothing that their love for each other couldn't overcome.

Then, in May of 1950, Bob Taylor left for Rome, where he was to star in Metro-Goldwyn-Mayer's epic production of *Quo Vadis*. And Barbara Stanwyck Taylor's world was about to be turned upside down.

CHAPTER 27

Even with all of the Hollywood hoopla surrounding Barbara Stanwyck's marriage to Robert Taylor, her private life was still one of the best-kept secrets in the industry. Just as she had when married to Frank Fay, Barbara extended every effort to give the impression that life in the Stanwyck–Taylor household was close to ideal. As carefully as possible, she and her unobtrusive press representative, Helen Ferguson, painted a portrait of a couple very much in love and very happy in their life together. Barbara and Robert appeared to be energetic, intelligent, and attractive individuals who conducted themelves both publicly and privately with a good deal more than a modicum of integrity, and to some extent this was true. Nevertheless, it seems obvious that there were a great many cracks in that portrait. As with so much of Hollywood's public image, all was not what it seemed.

Barbara's loss of her parents at such an early age and the subsequent abandonment of her and her brother, Byron, by their older sisters had a lifetime effect on her. Although she and Byron remained close until his death in 1964, Barbara's sisters seemed to remain at a distance. Byron had followed Barbara west in the early thirties, and they were often seen together. For a while Barbara helped him find work in the area until he was settled. Her sister Maude died before Barbara's move to Los Angeles, and all references to Mabel would seem to point to her death at about this same time. Barbara's third sister, Mildred, the one who supported her throughout her childhood, had settled in Brooklyn, and Barbara visited her whenever she made one of her infrequent trips to New York. There were few nephews and nieces, but Barbara is said to have helped those she had. In the case of Byron's son, Barbara was said to have paid for his college education. Nevertheless, the Stanwyck relatives were kept pretty much under wraps.

One of the most puzzling aspects of Barbara's personal life is her adopted son, Dion. There is little doubt that Barbara was fighting for Dion's best interest in the bitter custody battle with Fay, who was obviously incapable of offering the child a stable environment in which to grow. Although Barbara had seldom allowed the Hollywood press access to her son, there were many references to him in articles written throughout the thirties. Photographs of young Dion were off limits during his infancy and, in fact, seemed to have been denied the press until about 1936.

In the early days of Barbara's relationship with Robert Taylor, Dion became a primary topic in her interviews with the press or in the stories that were written about her. It was pointed out that Dion got along beautifully with Taylor, and the two of them were close friends. Photos appeared showing Barbara and the boy at Marwyck or showing Barbara, Bob, and Dion as a happy family unit. Later it became obvious that Dion had not been the happy youngster everyone believed him to be. In an article published in *Confidential* magazine, under his by-line (but probably ghost-written), Dion said:

> I never did get to know Fay well. He was always busy with his career and, by the time I started school, he and Mother were divorced. It was about that time that Mother and I began to have our differences. I used to cry myself to sleep at night in envy of

any boy who had a happy home and two loving parents. My mother was big box office. There were always parties and premieres she had to attend. There was her movie work during the day and social functions at night. And there were the trips for pleasure and the times she went on location that took her away from me. I know now that this is the life of a Hollywood star, but what reasoning can fill the void in a 5-year-old's heart when his father is gone and his mother is always busy?

Throughout the thirties and forties Barbara had been one of the busiest women in Hollywood. Between the years 1930 and 1950 she had appeared in sixty pictures, sometimes making as many as five pictures in one year. It is hard to understand how she would have had time for anyone, let alone a child. Barbara had desperately wanted her first marriage to work. It is obvious by her steadfast public support of him throughout their years together that she worked very hard at solving their problems, until Fay's alcoholism made her every attempt futile. Even if the boy had been adopted simply as a move to bring Barbara and Frank back together, it seems obvious, by her passionate struggle for the boy, that he meant a great deal to her.

Nevertheless, there seemed to be little warmth in Dion's upbringing, just as there had been little in Barbara's own childhood. Young Ruby Stevens had learned early in life that when she tripped and fell, there was no one there to help her up but herself. She had made it through her childhood virtually on her own, and after her divorce from Fay she found herself alone again. She had no time to shed tears publicly and had no sympathy for those who did. As far as Dion was concerned, she felt it was best for him to learn his lessons early in life while he still had the resilience of youth.

Vacations were taken alone or with Bob Taylor; there seemed to be no place for Dion with them. When doctors recommended a rest for her after the mental exhaustion of her custody fight with Fay, she "reluctantly" went away for two months without the child she had just fought for so desperately. When Dion came of school age, Barbara sent him to a private school in the San Fernando Valley. The school

144

was close enough that Dion could come home on weekends, but he wasn't sent for. Barbara's career was busier than ever now, and she and Taylor were inseparable. Dion recalled:

> I lived for the time when I could come home for vacation, but even then I found I could see little of Mother. She was at the peak of her career, a career that seemed to take up all of her time. Sometimes I would lie in bed, fighting sleep, so that I could say goodnight to Mother and tell her what I had done during the day, but she seldom came home before I fell asleep. I remember spending much of my vacation time hoping that the next day we might be able to spend some time together. We seldom did.

Dion hated life in the boarding schools, and his grades reflected the unhappiness he felt. He went from one private school to another, but his grades never improved. Nothing seemed to help, and Barbara grew more and more impatient with him. She had seldom accepted anything less than perfection from herself and continued to attempt to infuse Dion with the same drive and strength she had had as a child. As he continued to disappoint her, she declared even more adamantly, "I won't have him growing up to be a Hollywood brat."

According to Dion, his relationship with Bob Taylor hadn't been as ideal as the public was led to believe. He wrote in *Confidential*:

> I never really considered Mr. Taylor my father, although certainly I craved a father at that time. I was very unathletic, and I remember his disappointment because I didn't take an avid interest in sports. At first he tried talking baseball and football with me, discussing the games and complaining when his favorite team lost. But I just couldn't respond. These were things I had no knowledge of and the names and scores he talked about were completely foreign to me. After a while he gave up. I think he had a feeling I was Barbara's son and not his.

During the forties Dion was hardly mentioned at all. At times it was possible for the public to forget about Barbara's son altogether. He wasn't mentioned in her publicity and was seldom seen with his mother. By this time he had asked to be allowed to switch his name around, changing it to Anthony Dion Fay. He talked his mother into allowing him to attend public school in eighth grade, and although he claimed that his grades improved during that year, he was sent to Culver Academy in Indiana the following year. "That was the last time I was ever to live in my mother's home," he recalled later. The next summer he was sent to live with Bob Taylor's mother. The following summer Dion was shocked to find out that plans had been made for him to stay with friends of Uncle Buck Mack's:

> I had become totally unwelcome at home. I would no longer come home between terms. Mother had arranged to pay these people for my care and their home was to be my new home. Nobody ever asked if this was what I wanted or explained why it had been done. And for the next four years I neither saw nor heard from Mother.

Dion's motives in confiding so openly in *Confidential* magazine remain in question. He was aware, of course, of Barbara's strong penchant for privacy, yet he agreed to do the story. Published in 1959 at the time of his arrest for selling pornographic materials, the story ran under the headline DOES MY MOTHER, BARBARA STANWYCK, HATE ME?

As far as Barbara Stanwyck is concerned, her relationship with Dion has gone unexplained. "My personal life is my personal life," she says emphatically. It seems incomprehensible that a woman renowned on Hollywood's sound stages for her generosity and warmth could have a relationship with her son so devoid of those same qualities. The distance between mother and son seemed to widen in the early forties when Barbara's relationship with Bob Taylor first showed signs of vulnerability. It's possible that Barbara could cope with only one complex personal relationship at a time, and the strain of making her marriage to Taylor work was all that she could bear. Barbara may have felt that the atmosphere at home was too stressful and that a child as highly strung as young Dion seems to have been would be much better served by the disciplines of a private school. Whatever the causes, the constant increase in demands on her time by her career, the strains inherent in her relationship with Taylor, and the boy's long absences

146

while away at school, all may have worked to increase the gap between mother and son. With Dion away at school, it must have seemed to Barbara that her only involvement with him came when he was in some sort of trouble. From his earliest school days, Dion may have seemed to be unmanageable, thus the stringent disciplines and distance. It is certainly obvious that she was not as adept at handling personal crises such as the divorce from Fay and Taylor's tryst with Turner as she would have had the public believe. Under the hard-boiled facade of tough-talking Barbara Stanwyck still lingered vulnerable, battered Ruby Stevens, alone against the world's injustices.

When Barbara did see Dion again, after four years' separation, it was to take him out of Culver Academy just before he was to be expelled for poor grades—another disappointment and, Dion felt, "final proof of my unwillingness to amount to anything."

Dion continued to live with Buck Mack's relatives when not at school, and it was during this period that he received his draft notice. At this point the only contact Dion was having with his mother was through Mack. When Mack heard that Dion was going into the service, he talked Barbara into having lunch with her son. The meeting was a disaster. "We couldn't find much to talk about," Dion wrote later, "and when we did it just seemed to bring up sore points and started quarrels. As politely as a stranger I asked about her career. As politely and as distantly as the movie queen she was she answered and inquired how I had been." It was Barbara's last attempt at a relationship with her son, and to this day she has not seen him again.

Because of Barbara's incredible reserve and the impenetrable wall she had built around her marriage to Bob Taylor, it is hard to determine just what the state of that marriage was at any given time. She was certainly a woman with too much pride ever to admit that Bob's attentions may have wandered longingly to another woman, especially one younger than her own forty-three years.

Every marriage has its own struggles, and perhaps those that faced Barbara and Bob were no greater than anyone else's. The most apparent problem seemed to be that of their conflicting careers. Most of Barbara's work was done in the Los Angeles area, but work was harder to come by for Bob and it often involved distant locations. Months in London making *Conspirator* were to be followed by another long spell in Rome working on *Quo Vadis* and, already being mentioned, more time in Europe with Elizabeth Taylor to make *Ivanhoe*. To Barbara, these long-term separations were unbearable and were made even worse at the instigation of filmland's inveterate gossips. No one was free from their prying eyes, and Barbara was particularly vulnerable to the whispers emanating from the sound stages where Bob Taylor was working.

Taylor's passion for flying grew to be a thorn in her side. She feared flying and hated the fact that it was responsible for even more separations. Once, when Taylor was bragging to friends about the number of hours he had racked up in the sky, Barbara remarked dryly, "Now you can do everything the birds can do except sit on a barbed wire fence!" Later she told Louella Parsons, "I think our unhappiness started from the time he bought an airplane. Then he went on fishing and hunting trips with other men and was always away from home. I finally asked him if he thought I was making too many pictures and he insisted I keep on."

Despite the signs of dissatisfaction, when periodic rumors of trouble in their marriage came up, they were vehemently denied. Hedda Hopper got Barbara's brick-wall treatment often enough. Once when calling to check on a rumor of impending divorce, Barbara took the call. "Oh yes, Hedda. How are you? You heard Bob was divorcing me? He didn't say anything about it at breakfast, but wait a minute, I'll ask him." A few seconds later, Barbara was back on the telephone, "He says not today, Hedda. Sorry. Good-bye."

In May 1950, when Taylor left for Rome to appear with Deborah Kerr in *Quo Vadis*, Barbara was busy working with Clark Gable in *To Please a Lady*. *Quo Vadis* was to be one of Metro's biggest epics to date, and a long shooting schedule was planned. After completing *To Please a Lady*, Barbara announced that she would be going to Europe for two and a half months. "Of course I am lonely for Bob," Barbara told Louella Parsons. "When you have been married, and happily, for eleven years, you miss seeing his face and hearing him talk, even if some of the time you wish to heavens he would not litter up the background with fishing tackle and airplane paraphernalia."

Barbara would not be going straight to Rome, however. "I have made five pictures in eight months," she explained, "so I am going to take a little vacation before I go to Rome. Bob tells me it's so hot that both he and Deborah Kerr have lost pounds. So, I am looking forward to hearing the violins play at Monseigneur in Paris, swimming at Cap d'Antibes, and visiting some friends in London. Then I'll pay Taylor a visit. He's so busy with *Quo Vadis* he won't have much time for me and you know I am not very good at being idle."

Despite Barbara's seemingly relaxed approach to the forthcoming vacation, she flew to London instead of sailing as she usually did—an unusual move, considering Barbara's well-known aversion to flying and the amount of time at her disposal. Perhaps she was simply trying to make the most of her vacation, or she may have been in a greater hurry to reach Taylor's side than she admitted. Just possibly she had already begun to hear stories she didn't like about Bob Taylor's activities in Rome.

In spite of all this, Barbara's initial arrival in Europe was a quiet one, and there was little coverage of her vacation in London and Paris. Gossips waited with bated breath, however, for her arrival at the *Quo Vadis* location. Although Bob Taylor handled his personal life with his usual discretion, he was seen "swimming, dining and dancing with numerous Italian beauties," and it was generally presumed that these women were not all "just friends." Two names in particular seemed to come up more than any others, those of Italian starlets Marina Berti and Lia De Leo. De Leo had even gone so far as to tell the Italian press that Bob had told her he was tired of his wife and wanted to divorce her "after meeting me." It was expected that Stanwyck's arrival in Rome would bring enough fireworks for a lifetime.

Both Stanwyck and Taylor had too much class for such displays. Publicly, they were still a happily married couple, seen around Rome looking like young lovers. Privately, the truth may have been totally different. Rumors of what really happened in Rome remain unconfirmed, the wildest having Stanwyck find her husband literally in bed with one Italian beauty or another. The less sensational have the couple quarreling violently during Barbara's stay. The truth probably lies somewhere in between, but whatever happened, one thing seems certain: when Barbara Stanwyck returned from Rome in September 1950, her marriage with Taylor was over. All that remained was the public announcement.

Barbara sailed home on the *Queen Elizabeth* and told the press that she was still as much in love with Bob as ever. Rome hadn't been so great, she admitted, even though Bob was there. "They were shooting scenes with lions and bulls," she noted wryly, "and everything smelled to high heaven." Work on *Quo Vadis* would continue until November, it was reported, and until then, Barbara would anxiously await Bob's homecoming. Her stalwart performance was probably one of the best of her career, yet she never meant anything more than when she told reporters, "Bob is the only man in my life and always will be."

Bob did return home in November as planned, and he and Barbara went to Palm Springs for a few days. Then, after a few more days at home, they went to San Francisco where Bob underwent abdominal surgery for a double hernia that had been bothering him for some time. Although Barbara later admitted that the two hours Bob had been in the operating room had been among the most difficult she ever endured, she told the press, "Bob's condition is very good. The operation was a complete success. Due to his splendid condition he came through in very fine shape."

After the operation Barbara and Bob returned to their Beverly Hills home where he convalesced for a short period. Then at one in the morning on December 15, Barbara's close friend and publicity agent Helen Ferguson received a call from a very shaken Stanwyck asking her to come at once to the Taylor home. When Helen arrived, Bob met her at the door. Inside she found Barbara in "a tragically emotional condition." Barbara told her friend, "I want to make a statement. I am going to give Bob the divorce he wants." Helen later testified in court that it took two hours to calm Barbara down and that after doing so they prepared a statement for the press. Taylor remained nearby but said "hardly a word."

Hollywood was stunned later that day when Barbara and Bob issued a joint statement announcing their intention to seek a divorce. The statement read:

> In the past few years, because of the professional requirements, we have been separated just too often and too long. Our sincere and continued efforts to maintain our marriage have failed.
>
> We are deeply disappointed that we could not solve our problems. We really tried. We unhappily and reluctantly admit what we have denied to even our closest friends, because we wanted to work things out in as much privacy as possible.
>
> There will be a California divorce. Neither of us has any other romantic interest whatsoever.

Bob, it was said, was recuperating in Palm Springs from his operation, and Barbara was incommunicado at the home of friends. Louella Parsons summed up the reactions of Barbara's friends, co-workers, and fans when she wrote, "I don't know when the breakup on any marriage has come as a greater surprise."

Thirty years later Barbara would explain, "He wanted it and I'm not the kind of person who wants somebody if he doesn't want me. I just say, 'There's the door, you can open it. You've got a good right hand, just turn the knob, that's all you have to do. If you can't open it, I'll do it for you.' "

CHAPTER 28

Once the decision to separate was made public, Barbara's lawyers moved quickly. She filed for divorce in Los Angeles Superior Court on January 31, 1951, asking for the decree on the grounds of mental cruelty. The brief complaint read, "For some time past, the defendant [Taylor] has treated plaintiff [Stanwyck] with extreme cruelty and has wrongfully inflicted upon her grievous mental suffering." Barbara's lawyer stated further that she and Robert Taylor expected to sign a financial settlement and asked that the document be approved at the time of the trial. The trial date was set for February 21.

As was to be expected, the trial was well covered by the press. Nevertheless, to both Barbara and Bob's credit, it was never allowed to sink into the sensationalism that so often surrounded Hollywood events. Barbara took the stand first and testified to Superior Court Judge Thurmond Clark: "Shortly after Mr. Taylor's return from Italy in December he came to me and asked for a divorce. He said he had enjoyed his freedom in Italy and wanted to continue to be able to come and go without the restrictions of marriage." Asked her reaction to this, Barbara answered, "It shocked me greatly. I was ill for several weeks and under a physician's care."

Barbara's corroborating witness was Helen Ferguson, who had been with Barbara and Bob on the morning of December 15 and had helped prepare their statement for the press. Once the decree was granted, the Taylors' property settlement was submitted for approval. Although it was not made public in its entirety, Barbara's attorney did reveal that Taylor was relinquishing to Barbara his interest in their house at 423 North Faring Road, valued at $100,000. Additionally, Taylor had agreed to pay Barbara 15 percent of his gross earnings for the rest of her life or until she remarried. Although she meant it when she claimed that Taylor was the only man for her, she made sure he paid for the suffering he had inflicted on her.

As Barbara was about to leave the courtroom, she spotted her maid of many years, Harriett Coray, there to offer her support. As the two women embraced, Barbara cried softly. Then as she left, a reporter asked if she had plans to remarry. Looking him straight in the eyes, she snapped "No!" and continued through the crowd of press and photographers.

Then another reporter asked, "Is there any truth to the rumor that Mr. Taylor became interested in an Italian girl?" "That is for Bob to say," Barbara answered quietly. Then, accompanied by Helen Ferguson, she left the courthouse.

Sometime before the date for her divorce trial had been set, Barbara had agreed to appear in a satirical skit at the annual awards dinner given by the Writers Guild of America. When the dinner turned out to be a day or two after the trial, the dinner committee was certain Barbara would beg off. They had nothing to fear. Barbara was not only there, relaxed and beautifully gowned, but she was the only one of the four actresses involved who didn't need her script and never flubbed a line.

In fact, work became Barbara's most successful form of therapy, and she threw herself into it with renewed vigor. The first role she tackled after the divorce was in the film *The Man with a Cloak*, co-starring Joseph

Cotten and Jim Backus. The film, remembered by Jim Backus as a "pretentious piece of *merde*," was not up to the standards of most other Stanwyck films, but at least it offered the opportunity for Barbara to sink her teeth into a role. The divorce hadn't broken her stride professionally, and Backus remembers her as being "pleasant, charming, on time, knew her lines—in other words a complete pro."

Stanwyck's next film, *Clash by Night*, had a good deal more substance to it and really provided Barbara with something to work with. Her co-stars were Paul Douglas, Robert Ryan, and Marilyn Monroe. The script was based on the Clifford Odets play and involved Barbara as a restless woman who returns to her hometown where she marries a simple fisherman, played by Paul Douglas. Her restlessness continues, however, and she is involved in an adulterous affair with Robert Ryan. It is a dismal but well-crafted film, and Barbara's performance as the bitter and vulnerable Mae Doyle is wonderful. It won her a Laurel Award from the Motion Picture Exhibitors.

Marilyn Monroe's role in the film, as Barbara's future sister-in-law, was one of her first of any substance, and her notorious insecurity made her a somewhat difficult colleague. Barbara later spoke of working with the newcomer: "She was awkward. She couldn't get out of her own way. She wasn't disciplined, and she was often late, and she drove Bob Ryan, Paul Douglas and myself out of our minds . . . but she didn't do it viciously, and there was a sort of magic about her which we all recognized at once. Her phobias, or whatever they were, came later; she seemed just a carefree kid, and she owned the world."

On Marilyn's first day of work with Barbara, she reported to the set two hours late. Barbara had been there, as usual, since 6:00 A.M. Their first scene together was shot mainly over Marilyn's shoulder at Barbara. Marilyn blew her lines twenty-six times, and everybody waited for Barbara to blow up, but she remained calm. Later a member of the crew noticed Barbara watching the photographers crowd around Marilyn. "What do you think of her as an actress, Queenie?" he asked. Barbara simply smiled and quipped, "With a figure like that, you don't have to act!"

The director of the film, Fritz Lang, was known as a demanding man to work for, but Barbara had looked forward to the challenge. They both found the experience a rewarding one, and Lang later gave this example of why he enjoyed working with her so thoroughly:

One day before shooting in the morning, she complained to me about a scene and said it was very badly written and she could never play it. I knew the scene, which I thought was very well written, and said, "Barbara, may I speak very frankly and openly with you?" She said, "Naturally," and I continued: "I think the scene reminds you of a rather recent event in your private life, and that is why you think it is badly written and you cannot play it." Barbara looked at me for a second and then said slowly, "You son of a bitch"—went out and played the two-and-one-half-pages-long scene so wonderfully that we had to shoot it only once.

Barbara's last scene in the film was shot at midnight on the last day of production. She'd been there since 6:00 A.M. The next day she kept a scheduled appointment with a magazine interviewer and that afternoon was rushed to the hospital by ambulance with pneumonia. She had been fighting it off for the last three days of shooting but hadn't wanted to interfere with completion of the film.

After a brief recuperative period Barbara worked with Barry Sullivan and Ralph Meeker in a film entitled *Jeopardy*. Then, with Clifton Webb, she starred in Twentieth Century–Fox's production of *Titanic*, known throughout filming as *Nearer My God to Thee*. The film remains another of Barbara's most memorable, although she was actually onscreen less than usual. Her heartbreaking scene of farewell with Clifton Webb remains one of the most beautiful she ever filmed, and she looked lovely in the 1912-style clothes. She won another Laurel Award for *Titanic*.

Just as she had helped William Holden, Kirk Douglas, and other newcomers in the past, Barbara extended a helping hand to Robert Wagner during their scenes together in *Titanic*. Wagner was grateful, and years later spoke of Barbara's assistance: "Barbara was very helpful. She's a sensitive lady beneath that kind of sharp front. She changed my whole approach to my work—made me want to learn the business completely. She really started me thinking. It means a great deal when someone takes that kind of time with a newcomer."

The most difficult scenes to film in *Titanic* were those involving the abandonment of the ship, with dozens of cast members boarding lifeboats and then being "put out to sea." Barbara's performance throughout these scenes was never less than superb, but she admitted afterward that it had been less of a performance than a reaction to the re-creation of the tragedy. "The night we were making the scene of the dying ship in the outdoor tank at Twentieth, it was bitter cold. I was forty-seven feet up in the air in a lifeboat. The water below was agitated into a heaving, rolling mass and it was thick with other lifeboats full of women and children. I looked up at the faces lined along the rail—those left behind to die with the ship. I thought of the men and women who had been through this thing in our time. We were re-creating an actual tragedy and I burst into tears. I shook with great racking sobs and couldn't stop." The film was well received and won an Academy Award for its screenwriters, Charles Brackett, Walter Reisch, and Richard Breen.

Late in 1952, while Barbara was at work on *Titanic*, Stanley Kramer Productions announced that she would follow that film with Kramer's production of *Circle of Fire*. The film, originally entitled *The Library*, was to have been Mary Pickford's comeback vehicle, but Pickford backed out. Alas, Stanwyck wasn't destined to star in it either, and after she too dropped out of the cast, it was made as *Storm Center* with Bette Davis in the lead.

Jean Negulesco, director of *Titanic*, had so enjoyed working with Barbara that he had Twentieth Century–Fox sign her and Clifton Webb to share top billing again in the forthcoming film *Three Coins in the Fountain*. Signed to co-star were Jeanne Crain and Gene Tierney. Again, Barbara had to bow out before production began, and although Clifton Webb remained in the film, the three female leads were eventually played by Dorothy McGuire, Maggie McNamara, and Jean Peters.

Barbara's next film was Ross Hunter's tearjerker *All I Desire*, with Richard Carlson. It was Douglas Sirk's first experience directing

Stanwyck, and like each director before him, he was impressed with her professionalism. But there were also subtler qualities in Barbara's work that he found worthy of note:

> She impressed me all the time as someone—what can I say—someone who had a great experience, someone who had really been touched deeply by life in some way. Because she had depth as a person. That is exactly what we see on the screen of course and that is why she is a great star. There is nothing—nothing the least bit phony about her ever. Because she isn't capable of it. That insignificant little picture she did with me and she played it all out of herself. And yet she is so discreet—she gets every point, every nuance without hitting on anything too heavily. And there is such an amazing tragic stillness about her at the same time. She never steps out of it, and she never puts it on—but it is always there, this deep melancholy in her presence. I think she is more expressive and resonant than any other actress I worked with.

Even after obtaining their divorce, Barbara and Bob Taylor continued to see each other occasionally. In April, photos of them dining together appeared in many newspapers, and Barbara was asked if there were a chance of a reconciliation. "It's too early to say," she responded. "I admit I'm carrying a torch for Bob. However, there's a certain amount of bitterness that has to be ironed out." Meanwhile, Taylor was also being seen with other women, including screen ingenues Sybil Merritt and Lane Trumbel.

His contradictory behavior was puzzling. For Barbara's forty-fourth birthday, in July of 1951, he sent her a heart of diamonds on a platinum chain to match a pin he had given her in happier days. The night before leaving for England to begin work on *Ivanhoe*, he and Barbara had a farewell dinner at the Beverly Hills Hotel. While in London he was seen dating ballerina Yvette Kaltz, but he wrote and called Barbara regularly. "She's more beautiful than ever," he told friends. He arrived home from Europe laden with gifts for his ex-Mrs. and told the press, "I plan to see her. I have no predictions what will be."

Barbara's name was linked with others, too. Sears Roebuck heir Armand Deutsch and producer Norman Krasna were two of those seen escorting her to various restaurants and industry functions. Then, after appearing in a radio broadcast of *Hold Back the Dawn* with Jean-Pierre Aumont, she was rumored to be seriously involved with the handsome Frenchman. Aumont's wife, Maria Montez, had died in 1951, and he was considered a particularly eligible bachelor. "He's wonderful, but we didn't have any romance," she told reporters firmly. "He's never gotten over Maria." She might as well have added that she still hadn't gotten over Bob.

Photos of Barbara dining with Clifton Webb and Robert Wagner were cropped to show only Stanwyck and Wagner, and, again, rumors of romance blossomed. Wagner was furious. "It's all nonsense," he protested. "This silly gossip has certainly hurt my chance for a real friendship with a fine woman and a great actress." Barbara did spend a great deal of time with Robert Wagner during the production of *Titanic*, but she had always been attracted by young men who could learn from her professional experience, and she was always willing to help them out. One reason for this willingness on her part may have been simply that she enjoyed the companionship of these young men. She certainly was lonely much of the time. But it is doubtful that she ever solicited any romantic overtures from her protégés. Barbara remained close friends with both Robert Wagner and Jean-Pierre Aumont . . . and she remained unmarried.

Meanwhile, her continuing relationship with Bob never failed to raise eyebrows, but Barbara still denied that there was any reason to suspect a reconciliation. "We've gone back to getting on well and that's all," she explained emphatically. "We're good friends again. At last. It took some doing. But—no reconciliation. I am good and tired of conjecture. Conjecture is the cheapest thing in the world. We eat dinner together or go out to a nightclub and yackety-yackety-yack. People simply don't know what they're talking about. I know what I know; Bob knows what he knows. They don't."

Bob Taylor was soon seen escorting actress Eleanor Parker on a steady basis, and rumors of a remarriage between him and Barbara became yesterday's news. In February of 1952 Barbara's divorce became final. The Beverly Hills home on North Faring Road was sold and its contents auctioned, thus eliminating many remnants of Barbara's happier days with Bob. Barbara settled comfortably into a new house, purchased for $100,000, at 273 Beverly Glen Drive.

Over the next few years Barbara would work very hard at her career and even harder at picking up the pieces of her personal life. Nevertheless, despite hundreds of loyal admirers in the industry and millions of fans, she was a woman alone.

CHAPTER 29

With a life now devoid of husband and son, Barbara's close friends became even more important to her. She had always been selective about her friendships so there weren't many, but those she had embraced returned her friendship fervently and with an inordinate amount of loyalty. It was a small, elite circle. First and foremost was Helen Ferguson, a former actress herself. Ferguson now acted as publicity agent to such luminaries as Clark Gable, Loretta Young, Jeanette MacDonald, and both Barbara and Bob Taylor. She was the woman Barbara could turn to most easily.

Another close friend was Harriett Coray, Barbara's maid for many years. Barbara was one of the least class-conscious people in Hollywood and made no bones about her close friendship with Harriett, who was black. The sincerity of this friendship was made perfectly clear during location shooting for *To Please a Lady* in Indianapolis. When the film's business manager called Barbara to ask what type of accommodations she would require, Barbara told him she wanted a bedroom and bath for herself and the same for Harriett, with a sitting room between. The business manager explained that Gable had requested they stay at the best hotel in town, where blacks were not welcome. Barbara remained adamant. She wanted Harriett near her and requested that the business manager make the necessary arrangements. Later that day the producer of the film, Clarence Brown, called Barbara to assure her that Harriett would stay at the best "colored" hotel in Indianapolis. One can almost see the determined gleam in Barbara's eyes as she told the producer, "I'll tell you what you can do to solve the whole thing. You make a reservation at the best colored hotel in Indianapolis for two bedrooms and baths and a sitting room between, and that's where I'll stay with Harriett."

"Oh, Barbara, you can't do that," Brown protested.

"The hell I can't," Barbara said forcefully and hung up. As far as she was concerned, the subject was closed. When they reached Indianapolis, she and Harriett both stayed at the best hotel in the city with Gable and the rest of the cast.

Barbara's friendship with Jack and Mary Benny had continued since the thirties as had her relationships with Mr. and Mrs. Fred MacMurray, Mr. and Mrs. Joel McCrea, Joan Crawford, and William and Ardis (Brenda Marshall) Holden. After the divorce, Barbara found a close compatriot in Frank Sinatra's ex-wife, Nancy. Like Barbara, Nancy is a very strong, self-sufficient woman known in Hollywood circles for her decency and warmth. Once her marriage with the immortal crooner was over, Nancy settled into a quiet life built around the rearing of their three children, Nancy, Frank, Jr., and Christina. Nancy and the children accepted Barbara as one of their own with open arms, and she found their friendship a source of great strength. One post-divorce tale Barbara enjoyed telling involved young Frankie, then around eight years old.

One evening Frankie asked her, "Hey, Barb, were you ever married?"

When Barbara admitted that she had been, Frankie asked to whom, and she replied, "Bob Taylor."

Then Frankie asked, "Where is he?" Barbara hesitated long enough for Frankie to size up the situation knowingly and exclaim, "Oh, you got rooked, too!"

"I'm concentrating on work," Barbara told Hedda Hopper after her divorce had been finalized, "and this is what it takes. Serenity, beauty, quiet, friends when I want them, and the valuable state of being alone which a creative person must have in between." A great deal of Barbara's strength came from those who rallied round her after the divorce, and she touched upon this in a column that Edward R. Murrow asked her to write:

> I believe in God. I am forever grateful to Him for His patience with me, and His tolerance, and His forgiveness. Not too long ago, unhappy and bitter—I left Him. But He never left me. He was there, always helping me—in the untiring devotion of two friends—guiding me gently back to the path of belief and back to the habit of daily prayer.
>
> I still believe in never taking anything for granted in this very human world. I believe that men should not be afraid of sentiment.
>
> I don't believe that people want to be bad or hurt others. Most of the time when people have been hurt badly themselves they lash out at everyone else. We don't have His kind of forgiveness and it's very difficult to learn to "Turn the other cheek." I have not learned this as well as I should nor as well as I want to—but I am trying. I do believe that this is a lesson I must learn so I may become a better person—and as I learn my lessons, I may be able to help someone else as I have been helped. I believe that this is the only way I can prove my gratitude to God and my appreciation of all the help I've had from people of greater faith and wisdom than mine.
>
> I believe we must believe in God. I believe that without this we will have no world.

It was Barbara's friends who helped give her the strength to bear the news of Robert Taylor's marriage to actress Ursula Thiess in May of 1954, and her telegram of congratulations was the first to reach the newlyweds.

Barbara continued to work as hard as ever, and her next film was a "dinky little western" produced in 3-D, *The Moonlighter*. Barbara's co-star was Fred MacMurray, but the two talents were wasted in this film. She replaced Lauren Bacall in *Blowing Wild* with Gary Cooper—not a high point in either of their careers.

Her next film, *Executive Suite,* was a good deal better. No other studio could put together all-star casts as well as Metro-Goldwyn-Mayer; and their lineup for this film was superb. Its producer was the distinguished John Houseman, and the director was Robert Wise. The cast included June Allyson, Fredric March, Walter Pidgeon, Shelley Winters, Paul Douglas, Louis Calhern, Dean Jagger, Nina Foch, and, at the top of the list, Barbara Stanwyck and William Holden. Barbara's role in the film wasn't as large as some, but it was a strong one and she wanted to do it, "no matter how short it was." A large part of this decision was probably based on the opportunity to work with Bill Holden again. Their one powerful confrontation scene was probably the best in the film.

Barbara's wardrobe for the film was designed by Helen Rose, now twice an Oscar winner. One day during the filming of *Executive Suite,* Rose stopped by the set only to find that Barbara had done the whole day's shooting with her dress on backward. Barbara was horrified and embarrassed. Reshooting the day's work would be very expensive. There was no need to worry. Helen Rose saved the day when she exclaimed, "I like it better, it looks great!"

"Helen Rose is not only a great designer," Barbara later proclaimed, "she's a hell of a lady!"

Executive Suite was one of the most successful films of 1954, and it appeared on many of the "ten best" lists. Barbara's performance won her her third Laurel Award. The film was followed by *Witness to Murder,* a frantic film in which Barbara inadvertently witnesses a murder and, in trying to convince the police, ends up in a psychiatric ward. It was a film Barbara could easily have done without.

CHAPTER 30

Although Barbara Stanwyck never gave less than her best in any film, those films made during the mid-fifties left a great deal to be desired. It was the same story with many of the most important stars of the thirties and forties. Bette Davis, Joan Crawford, and Gary Cooper found themselves in the same predicament. Good scripts had disappeared. Most of the long-term contracts between the studios and their stables of stars had expired, and careers began to crumble.

To her credit, Barbara held on longer than most. "I'm an actress and an actress acts," she explained, so when the good parts were few and far between, she filled in the gaps with some less distinguished films. Barbara was once asked how she could allow her talents to be squandered in such films as some of those she made during this era.

The answer is simply that you make a horrible mistake. You get taken in by what seems like a basically good idea and a sort of rough, temporary screenplay and you sign on to do the picture without ever having seen a completed script. Within one week after the start of shooting, everybody on the set knows that the thing is just not jelling. But by that time you're hooked. So you do the best you can—and you privately hope that nobody goes to see it.

One of these was *Cattle Queen of Montana* in which she played opposite Ronald Reagan. The film was based on the true story of a woman who drove a herd of cattle from Texas to Montana. Most of the film was shot on location in Glacier National Park in Montana during extremely cold weather, and Ronald Reagan remembers Barbara's courage through some very difficult scenes.

> I remember one day when the scene called for me to come riding out of the woods while Barbara was swimming in a lake. There was a double on hand to do the scene for her, but Barbara's instinctive knowledge of screen technique told her that it would be a better scene if her face could be seen rather than a double being shot from a distance. So, into the icy water she went.
>
> Movie scenes are never filmed in a few minutes. There is always a reason for doing it over and over, then over again. But not one whimper out of Stanwyck. If the scene called for her to ride, she rode and she rode well. And, when we had to run through the woods, dive over a log and then turn and start blazing away at the bad guys, she dived over the log.

Some of the Blackfoot Indians in Glacier National Park appeared in *Cattle Queen of Montana* and were impressed by Barbara's incredible stamina and hard work. In admiration they gave her their tribe's most revered name, Princess Many Victories III, and the braves made her a member of their Brave Dog Society. During the induction ceremony they stated, "To be a member of our Brave Dog Society is to be known as one of our brave people. Princess Many Victories III is one of us."

Barbara's next film, *The Violent Men*, had little more to offer than the chance to see her work with Glenn Ford and Edward G. Robinson. *Escape to Burma* with Robert Ryan was no better.

There's Always Tomorrow was another of Ross Hunter's glossy remakes of a thirties soap opera. Nevertheless, it was tastefully put together, and the casting of Fred MacMurray and Joan Bennett opposite Barbara helped raise the film above many others of the genre. This was Barbara's fourth film with MacMurray, and their easy rapport was a pleasure to watch.

Barbara had never appeared in a full-fledged musical. There were few that seemed appropriate for her to pursue, but in 1956 Columbia Pictures announced that it would be producing a film version of John O'Hara's *Pal Joey*. The play had been a musical hit on Broadway with Gene Kelly as Joey and Vivienne Segal as Vera Simpson, the socialite who falls in love with him. The film was to star Frank Sinatra, and although Harry Cohn wanted Marlene Dietrich for the female lead, Barbara let him know that she wanted the part badly. However, neither was chosen as Vera; Cohn eventually cast Rita Hayworth, feeling that her obvious sexuality was more appropriate.

Meanwhile, Barbara had to make do with a few more less-than-worthwhile properties such as *The Maverick Queen* with Scott Brady, *Crime of Passion* with Sterling Hayden, and *These Wilder Years*. At least *These Wilder Years* gave Barbara the chance to work with James Cagney, but even their talents couldn't save the film. *The New York Times* noted that:

> Mr. Cagney and Miss Stanwyck go at it with becoming restraint and good-will. But the story is hackneyed and slushy and Roy Rowland's direction is so slow and pictorially uninteresting that the picture is mawkish and dull.

Trooper Hook was the sixth film in which Barbara worked with Joel McCrea, and as in her collaborations with Fred MacMurray, there was an easy rapport between them obvious to the audiences. Barbara's role in this film was a departure from anything she had portrayed to date. She played the part of Cora, a white woman who, during her imprisonment by an Indian chief, gives birth to his son and then suffers an estrangement from her own people because of her love for the half-caste child. Her performance is both gentle and strong, and director Charles Marquis Warren later called her "the most magnificent actress I ever worked with and, I think, the finest actress Hollywood has ever turned out."

Marilyn Monroe had wanted the lead in the Samuel Fuller film *Woman with a Whip*, but Fuller had written the script with Barbara in mind and insisted she be cast in the part. Fuller's films are notorious for violence, and this one was no exception. Fuller's script called for Barbara to be killed in the end, but Twentieth Century–Fox insisted she live and also demanded that the title be changed to the less perverse-sounding *Forty Guns*.

Barbara was fifty years old when she completed *Forty Guns* in 1957 but seemed as vigorous and vital as she had twenty years earlier in *Stella Dallas*. She had made eighty-one films in thirty years but still looked forward to each new film with enthusiasm. "My work is responsible for all the good things that have come into my life," she has said. "I feel most completely alive when I'm starting a new picture." After *Forty Guns*, however, she would not make another film for five years.

Refusing to sit on her laurels, she set her sights on the opportunities presented by television, and in just a short time she was to conquer that medium as well.

CHAPTER 31

Barbara wet her feet in the magic waters of television rather slowly. Her first appearance on the small screen had been as a guest on Jack Benny's series in 1954. This was followed by two appearances as guest hostess on Loretta Young's series in late 1955, during Miss Young's recovery from surgery.

Over and over again Barbara had vowed that Westerns were her favorite type of film, and during the fifties she had appeared in quite a few. Television gave her an even greater opportunity to ride the West. During the 1958–59 season she made four appearances on *Dick Powell's Zane Grey Theater* anthology series, and in early 1959 she was the star of Jack Benny's famous takeoff on the film *Gaslight*, entitled *Autolite*.

Throughout the fifties Barbara's agents received numerous offers from each of the networks asking her to star in her own series, but none was willing to give Barbara what she desperately wanted, a Western series of her own. Again and again they told her the same story, Westerns were beneath her, she deserved something classier, something prettier. "I'm too old and too wealthy to swallow that stuff," she protested. "They don't understand what it is I want to do anyway. I want to play a real frontier woman, not one of those crinoline-covered things you see in most Westerns. I'm with the boys, I want to go where the boys go." Nevertheless, all of Barbara's arguments seemed to be in vain.

One of her appearances on *Dick Powell's Zane Grey Theater*, in an episode entitled "The Freighter," was meant as a pilot for a Western series. "I don't care what you or anyone else thought of it," she told one reporter, "I loved it." Unfortunately the networks felt differently. "The boys in the flannel suits said they didn't see how we could go for thirty-nine episodes," Barbara fumed. "That's silly. I've got enough books on Western lore at home for a hundred episodes."

As the Hollywood film industry ground to a halt, many of the greatest stars of the thirties and forties found refuge in television, many of them hosting anthology series. Loretta Young had been one of the first to make the move, and the immediate success of her series made it a prototype for many of those to come. Each of Miss Young's shows opened with her making a glamorous entrance in a stunning gown and then speaking briefly about the forthcoming show. Then the drama would begin with Loretta Young starring in about half of them and celebrity guests starring in the others. Afterward Miss Young would return to say good-night.

With the dearth of quality films being offered her, a similar series seemed to be a natural route for Barbara to take. It was just such a series that the networks wanted Barbara to do, but all backed off at Barbara's demand that she be given completed scripts to approve before signing a contract. She had no intention of finding out after making her commitment that she would have to deal with inferior material. Finally, her management representatives, the Jaffe Agency, took the situation in their own hands and, at great expense, purchased stories and had teleplays prepared to submit to Barbara. Their strategy worked, and in January of 1960 Barbara and NBC-TV jointly announced that she would be starring in the fall in *The Barbara Stanwyck Theater* to be shown on Monday evenings at 10:00. The prospect of her own series excited Barbara, and she assured the press that she would personally take responsibility for the show's quality.

"We are prepared to offer top prices for scripts," Barbara told reporters. "The foundation of any good show is the story, not the star. We have found several potential stories for our series, and I hope I don't louse them up. They just don't seem to make movies for the female stars anymore—the Colberts, the Crawfords, and the Dunnes," she said. "I haven't the vaguest idea why. Motion pictures have great roles for men these days, even if the characters are a little mixed up. For my series, I hope to locate scripts with meaty roles for women, but that doesn't mean I intend to avoid stories centering around the male lead. If the story is good, I'll be happy to play an also-ran; I've no particular desire to be 98 percent of the script. In fact, I'd rather have a 50-50 situation, because then there would have to be an awfully good actor with me, and I need all the help I can get."

Asked why she was switching to television, Barbara was her usual honest self. "Simple, I wasn't working and I wanted to work. What else is there for me to do? I have no hobbies. I suppose that makes me an idiot, but there it is. You're supposed to paint or sculpt or something. I don't. I like to travel, but a woman can't travel alone. It's a bore. And it's a darned lonesome bore." Nevertheless, excitement aside, Barbara remained wary of too much optimism. "Friends and acquaintances have been saying to me, 'I see you're going into television—how nice,' " she remarked wryly. Then she added, "How nice remains to be seen."

Of the thirty-nine segments of *The Barbara Stanwyck Show*, Barbara appeared in all but four. The first segment was called "The Mink Coat" and featured in a small role a young newcomer by the name of Jack Nicholson. Four Western scripts were slipped in to satisfy Barbara. Three other scripts, developing a character by the name of Little Joe, were submitted as a pilot for another series starring Stanwyck, but the concept was turned down because of difficulties connected with its Hong Kong locale.

One of these stories about Little Joe, entitled "Dragon by the Tail," even found its way into the *Congressional Record*. In a speech reminiscent of those made during the Red witch-hunts of the early fifties, Repre-

170

sentative Francis E. Walter, chairman of the House Committee on Un-American Activities, told Congress that Communists were "openly moving back into" the Hollywood movie industry. "A number of frequently identified Communists are back at work writing, producing, or otherwise associated with films, some of which are only thinly-disguised Communist-serving, anti-U.S. propaganda." Then, citing Barbara Stanwyck as a real patriot, Walter spoke of her performance in "Dragon by the Tail," in which the script called for her to defend the United States against a Communist agent. Barbara was so carried away by the script, Walters reported, that she forgot her lines and had to ad-lib. She concluded the scene in tears while emphatically stating, "Loving your country is never out of date."

Although Barbara was pleased to have the show noted for its patriotism, she refused to take credit for it herself. "I only ad-libbed two words," she explained and then cited the work of screenwriter Albert Beich. "He was writing for and about America as it should be done. It was part and parcel of the show. I didn't intend to cry, to get emotionally involved. If the writing had not been good, I wouldn't have been carried away even though I do get emotional when I see someone wave the American flag."

For the most part *The Barbara Stanwyck Show* was consistently well reviewed and drew good ratings. Therefore it was no surprise when, in May of 1961, the Television Academy of Arts and Sciences honored her with an Emmy Award as Outstanding Actress in a Series.

Later in the month, however, Barbara did get hit with a blockbuster of a surprise when NBC announced that her show was not being picked up for the next season. Barbara was heartbroken and in subsequent interviews expressed a great deal of anger and confusion:

As I understand it, from my producer Lou Edelman, they want action shows and have a theory that women don't do action. The fact is, I'm the best action actress in the world. I can do horse drags, jump off buildings, and I have the scars to prove it.

When asked, Barbara was at a loss to explain who "they" were:

I don't know who "they" are and no one else seems to know any of the individuals who make up the group. They're just referred to as "they" in all conversations. Apparently it's a word applied to certain New Yorkers with a deliberate corporate lack of identity. It's ironic though that after all the romancing of me that took place trying to get me to do a show that was a success, now they've decided to drop the show after a year.

When Barbara was told that there was a movement among her fans to keep the show on the air and that hundreds of letters were reaching NBC protesting the cancellation, she remarked bitterly, "What's the difference, no one at NBC can read."

CHAPTER 32

Perhaps no one individual knew Barbara Stanwyck better than Buck Mack. Uncle Buck, as she called him, was one of the few people who had known her since her days as Ruby Stevens in New York; he more than anyone else had been with her through her triumphs and her tragedies.

Mack had been living with Barbara since her divorce from Frank Fay in the mid-thirties when she invited him to help out at Marwyck. When Barbara married Bob Taylor and moved to Beverly Hills, Buck Mack went with them, and after her divorce he stayed with her.

Barbara Stanwyck is one of the most anonymous of Hollywood's philanthropists, and often it was Buck Mack who brought various charities to her attention or carried out her gestures of kindness. If Barbara read of a family that had lost all their possessions in a fire, it was Buck who would bring them her anonymous cashier's check. Each Christmas, Barbara would send Uncle Buck to the Brown Derby to determine surreptitiously which of the regulars were down on their luck and then have baskets of food delivered to their homes. And each Christmas, she picks up the tab at the Brown Derby for thirty or forty Hollywood veterans who can't afford to go anywhere else.

Mack was a stabilizing influence in Barbara's life and someone she could always turn to whom she knew would level with her. "He's the only one who tells me the truth about my pictures," she remarked. "If he thinks it's a stinker, he says so."

In the late fifties Buck Mack developed serious problems with emphysema, and Barbara took personal responsibility for his care. She attempted to get him a live-in nurse, but Buck Mack insisted he could care for himself and, incredibly, for two years he did. Then, when he no longer could function on his own, he insisted that Barbara take him to the Motion Picture Country House and Hospital.

Barbara visited Buck twice a week when she wasn't working, and on the weekends when she was working, she would be with Buck on Saturdays and Sundays. They would spend the days of Barbara's visits strolling through the gardens until Buck could no longer walk. After Buck was confined to bed, he and Barbara would reminisce for hours about the good times and the bad. Often, Uncle Buck would think back to the "funny little gal with shining shoe-button eyes and brown pigtails" who told him joyfully, " 'I'm going to be a star. I'm going right to the top and nothing is gonna stop me!' "

In July of 1959 Buck Mack took a turn for the worse. Barbara went to the Country House every day and stayed until evening. She called his only living relative, a brother in Ohio, and brought him out to Los Angeles. For a while in September, Buck seemed to rally, and Barbara cut her visits back to two or three a week.

On Friday, September 29, Barbara was sitting at the hairdresser's under a dryer when she suddenly felt she should go out to see Buck, although she hadn't planned to go again until Saturday. Leaving the beauty salon, she made a beeline for the Country House. At first, when she got there, Buck seemed to recognize her. "Is it Saturday?" he asked, knowing that she had promised to come back then. "Yes," Barbara told him, not wanting to confuse his already fragile condition. Then his mind clouded further. "Where is the Queen?" he kept asking. "Why doesn't she come to see me?" "I'm here, Uncle Buck," Barbara would reply, but Buck couldn't hear. That evening he was given last rites. The next morning at seven, Barbara's phone rang. It was the head nurse calling to tell her that Uncle Buck had died during the night.

Again, Barbara called Buck's brother in Ohio and offered to fly him back for the funeral, but his brother was too sick to come. Barbara handled all the funeral arrangements and made sure that Buck's wish for a high mass was fulfilled.

Barbara hadn't seen her son for eight years when, in April of 1960, newspapers and scandal sheets reported that Anthony Dion Fay had been arrested for attempting to sell pornographic materials to teenagers. Dion had been married in the middle fifties, and at the time of his arrest he was living at 4714 Slauson Avenue with his wife and two-year-old son.

Uncle Buck had been Barbara's only contact with Dion since the breach in their relationship years before. It had been Buck who had told her of Dion's marriage, and although Barbara had sent her son and his wife a bedroom set at the time, there had been no reconciliation. Barbara's reaction to her son's arrest is unknown, and it seems there was no communication between them at that time. Nor was Barbara in touch with him a year later when Frank Fay died on September 25, 1961, after rupture of the abdominal aorta. Fay's estate, estimated at $200,000 at the time of his death, went to Dion. When asked about Dion's whereabouts, Barbara would only mumble, "Oh, he's long gone" and then change the subject.

With Buck Mack's death, Barbara's circle of friends drew even closer. There had been few additions over the last few years. Columnist Shirley Eder had been introduced to Barbara by Renee Godfrey, and Shirley and Barbara became extremely close although Shirley lived in Detroit. Designer Nolan Miller began creating a great deal of Barbara's personal wardrobe, and he, too, became close. Nancy Sinatra and Helen Ferguson seemed to remain closest. Remarkably, from the mid-fifties on, there was not even a rumor of a romance of any sort. When a reporter asked if she ever went out dating, she responded glibly, "Oh, yes, sometimes I have to go to something or other. When I do, I just call good ol' Butch [Cesar] Romero and he says rather reluctantly, 'Well, if you HAVE to go, I'll take you.' He does that for all of us old broads."

On the whole, Hollywood parties bored Barbara. She had been an integral part of the town now for over thirty years, yet she still felt uncomfortable among such a crowd. Academy Award-winning actor George Kennedy remembers watching Barbara's discomfort at just such a party during his early days in pictures:

> In the days when I thought it important to go to some Hollywood parties, it was always difficult because I'm basically quite shy. I would have some drinks in order to get enough courage to go, and even then would seek out a commiserate spirit and sit with him until I figured I'd put in enough of an appearance. Then I would leave.
>
> Under just such circumstances I was sitting with Edgar Bergen at the home of Anita Louise and Henry Berger. He was even quieter than I was, but he did talk, and I did (quite admiringly) listen.
>
> Miss Stanwyck entered. Like many of the "GIANT" ladies of the screen, she was hardly a giant. I could see as she acknowledged the immediate and usual fawning that she was uncomfortable. She finally sat. The fawners went on to the next one through the door. And Bergen and I watched her awhile, from across the room. And she just sat. The hubbub went on—she said an occasional word or two to her escort—but mostly we realized she was even shyer than we were, and like us was waiting for an opportunity to leave. So she sat.
>
> So tall. So regal. I said to Edgar, "That's a great star." He said, ". . . A giant."
>
> I think she was taller than anybody there, even sitting down.

Meanwhile, when not working, Barbara kept busy by reading three or four books a week and watching an endless number of old films on TV: "I have no willpower. I watch all the old movies on TV, including some of mine. I see *Stagecoach* every time it's on, and have seen *Woman of the Town* starring Claire Trevor, at least ten times. I'm an addict. I have no courage. But it does make me angry that they cut these movies. They cut key scenes. One of mine, *The Other Love* with David Niven, had a dramatic scene at the end, where I'm dying of consumption. Just before my death, Niven is talking to me. He knows I'm dying and I know it. It was very difficult doing. On TV, right in the middle of the scene, when David is talking and I'm gasping for breath, they end it, cutting out the death. I look like an idiot."

The intimate details of her life continued to be an area she kept well guarded, and when Ralph Edwards approached Helen Ferguson about arranging to surprise Barbara on *This Is Your Life*, Helen managed to talk him out of it, knowing how horrified her friend would have been at such an infringement on her privacy. "If Edwards ever tricked me into that," Barbara later warned, "I'd just say right there, 'Brother, that's your trouble, not mine,' and I would walk out." Wisely, Edwards never pursued the idea.

During the early sixties there were rumors that Barbara would return to the Broadway stage. Whether Barbara had ever expressed an interest in appearing again in live theater, she was quick to give them thumbs down at this time. "I'm a coward," she explained. "When somebody sends me a play script I don't even have to look at it, I break out in hives. I don't think I could ever survive the dress rehearsal. I couldn't even do live TV, that's how scared I am of an audience. I think I made a mistake staying away from a live audience so long, but I love films. Of course, I work with crews of forty to sixty when I make movies, but that's like a family affair. Actually, I'm working with the sons and the daughters of the crews I worked with in the old days."

As for motion pictures, Barbara claims to have received no offers between the completion of *Forty Guns* in 1957 and her acceptance of a role in *Walk on the Wild Side* in 1962. This film was based on Nelson Algren's rather torrid novel of the same name and was set, for the most part, in a ritzy New Orleans bordello, the Doll's House. The cast included Jane Fonda, Laurence Harvey, Capucine, Anne Baxter, "and," as the credits read, "Barbara Stanwyck as Jo Courtney." Barbara's role was that of the madam of the Doll's House, and she relished it, telling reporters, "Chalk up another first for Stanwyck!"

The set of *Walk on the Wild Side* was not a happy one. There are unconfirmed rumors that Blake Edwards had begun the directing chores but was replaced by Edward Dmytryk within the first few days. Possibly this was the cause of the tension. Anne Baxter recalls, "The atmosphere on the set was ghastly, just ghastly. Indescribable. The royally spoiled male co-star had made some charming, scathing remarks about the lack of talent to do with one of the other female stars and she was in tears most of the time. He fought with the director and stalked off the set and was never on time. One day, he kept us waiting one hour and a half. Highly professional Barbara was furious. So was I. But I had lied rather baldly about an increasingly pregnant self and was keeping a rather low profile. Well, when he finally drifted back on the set, Barbara chewed him out with such icy grace that I wanted to cheer. He never did it again. Never."

The "royally spoiled male co-star" Anne Baxter speaks of was Laurence Harvey. Some years after making the film he was asked for his recollections of working with Barbara and responded in an adroit but gentlemanly manner: "Miss Stanwyck is one of the most startling and professional women I have ever worked with. She had a great air of honesty and directness about her, and her relationship with cast and crew was totally unpretentious . . . in fact I could never quite decide what side of the camera she was working on!"

Unfortunately the film didn't live up to the potential promised by its script. Barbara's performance was wonderful, fluctuating subtly between cruelty and vulnerability in her portrayal of the hard-bitten madam no longer attracted to her husband but desperately in love with one of her girls.

There was a good deal more television work awaiting Barbara, including two memorable appearances on *The Untouchables* and four on *Wagon Train*, which was one of her favorite television shows. By now Barbara had sort of adopted the many stunt men and women she had worked with through the years, and on shows such as *Wagon Train* she enjoyed a wonderful working relationship with them and began referring to them as "my own special people."

Barbara didn't make another film for two years and then suddenly in a surprising piece of casting turned up with Elvis Presley in *Roustabout*. Barbara was surprised when Hal Wallis called her with a part in

Presley's film but later explained that, "The idea of working with Mr. Presley intrigued me because that would bring me into a younger audience than I'm accustomed to. And I thought this would be rather fun."

Barbara did have reservations about what sort of professional attitude she would find in the singing sensation but was pleasantly surprised and, as usual, didn't hesitate to say so: "So many people expect the swelled head and all that sort of thing. As a matter of fact, very honestly, so did I. It is not the case. Elvis was a wonderful person to work with. His manners are impeccable, he is on time, he knows his lines, he asks for nothing outside of what any other actor or actress wants."

Even *The New York Times* was pleased with the film and said in its review: "It has three assets. One is Mr. Presley, perfectly cast and perfectly at ease, as a knockabout, leathery young derelict who links up with a small-time transient midway. It also has, as the carnival owner, the professional seasoning of Barbara Stanwyck. Welcome back, Miss Stanwyck, and where on earth have you been? And while the carnival canvas yields little in the way of dramatic substance, it does cue in 11 songs."

CHAPTER 33

For years Barbara had included among her circle of close friends director Peter Godfrey and his wife, Renee. The three of them would often have dinner together on Friday nights until Peter became seriously ill with Parkinson's disease and went to stay at the Motion Picture Country Home and Hospital. Then, in May of 1964, Renee Godfrey died suddenly, leaving three daughters to fend for themselves—Barbara, who was seventeen, and fourteen-year-old twins, Jill and Tracey. Mrs. Katherine H. Danzig and Barbara were appointed as legal guardians of the Godfrey children. It was a responsibility that Barbara took very seriously.

Their father died just a short while later, and the girls grew very close to Barbara. Not only did she see that their physical needs were taken care of, but she became a constant source of encouragement and guidance to them, and she considered them an important part of her family.

Unfortunately, Mrs. Godfrey's death was not the only sadness to touch Barbara that year. On December 14, 1964, her brother, Byron Stevens, was stricken fatally by a heart attack while filming a television commercial at the El Caballo Country Club. He was sixty years old. Years earlier Barbara had helped Byron get started in films as an extra, and he had made a good living in films since the thirties. At the time of his death he was a director of the Screen Extras Guild. Byron was survived by his wife of many years, Caryl, his son, Brian, and a five-year-old grandson, Michael. Now Barbara's closest remaining relative was her sister Mildred.

After the cancellation of *The Barbara Stanwyck Show* there were a great many attempts to find another series for her, but it took some time to get one off the ground. Barbara's two appearances on *The Untouchables* had been considered pilots for a series to be called *The Seekers* about a woman heading the FBI's Missing Persons Bureau, but again, Barbara was disappointed: "We could have gone all over the world looking for missing persons. That's what I liked about it. The idea was varied and we were using case histories of missing persons. A lot of the histories were tragic but many were funny. The show didn't have to be grim."

Then there were Jackie Cooper's futile attempts to sell a series entitled *Calhoun*, starring himself and Barbara. It was an experience that would leave Cooper bitter and disillusioned and would be immortalized by Merle Miller in his book *Only You, Dick Daring!*

By 1965 Barbara Stanwyck was fifty-eight years old and a certified Hollywood legend. Work was as much a part of her life as ever. During her career she had appeared in more than her share of classic films and had racked up four Academy Award nominations. Nevertheless, she didn't sit at home refusing all but the choicest roles. Financially she was secure enough never to work again but emotionally she needed to work. "I'm not giving up," she stated unequivocally. "I couldn't retire to a life of leisure. That would drive me mad. I'm ready to work anytime and everybody in the business knows it. I'll take any part that comes along. I don't care about the money or the size of the role. All I care about is working."

"To hear people talk about me," she complained, "you'd think I was some sort of freak living with my memories, in a vine-covered mansion, hidden away from the world. I'm supposed to be a hermit, a loner nursing a broken heart because I lost Robert Taylor. That's ridiculous. My divorce from Taylor was nearly sixteen years ago. If I'd been holding up a torch that long, by now my arm would have withered! I don't think anyone's hilariously happy living alone, but you learn to adjust."

Barbara's life had been one of many adjustments, and she had always been a woman who met them head-on with very few glances over her shoulder. Her relationship with Robert Taylor is a prime example. Once the rumors of a reconciliation were put aside and after Taylor had settled into his marriage with Ursula Thiess, Barbara and Bob were able to establish a friendship based on mutual respect and a sincere affection for each other. Although there was no socializing between them after Taylor's remarriage, neither ever spoke negatively about the other for publication or otherwise. Barbara's proud protestations aside, it is doubtful that she ever grew out of love with Bob Taylor.

Producer William Castle was well aware of the legendary status of the Taylor–Stanwyck romance and of their continuing friendship and thought they would be a powerful box-office draw if they co-starred in a film. With just such an idea in mind, Castle approached Barbara with the script for a film entitled *The Night Walker*. Barbara had resisted joining such contemporaries as Bette Davis and Joan Crawford in the horror genre, although she had been tempted to appear with Davis and Olivia DeHavilland in *Hush . . . Hush, Sweet Charlotte*. *The Night Walker* was just such a film, though, and Castle promised a first-class production.

After getting Barbara's commitment to the film, Castle asked her what she thought of the idea of co-starring opposite Bob Taylor. "I said it was fine with me but he'd better ask Bob. That was all there was to it," she said later. Taylor accepted the part readily and explained to the press, "Any actor who would turn down a chance to play opposite Barbara Stanwyck, under any circumstances, would have to be out of his head. She's certainly one of the pros in the business. I'm very enthusiastic about the film. It looks like it will be a pleasant experience."

Production of *The Night Walker* proceeded without incident. Between scenes Stanwyck and Taylor chatted amiably, and Ursula Taylor visited the set often with no apparent problem. It is said that the second Mrs.

Taylor wished to become better friends with Barbara and kept pestering Bob to invite her for dinner. Bob vetoed the idea, telling Ursula, "You don't know Barbara like I do." Producer/director William Castle was pleased with the pleasant atmosphere on the set and especially with Barbara's influence: "Her very presence on a set inspired. Her feeling of camaraderie toward everyone she worked with—and the love of the entire crew, as they called her Missy, was something to behold. I used to watch in awe and amazement as the electricians, high up in the rafters, shouted down, 'Hi, Missy!' She would look up and shout back with warmth."

As for Bob Taylor, when asked what it had been like working with his ex-wife, he responded, "It's as if we were never married."

CHAPTER 34

Stanwyck's lobbying for a Western series eventually paid off, and in January 1965, ABC announced that the next season would find Barbara Stanwyck starring in *The Big Valley* on that network.

The premiere of *The Big Valley* had been developed for Barbara in 1961 by Lou Edelman, producer of *The Barbara Stanwyck Show*. Edelman had been unable to interest the networks in a Western series starring Stanwyck, and in late 1963 he sold property to the producing team Levy–Garner–Laven, the men responsible for *The Rifleman*. They, in turn, struck a deal with ABC in late 1964 and then asked Barbara if she would still be interested in starring as the widowed owner of a big California ranch circa 1870.

Although *The Big Valley* was developed along the lines originally planned by Edelman some years before, Barbara was somewhat dismayed to find that her character, Victoria Barkley, was a little tamer than the two-fisted dame she had in mind. Before agreeing to star in the series, she made sure the producers understood the conditions involved in her acceptance of the role: "I'm a tough old broad from Brooklyn," she told them. "Don't try to make me into something I'm not. If you want someone to tiptoe down the Barkley staircase in crinoline and politely ask where the cattle went, get another girl. That's not me."

The Big Valley was the saga of Victoria Barkley and her family, which consisted of three sons, a daughter, and the illegitimate son of her deceased husband. Cast in these roles were Richard Long as Jarrod Barkley, the oldest son and a lawyer; Peter Breck as Nick Barkley; Charles Briles as Eugene Barkley, the youngest son and a college student; Linda Evans as Audra Barkley, the beautiful daughter; and, finally, Lee Majors as the bastard son, Heath Barkley. Despite the inexperience of Lee Majors and Linda Evans, it was a strong cast and one Barbara found she could work well with.

Throughout her career Barbara had been interested in helping the inexperienced, and during the show's first season she showed just such an interest in Lee Majors, much to the consternation of Peter Breck, who felt she was showing undue favoritism. Breck needn't have worried. Once Majors seemed to be in control and gained more confidence, Barbara's relationship with the three men evened out, and over the next four years all three of Barbara's "sons" grew to respect her inordinately. (The part of the youngest son was subsequently written out, early in the series.)

Linda Evans, Barbara's daughter in the series, had made some small appearances in series such as *Bachelor Father*, but she too was a novice, although she was wise enough to watch Barbara carefully and learn from her. Seventeen years after the start of *The Big Valley*, Evans would be one of television's superstars because of her role in the drama series *Dynasty*. A close friend of Barbara's, she recently spoke of the star's effect on her own career:

> I absolutely love her. She really is like a mom to me. I still call her. We still talk to each other. As a matter of fact, about eight months ago, Lee Majors, Missy, and myself had lunch together and had a wonderful time. She taught me the most important thing in my career, which is to be a professional. She never liked

pampering. She was always there a half an hour earlier than when she was supposed to be, completely prepared and ready to do her job and said to everybody else, 'you'd better be too,' and that's the way I've been and when I work with people, they always say 'you can tell who taught you about the business because you're very professional.' I'm very grateful to her for that.

Barbara's position on the set of *The Big Valley* was undisputed. She was "the Queen" but never to the point of interfering with the director's place in the work. She was a pro and those around her knew it. Subsequently, when she opened her mouth, everyone listened. Once, when an assistant director was attempting to get quiet on the set and couldn't, Barbara stepped in to help. "Qui-et!" she yelled in a voice that reverberated through the sound stage. The response was immediate. Total silence. Then Stanwyck smiled. She wasn't angry with anyone. She just wanted quiet; she got it.

On another occasion, Majors and guest star Pete Haskell took a somewhat longer-than-warranted lunch during a shooting day. When they returned, Barbara was infuriated. Not at Haskell, who was unaware of Stanwyck's demand for punctuality, but at Majors, who should have known better. Majors stood corrected.

During the run of *The Big Valley* no one could solicit Barbara's ire more easily than those who compared her series to *Bonanza*, NBC's long-running Western saga of the Cartwright family. Although the popularity of *Bonanza* was probably a major part of ABC's decision to proceed with *The Big Valley*, Barbara considered such comparisons foolhardy. "Fine, let them compare us to *Bonanza*," she argued. "You've got to be compared to something, so why not *Bonanza*? I'll tell you this, though," she went on, "we get mad at each other in our show, and make mistakes. Lorne Green is the Loretta Young of the West. That's not for me."

Later Barbara explained further: "I have been quoted as saying that I thought Lorne Greene in *Bonanza* was the 'Loretta Young of Western Soap Operas.' I think I've been slightly misquoted. What I did mean was that I felt he was far too pontifical. When he passes judgment— that's that! When Lorne Greene has an opinion, it has to be right.

Well, damn it all! I've had my own ranches. I am a horsewoman. I ran ranches and herds and bred livestock years before Lorne Greene even knew what a saddle looked like. And you don't run ranches anywhere by being pontifical about any bit of it. Nobody on any ranch can ever tell what's going to happen next. You just can't afford to become too opinionated or too conceited. If you do, you portray the West badly, and you do the West an injustice. The West was tough, hell-country, full of fights and wrongs and hardness. Pontifical wiseacres did not survive long out there!"

Comparisons aside, *The Big Valley* was successful enough to be renewed for the next season and two more after that. All in all, there were 112 episodes involving an incredibly talented list of guest stars, including Anne Baxter, Diane Baker, Milton Berle, Colleen Dewhurst, Maurice Evans, Julie Harris, Carol Lynley, Leslie Nielsen, Pernell Roberts, Tom Tryon, Katharine Ross, George Kennedy, Peter Haskell, and Bradford Dillman.

Barbara's stamina amazed everyone, as usual, and she insisted on doing most of her own stunts. In one case the script called for her to be dragged through the street on the end of a rope tied to a horse. Director Virgil Vogel cleared a path 50 feet long and instructed Barbara to let go at the end of the clearing. Not Barbara. She held on for 150 feet with two cameras on her. "It was a great shot," Vogel exclaimed.

Barbara's position as one of the Grand Dames of Hollywood was somewhat softened by the fact that she was working a great deal more than any of her contemporaries. Fan magazines were again full of stories about her, published under titles promising sensational intimate details about her life. "We Find Barbara Stanwyck's Missing Family," cried one. "The Lady Shoots Straight from the Heart," promised another. Through all of it Barbara continued to hold her head high, meeting reporters' questions with honesty and integrity but allowing few glimpses of the woman behind the star.

She admitted that the "new Hollywood" left a great deal to be desired and complained that there were few actors around to compare with those of the past, such as Clark Gable, Henry Fonda, and Bette Davis. "I don't know quite what has happened," she said. "There are one or two actors who have it in them. Natalie Wood, of course, is a star. I think Suzanne Pleshette will become one certainly. Of the young men, there's Steve McQueen, who is one of the very few who has managed the transition from the smaller screen to the wider screen of pictures. James Garner—well, he's made the transition but I have my doubts."

The ingratitude of those gaining immediate fame on series television was something that Barbara couldn't tolerate, and when Dan Blocker of *Bonanza* complained about his $10,000-a-week salary, it was more than Barbara could bear. "What so-called artist is this who feels he is wasting his talent for $10,000 a week?" she asked angrily. "He seems to feel the public loves him for himself as an actor. But what was he before playing Hoss? The love the public has given him is due to the role, the script, the actions of the person he is employed to portray. If he is now a multimillionaire, as he says he is—and from this part—what a shame he should continue to fool the public and to accept the love they give him."

Barbara knew that without the public she would have remained Ruby Stevens. She was not hesitant to reveal her feelings that stemmed from this knowledge: "With any actor, or actress, our dedication proves that we are servants of the public. The question of money and fame—surely, all these are secondary in importance to the true artists who have given their lives to the stage or screen. And to use terms like *selling one's self*, isn't that an insult to the public that watches and likes a show and pays for it all? I probably won't be able to look at him [Blocker] again, not in any role he plays. I think I'll probably feel he is just 'prostituting himself' again in playing this next role—any role. How can one avoid remembering some statement like that each time? But it is a fact that the public loves Hoss and has made Dan Blocker a rich man. It is like spitting at an audience that's standing and applauding. That's how I feel."

The Big Valley brought Barbara more recognition and greater honors than she had had in years. In 1966 *Photoplay* magazine presented her with its Editors' Award, which was engraved: "To the 'Eternal Star' whose glamour, talent and professionalism both on and off the screen have thrilled millions of fans throughout the years."

In 1967 and 1968 *Photoplay's* readers voted her "The Most Popular

Female Star," and *TV Radio Mirror's* Television Critics Poll honored her in 1966 as the "Best Dramatic Actress in Television." The National Academy of Television Arts and Sciences awarded her her second Emmy in 1966 as "Outstanding Actress in a Dramatic Series" and nominated her again in 1967 and 1968.

On November 21, 1966, Barbara received what was probably the greatest honor of the many she had earned up to that time. She had been asked by the Screen Actors Guild to present an award to Governor Ronald Reagan at the guild's annual membership meeting. Barbara was standing in the wings waiting to present the award when she heard Reagan begin speaking about the award she thought she was presenting to him. Stunned and unbelieving, she stood stark still as Reagan spoke:

> The Screen Actors Guild Award is not presented just for longtime excellence onscreen. It should be called, perhaps, an above-and-beyond award, because it is given for outstanding achievement in fostering the finest ideals of the acting profession.
>
> The individual to be honored has given of herself in unpublished works of charity and good citizenship. I think there are few among us of her fellow performers or in the public who have any comprehension of the extent of this artist's devotion to those who are handicapped by blindness, human misery, and poverty, both here and abroad.
>
> So for performance of our craft, as well as for performance as a citizen, this . . . award is being presented from actors to an actor, and I am very proud to present someone whom so many of us have worked with. We have known her in this profession as truly a professional and an exponent of our art and craft of the best. Barbara Stanwyck.

Barbara was crying and visibly shaken as she approached the microphone to a standing ovation. Acknowledging Reagan's kiss, she quipped, "That's the first time I've ever been kissed by a governor." Then, holding back her tears, she told the crowd: "I am very, very proud at this moment. I love our profession very much. I love our people in it. I always have and I always will. And whatever little contribution I can make to the profession, or to anything, for that matter, I am very proud to do so. It is a long road. There are a lot of bumps and rocks in it, but this kind of evens it all out, when an event like this happens in your life. From a very proud and grateful heart, thank you very much."

CHAPTER 35

Straight as an arrow, patriotic as an American flag waving in the breeze, Barbara Stanwyck has no tolerance for drugs, draft evaders, or hippies. "The great unwashed," she called them. "I think the hippies are a very small minority," she said once, "who make a very large noise. If their movement is based on love, why do they show so much violence?"

As Stanwyck's career flourished in the late sixties, her personal life was analyzed more closely than ever, and a great deal more attention was given to Dion's absence from that life. As usual, Barbara offered no specific explanation, but during an interview with Dora Albert for *Coronet* magazine she offered more insight than ever before into the reasons for her estrangement from Dion. "There are certain children who are born outlaws, just as there are outlaws in horse breeding. You do everything you can for them and they remain bad: finally you try to see to it that they don't break your heart any longer. After you've done everything you can think of, there is finally a point of no return. You can shoot outlaw horses but not kids. The only thing you can do when you have tried everything, and nothing has worked, is to save yourself. When you have tried to save them and you can't, all you can do is to pray for them and put them in God's hands."

The Big Valley was canceled in the spring of 1969, and Barbara was undoubtedly disappointed. But the show had had a healthy four-year run, and Barbara had few regrets. Actually she had no time for regrets because in June of 1969 she was hit by a much greater heartbreak.

During the summer of 1968, Bob Taylor's doctors found that he was suffering from lung cancer. Initial treatments were futile, and in October 1968 his right lung had to be removed. Then, on May 16, 1969, he was taken to St. John's Hospital in Santa Monica, where doctors reported he was "undergoing treatment for an infection of the left lung." Then, while still undergoing treatment at St. John's, Taylor received the news that his stepson, Michael Thiess, had died of a "possible intentional overdose of narcotics." Both of Taylor's stepchildren, Michael and his older sister, Manuela, had been troublesome children, and only a year before Michael had attempted to kill himself by cutting his wrists.

Just twenty-three days later, on June 8, 1969, Bob Taylor succumbed to lung cancer. Barbara Stanwyck was devastated. Seventeen years before she had told the press emphatically that Bob Taylor was the only man for her . . . the only man she would ever love. Hollywood's cynics were doubtful, sure that with time Barbara would forget her vows of devotion and remarry. But Hollywood's cynics hadn't reckoned with Barbara Stanwyck's iron will. Seventeen years after Hollywood's "perfect marriage" ended in divorce, Barbara remained unmarried. Reporters who asked about the possibility of a marriage in her future were told quietly but firmly, "I've had that!" Now Robert Taylor was dead.

Barbara seldom looked back to the past, but it is inevitable that the tears she shed at Taylor's passing were not only for the death of her friend, but for the hopelessness of her love for him and the ending of a marriage she had always looked on as "forever."

She wanted desperately to attend his funeral but feared her presence would turn the ceremony into a three-ring circus. She remained undecided, arguing herself into and out of one decision or another, until a call came that made it easier for her to make her decision. Barbara's business agent for the last twenty years had been Morgan Maree. During the preparations for Bob Taylor's funeral, Maree received a call from Ursula Taylor asking him to tell Barbara that she wanted her at Bob's funeral and that she would like her to join the family in their private room at the church and to return home with them afterward. Barbara was touched by Ursula's invitation but nevertheless couldn't make up her mind until the morning of the service.

Barbara decided to go to the funeral but decided against wearing black. That privilege belonged to Ursula Taylor, as far as Barbara was concerned. She dressed in a yellow suit and was accompanied to Forest Lawn by Morgan Maree's son, Andrew.

Ursula Thiess, in mourning for the second time in two weeks, was accompanied by Morgan Maree and Governor Ronald Reagan. Barbara declined to join Taylor's family at the service. She felt it would be awkward for Ursula to explain her presence to the Taylors' children, Terry, then fourteen, and Tessa, ten. Barbara sat in the chapel with the rest of the mourners. She tried not to cry, but Taylor's death was more than she could bear. Taylor's eulogy was delivered by Ronald Reagan, who told those gathered, "Perhaps each one of us has his own different memory, but somehow they all add up to 'nice man.' " Barbara cried desperately during the eulogy, calling a great deal of unwanted attention to herself. Swarms of reporters and photographers waited outside to cover the celebrity-studded crowd. As Barbara left the service, flashbulbs popped like fireworks. Barbara wore dark glasses, but tears continued to roll down her cheeks.

As Barbara and Andrew Maree were getting into her car, Morgan Maree approached with a message from Mrs. Taylor. "Ursula insists you come back to the house," Morgan told Barbara. Barbara agreed to return to the Taylor home. When Barbara walked into the Taylor house in Mandeville Canyon, Ursula Taylor greeted her with her arms open. As they embraced, Ursula said, "Bob's two wives." For a while Barbara tried to sit quietly alone in a corner, but she was uncomfortable listening to everyone reminisce about their days with Bob. Before leaving, Barbara was joined again by Ursula, and the two of them went outside, where, arm in arm, they spoke for half an hour, walking up and down the driveway. Then Barbara got in her car and drove away.

Sometime after Bob Taylor's funeral Barbara received a package from Morgan Maree's office. Bob had requested that specific items be returned to Barbara after his death. Included in the package were a photo album filled with pictures of Barbara and Bob taken during their European vacation in 1947, two money clips, a platinum-and-gold cigarette case Barbara had given Bob before their marriage, and a gold cigarette lighter inscribed, "To Lt. Robert Taylor with my admiration and my love from Mrs. Robert Taylor."

CHAPTER 36

The seventies were to be a decade of privacy and inactivity for Barbara Stanwyck—but they didn't start that way.

Hollywood had been stunned when Bill Lennon, the father of the Lennon Sisters, was shot in cold blood while playing golf. His assailant, Chet Young, had recently been released from a California mental institution and was obsessed with love for Bill's daughter Kathy. Since the days of Mary Pickford and earlier, beloved women in the entertainment business had been subjected to sick young men obsessed with love for them.

Two months after Bill Lennon's murder, Barbara's own nightmare began. This time, the fan was a forty-five-year-old transient from Ohio by the name of Henry Roy Balmert. Just like Chet Young before him, Balmert was possessed by an unreal love for a woman he had never met, and thanks to the sidewalk map salesmen in Hollywood, it was easy for Balmert to find Barbara's address. Once he had found her house, Balmert was able to begin what was to become a reign of terror over Barbara Stanwyck.

Balmert would wait for hours outside Barbara's Beverly Hills home waiting to catch a glimpse of the unwitting object of his attentions. On one occasion when Barbara opened her front door to bring in the newspaper, Balmert jumped out at her and shouted, "I'm here, Barbara, baby, I love you." Barbara was terrified and jumped back into the house. Slamming the door and locking it quickly, she warned Balmert, "I'll report you to the police if you don't leave." Balmert left.

Still shaking, Barbara waited twenty minutes before opening the door for the paper. As she opened the door, Balmert spotted her from across the street and ran over to her again. Barbara grabbed the paper and ran inside, again locking the door behind her. This time she called the police, but Balmert came back again and again. Barbara brought charges against Balmert, who was sent to Atascadero State Hospital. When a judge, acting on the recommendation of two psychiatrists from the hospital, decided to commit Balmert as a "mentally disordered sex offender," Balmert was informed of his rights. It was his prerogative to demand a jury trial on that issue before he could be sentenced as a mentally disturbed sex offender. As required by law, he was granted that hearing, and his commitment was held in abeyance pending the jury's verdict.

When Barbara took the stand during the jury trial at Los Angeles Superior Court, the rules of evidence did not permit her to testify to the mental anguish she suffered because Balmert's unwanted attentions developed so closely on the heels of the murder of Bill Lennon. Nevertheless, she told judge and jury plaintively, "I don't know when I'm going to open the door and find him there. I don't know when he's going to jump out at me and grab me." The jury was sympathetic, but Balmert's performance seems to have outshone Barbara's testimony. He swore that the time he had spent in jail had taught him a lesson and that he would never again go to Barbara's home. "She doesn't love me," he said, "and I won't force myself on any women that won't have me."

It took the jury less than an hour to agree that Balmert was not a mentally disordered sex offender. That did not mean he was not guilty of the crime of which he was accused. It meant that the jury had found

196

no basis, under law, for classifying him as a sex offender—no matter what the acknowledged potential for such behavior—because no evidence had been presented nor had any accusation been made of an actual sexual approach. To the dismay of Deputy District Attorney John Hoyt, Balmert was let go, with strict terms of probation.

Promises aside, it wasn't long before Balmert was back at Barbara's, harassing her as before. He was found sleeping in her garden and was roused and bodily ejected by Barbara's staff. He swore he would return. At another point a hysterical Stanwyck telephoned police to tell them that Balmert was cutting through her screen door. That day Balmert was taken into custody again.

Barbara Stanwyck eventually escaped Balmert's terrifying love by selling her house and moving to another in the Trousdale Estates area of Beverly Hills. It was a smaller one-story house, but with the help of Nancy Sinatra's daughter, Tina Michael, she decorated it beautifully, using bright, cheerful colors full of vitality and filling it with her favorite form of artwork, winter scenes of every type.

There wasn't a great deal of work for Barbara in the seventies, although she did star in three movies for television produced by Aaron Spelling. The first of these, made in 1970, was entitled, *The House That Wouldn't Die*. It co-starred Richard Egan. Second was *A Taste of Evil*, made in 1971 and co-starring Barbara Parkins. Then, in November of 1971, Barbara began work on *Fitzgerald and Pride*, the pilot for a projected series about a liberated woman lawyer and her young law partner, played by James Stacy. Although Barbara wasn't feeling very well, she said nothing to the producers and began shooting as scheduled. The first two days proceeded without incident, even though one scene called for Barbara to stand in the rain for hours. Then disaster struck.

Barbara returned home on the evening of the second day's work and realized that she really wasn't feeling well at all. At first she tried to convince herself that she had a touch of the flu. She hated to disrupt filming and could easily have convinced herself of anything, but then the stabbing pains in her left side became unbearable. She realized that it was possible that something very serious was wrong with her. Urgently, she called Nancy Sinatra and asked, "Could you come over and take me to the hospital?" Nancy rushed to Barbara's in minutes and took her immediately to St. John's Hospital, where doctors determined that she was suffering from a ruptured kidney wall and required emergency surgery to remove one kidney.

Nancy Sinatra remained with Barbara throughout the ordeal. Nancy, Jr., a young woman well known among her friends for her compassion and loyalty, stayed at St. John's for thirty hours, teary-eyed, as she wondered whether her Aunt Barbara, then sixty-five years old, would survive the crisis. Shirley Eder, Barbara's close friend from Detroit, immediately flew west to be by her side.

The operation was a success, and the next day doctors announced that Barbara would remain in the hospital for two weeks and would then require a few months to convalesce at home. Meanwhile, flowers and cards from all parts of the world lined the hallways. "Never has St. John's Hospital seen such a demonstration of regard, esteem, and love for a patient as we have witnessed for Miss Stanwyck," a nurse remarked. "Our switchboards were tied up with incoming calls constantly, asking for reports of her condition. People milled around day and night, waiting for word of her progress. Miss Stanwyck is one of the bravest women, and one of the nicest, I have ever met here, and we have had many celebrities as patients."

Days later Barbara told friends, "I'm very fortunate under the circumstances. Plenty of people survive with one kidney. I'll be fine."

Ironically, just three years before, Barbara had helped a teenage girl whose kidneys had ceased to function and who faced certain death. Sixteen-year-old Marianne Baretta had less than four weeks to live when Barbara learned of the girl's desperate need for help. At that time there was not one artificial kidney machine available to save her. Doctors had said that unless she could have the use of a kidney dialysis machine, ten hours a week, at a cost of $7,000, or a kidney transplant operation, which would cost $40,000 if a matching donor could be found, the young girl was doomed to die within thirty days. Stanwyck got behind a major fund-raising effort for the girl and contributed generously herself. "I'm concerned for the child," she said. "I'm asking the Man Upstairs to help."

Obviously, Barbara would not be able to proceed with production of

198

Fitzgerald and Pride for some time, and it was impossible to hold the film for her, so the producers approached Susan Hayward to step into the role, and she did so happily.

Nolan Miller had been hired to design Barbara's wardrobe for the film and continued in that capacity for Susan Hayward. He was, of course, a close friend of Barbara's, and Susan knew this. Throughout production of the film she showed great concern for Barbara's well-being, although the two actresses had never met. Miller later told of Susan's concern:

> The minute I'd walk on the set, she'd ask, "How is she? Have you checked on her today?" She really kept tabs. Then Susan started sending Missy little notes and flowers. Susan called me and asked what Missy's favorite flower was and I said, "Red or pink roses." Then she called Flower Fashions and ordered roses. When Harry Finlay, the owner, asked how many she wanted to send— one dozen, two—she said, "No, I want to send *roses*, that means at least twelve dozen." The doctors wouldn't allow Missy to keep flowers in her room—she'd been getting so many—but when she saw Susan's arrangement she insisted on keeping it for a while to really look at it; they had to set up a table in the corner. It looked like a bush, it was so huge.

Susan Hayward was taken ill not long after this, and doctors had to report the horrifying news that she had brain tumors. She fought her battle against cancer with all the determination and spirit so apparent in her personality over the last thirty years, but by early 1974 it was apparent that she was losing. Nevertheless, mustering her courage, Susan agreed to appear at the Academy Awards as a presenter on April 2, 1974. It was an incredible undertaking considering the state of her health, but with Frank Westmore to do her makeup and Nolan Miller designing her gown, she managed to look as beautiful as the Susan Hayward audiences remembered. Immediately before she walked on stage on the arm of Charlton Heston, her doctor gave her a massive dose of Dilantin to prevent a seizure, and then, shaking badly, she went to the podium to a thunderously emotional ovation. Afterward she commented, "Well, that's the last time I pull that off."

199

That evening Barbara was escorted to the Awards by Nolan Miller, who received a call from Susan Hayward the next morning. Hayward told him that she had glimpsed Miller and Stanwyck together at the ceremony and had spent the rest of the evening trying to find them so that she could be introduced to Missy. Not long after the Awards, Miller mentioned to Susan that he was taking Barbara to the Getty Museum for a private tour before its opening. Hayward said she would love to see the museum, and so she and her nurse, Carmen, went along.

"It was so funny," Miller recalls. "When I introduced Missy and Susan, they were very formal about it. 'Hello, how are you,' in very elegant tones of voice. At the end of the afternoon, when we walked Susan and Carmen back to Susan's limousine, they were both hugging and kissing, with tears and the whole thing. Then the earlier situation reversed itself. Missy was calling me to ask, 'Did you speak to Susan? How is she?' She would write Susan little notes. But they never saw each other again. They'd talk about having dinner. A couple of times we'd be getting ready to pick Susan up when Carmen would call and say, 'I think you better not come, she's having a bad day.'"

Susan Hayward had been right; the Academy Awards was her last public appearance, although she fought cancer for almost another year. On March 14, 1975, she died.

After Barbara's recovery she made the third of her films for Aaron Spelling, this one entitled, *The Letters*, telecast in 1973, with Leslie Nielsen and Dina Merrill appearing opposite her.

On April 28, 1973, at a black tie, candlelight ceremony, Barbara Stanwyck was inducted into the Hall of Fame of Great Western Performers in the National Cowboy Hall of Fame, Oklahoma City. Barbara was honored with the Wrangler Award, presented to her that evening by Joel McCrea and by the fact that the Hall of Fame would have a portrait of her commissioned for the occasion. She later said that the evening was one of the most memorable of her career.

CHAPTER 37

One of the most exciting ad campaigns, begun in the late sixties and running to this day, has been the one put together by Peter Rogers for Blackglama Minks. Under the caption WHAT BECOMES A LEGEND MOST Rogers has featured exquisite black-and-white photos of the decades' greatest stars, including, among others, Judy Garland, Barbra Streisand, Claudette Colbert, and Bette Davis. The photos show these women clad in some fabulous Blackglama minks, which, incidentally, served as their compensation for appearing in the ads.

Joan Crawford had been one of the earliest to cooperate with the campaign, and she urged Barbara to agree to be included. Barbara readily agreed, and Crawford continued to act as go-between, making all the arrangements. Rogers felt some apprehension at meeting his latest legend. "The plane was late and I was smoking too much," he recalls, "half expecting the tough bitchy broad of a dozen films to descend on me. Instead, out steps a gracious, rather retiring publicity-shy lady."

Peter Rogers and Barbara headed for the Plaza Hotel, and as they endured torrential rains, rotten traffic, and problems with Barbara's room, Rogers gritted his teeth, "still waiting for the full star tantrum." But it wasn't to come, and he found Barbara "the perfect lady."

The next day, at the studios of photographer Richard Avedon, Barbara was dressed in a very complicated Blackglama toga. She and Avedon proceeded with all the usual glamour shots, but somehow it just wasn't working. Barbara suddenly turned to express her displeasure, and Avedon shot again. The result: "a tough, no-nonsense" photo in which Barbara was obviously letting loose with an unprintable expletive. Avedon hated the shot, but Rogers disagreed. The decision was left up to Barbara.

She and Rogers met for lunch in the Plaza's Oak Room, and he showed her two photos from the shoot: one, a typical glamour shot, the other, the shot of her spouting off. "You have a choice," Rogers told her. "You can look like your average Hollywood star. Or, you can look like Barbara Stanwyck." Barbara agreed with Rogers and told him, "Run it. I've never seen that word spoken on a page before."

Barbara seemed to accept her relative inactivity with aplomb. Perhaps the kidney operation had slowed her down somewhat, but she still kept busy at home. "I live like a housewife, a housewife who works at it," she said. "I'm a dirt-chaser at heart. I enjoy it. Besides, changing beds and waxing floors is great exercise—wonderful for the figure."

If her career was over, it was something she would have to live with, and she sought no sympathy: "You have to know when you've had your hour, your place in the sun. I pity an actor who doesn't understand that. People talk about my 'career,' but *career* is too pompous a word. It was a job, and I always felt very privileged to be paid for doing what I love doing. I still look forward to living. I wake up looking forward to each day. Whatever comes, I'm alive. I'm existing. I'm a part of it. I couldn't stand being passive; I couldn't play the placid girl. I'm not Lady Bountiful. There's no halo around my head. But there's always someone in trouble, and if anyone needs help, I'm there.

"If I have one regret, it is that I did not return to the stage decades ago. I had become a minor stage star in *Burlesque* before United Artists brought me out for *The Locked Door* in 1929. But I fell in love with film.

Besides, how do you keep a marriage together if you're back there and he's here? Now I'm scared to try. Now I'm a coward. They keep asking me, and I wish I had the courage."

The Academy of Motion Picture Arts and Sciences was celebrating its fifteenth anniversary in 1977, and to commemorate the event the organization planned to make its annual television awards ceremony, on April 3, 1978, a superlative event. Producer Howard Loch and Director Marty Pasetta invited an extraordinary list of Hollywood's greatest stars to participate and, in doing so, ended up with the most memorable show in the Academy's history. Among those guests were William Holden and Barbara Stanwyck, set to present the Academy Award for Best Achievement in Sound.

In introducing Barbara and Bill Holden that evening, Bob Hope said, "There's a lot of gold being given out tonight, but Hollywood will never run out of it as long as we have treasures like the next two stars. He made his sensational screen debut in *Golden Boy*, and we'll never forget his leading lady whose performances are never less than twenty-four-carat. The Golden Boy and his Golden Girl are together again tonight. William Holden and Barbara Stanwyck."

Then Barbara and Bill appeared at the top of the grand staircase. Holden, in black tie, looked distinguished but somewhat older than his sixty years. Barbara, on the other hand, was stunning. Dressed in a black gown studded with rhinestones, and wearing her sensational corsage of diamonds, she appeared to be ten years younger than the seventy-one years she admitted to. The audience gave them perhaps the greatest ovation of an evening of great ovations.

Once settled in at the podium, Holden departed from the script, telling the audience, "Before Barbara and I present this next award, I'd like to say something. Thirty-nine years ago this month, we were working in a film together called *Golden Boy*. It wasn't going well because I was going to be replaced. But due to this lovely human being and her interest and understanding and her professional integrity and her encouragement and above all, her generosity, I'm here tonight."

Barbara was overwhelmed by Bill's impromptu public acknowledgment, as well as the tremendous roar of approval. It was one of those rare instances when she was caught with her guard down, and turning toward Holden with tears in her eyes, she cried, "Oh, Bill." Then, she almost seemed to be comforting him as they embraced and she told him, "I didn't know." Then, with her head down, she blinked back the last of her tears and took a deep breath before beginning the award presentation she was there for. After they took turns reading the nominations, she turned once again to Holden and, handing him the envelope said, "And here, my Golden Boy, you read it."

Although William Holden had spent a great deal of the past twenty years in Europe, he and Barbara had remained close friends. Barbara was, undoubtedly, aware of the hopeless battle Holden had been waging against alcoholism for many years, and it is possible that Holden had confided in her of the many demons that haunted him. It was, perhaps, these same demons and insecurities that she had in mind during their embrace. Perhaps not. In any event, she was obviously appreciative of the sentiment involved, and the affection she and Bill Holden felt for each other was readily apparent.

As Barbara grew older and worked less, she seemed to get even more recognition for the work she had done in the past. One of the nicest of these tributes came from the Film Society of Lincoln Center, New York, in April 1981. When Barbara was first approached by the Film Society, she tried to turn them down or at least put them off. Then the group shrewdly solicited Shirley Eder's help and asked her to help convince Barbara to accept their tribute. Shirley was successful, and April 13, 1981, was set for the ceremony to be held at Avery Fisher Hall.

Barbara arrived in New York a few days earlier and agreed to more than her usual quota of interviews. She was seventy-four years old, but she looked as beautiful as ever. Age hadn't forked her tongue either. That same Stanwyck forthrightness was as apparent as ever when she told Rex Reed:

> I could understand if they picked Katharine Hepburn, but of course, she wouldn't do it. But when they asked me, I thought at first it was a mistake. I thought they got me mixed up with Bette Davis. Attention embarrasses me, I don't like to be on display. I

was always an extrovert in my work, but when it comes time to be myself I'll take a powder every time. The woman who came to the airport to meet me couldn't find me because I was hiding behind a post. I never got an Oscar. I never had an acting lesson. Life was my only training. Eighty-five movies, yes. But that wasn't eighty-five great movies, honey. There were some real clinkers in there, oh Lord, yes.

On the evening of April 13, 1981, Barbara was escorted to Lincoln Center by William Holden. She was a vision. Her hair was gleaming white and softly curled; there were pearl-and-diamond earrings dangling from her ears, and she wore a fabulous white gown covered with silver sequins and bugle beads. The whole package was wrapped with a white mink stole.

It was a star-studded evening of accolades that included tributes from Anne Baxter, Joan Bennett, and Frank Capra. Henry Fonda, who had called Barbara "the great love of my life," was in a California hospital undergoing tests but had threatened to fly in anyway until Barbara told him she would murder him if he did. Nevertheless, his telegram was read from the stage. "Dear Barbara: Can't be at your marvelous evening because I'm having hospital tests. I'm feeling fine but my only sadness is not being able to be with you at the Film Society of Lincoln Center's Tribute. Shirley approves of my forty-year love for you, Barbara, and she and I will be honoring you in California. We send our very special love." Another telegram, from President Ronald Reagan, read in part . . . "You are a woman whose strength of character, vitality and energy permeate every word you play. Long before it was fashionable, you were a paradigm of independence and self-direction for women all over the world."

Perhaps no tribute so well expressed the industry's feelings about Barbara as William Holden's. After speaking briefly of Barbara's help during the making of Golden Boy, Holden summed up his comments by telling the crowd, "So, if anyone ever needed a term for courtesy, and consideration, generosity, and, above all, professionalism, they would only need two words. One, Barbara, and the other, Stanwyck.

Appreciation has two sides. That of the recipient and the other is the one that expresses it. And tonight, I'm expressing it for all of us. I love you, Queen."

Barbara came out immediately after Holden's tribute, and was greeted by an ovation that seemed to go on forever. After thanking the Film Society, she told those gathered: "When the Film Society first notified me about this event, I thought they made a mistake. I thought they meant Barbra Streisand. Well, we got that straightened out. And then I thought that I had to tell them that I had never won an Academy Award. So, we got that straightened out. They said that didn't make any difference to them." Then, after thanking those behind the scenes who had helped her through the years, she thanked everyone there "for a beautiful memory."

CHAPTER 38

"You know as well as I, Queen," Bill Holden told Barbara, "as we get older, the parts get harder to find. I don't know how much longer I can continue. A couple of years, I think. Then I'll go live in Africa. Oh, I'll keep the Palm Springs house; I'd never sell that. And I'll always come back to visit my sons and my mother. But I think Africa will be my real home."

This conversation was at a dinner party at the home of Nancy Sinatra in October of 1981. Holden was depressed. He had looked forward to starring in the film version of *That Championship Season*, but that seemed to be on hold indefinitely and, just recently, his close friend Charles Feingarten had died. Holden wanted to visit Feingarten's widow that evening, so he and Barbara left the dinner party early. Holden took her home, and when they parted that evening, Barbara said, "Good night, Golden Boy. Take care of yourself."

Just three weeks later, on November 16, 1981, Barbara was at home when she received a call telling her that William Holden had been found dead in his apartment at the Shoreham Towers in Santa Monica. "N-n-no, it can't be," Barbara stuttered. "Are you sure it's Bill?" There was no doubt. Bill Holden was dead at the age of sixty-three.

Shortly after the dinner party at Nancy Sinatra's, Barbara had undergone a nightmare of her own. At about one o'clock on the morning of October 27, Barbara was roughly awakened from her sleep by a man in a ski mask holding a revolver and shining a flashlight in her face. Barbara's first reaction was to switch on her bedside lamp. The intruder responded by belting Barbara over the head with the revolver. "I told you not to look," he yelled, "or I'll kill you." The thief then insisted that Barbara show him where she kept her jewelry. Wisely, she realized that it wouldn't be worth her life to protect the valuables, so she cooperated. Then, savagely throwing Barbara in the closet, he told her, "If you come out, I'm going to kill you." Blood from her head injury was streaming down Barbara's face into her eyes, and she felt as if she were losing consciousness, but she was still able to think quickly enough to jam her thumb between the closet's sliding doors, thus preventing the lock from catching. Then she waited until the silence confirmed the intruder's escape and called the police.

It had been a frightening and horrifying experience for Barbara, but most upsetting had been the thief's escape with Robert Taylor's platinum-and-gold cigarette case. She was still on the mend, emotionally and physically, when she had gotten the news of Bill Holden's death.

More honors followed Barbara's Lincoln Center Tribute, but it was work that kept her moving. In 1982 she accepted the role of Mary Carson in David Wolper's mini-series *The Thorn Birds*, based on Colleen McCullough's bestselling novel. "As scripted, the role of Mary Carson was the best I have read in two years," Barbara admitted, and she was anxious to sink her teeth into such a bitchy role.

McCullough's novel of love and lust on a remote Australian sheep ranch known as Drogheda had captured the imagination of millions, and the mini-series based on her story was one of the most eagerly awaited in television history. Appropriately, producers Stan Margulies and David Wolper spared no expense in mounting their production. Leading their cast was Richard Chamberlain, one of television's most magnetic stars. Appearing opposite him was the beautiful Rachel Ward. And, in supporting roles: Jean Simmons, Richard Kiley, Christopher Plummer, Ken Howard, Earl Holliman, Philip Anglim, Mare Winningham, and Barbara Stanwyck.

Barbara's excitement over winning the role of Mary Carson turned to furor when she received the script. The character of Mary, as written in McCullough's novel, had been that of a tough, no-nonsense, rich bitch who manipulated the lives of those around her with a heartless deceit. A great deal of the first half of the novel revolved around Mary's sexual obsession with a young priest, Father de Bricassart (played by Chamberlain), and her determination to destroy him because of his disinterest in her.

As far as Barbara was concerned, the script Margulies had sent her had weakened her character by eliminating or softening those scenes that had been Mary's strongest. In the heat of anger she called Margulies and told him, "There is no way this is going to be a polite call." She proceeded to bawl out Margulies for tampering with her role and said that although she had obviously made a mistake in accepting the part, she would honor her contract. "I have never slammed down a telephone on anyone," she said in conclusion, "but I am telling you now, the conversation is over!"

Margulies reviewed the script and found that Barbara was right. The guts had been torn out of her part. The missing scenes were restored. Later Margulies told the press admiringly, "I've had my ass chewed out by people over the years, but she ranks in the top two percentile."

The series went into production in June of 1982, and once at work, Barbara charmed cast and crew, as usual. Although newcomer Rachel Ward felt awkward around Barbara at first, she soon joined the bandwagon. As for Richard Chamberlain, he had nothing but raves for Stanwyck: "Barbara was amazing," he said enthusiastically. "On the first day of rehearsal she knew all her lines. She could stand longer than anyone on the set, and she was terrific on horseback, even though she hadn't ridden since *The Big Valley*. She's very conscious of her eyes and knows just when to look at you in a scene. She has great legs and isn't hesitant to show them—a little flash now and then. And that voice! It's like a million-dollar case of laryngitis."

Barbara's performance in *The Thorn Birds* was a tour de force. Many critics found her the best part of the show and thought her performance to be among the best of her career. Never were her still consummate skills as an actress as apparent as in her final scene when she confesses her love to Chamberlain and damns him to hell for his disinterest in her. Fiercely she rants at him in a voice full of pain and bitterness: "Let me tell you something, Cardinal de Bricassart, about old age and about that God of yours. That vengeful God who ruins our bodies and leaves us with only enough wit for regret. Inside this stupid body I am still young. I still feel. I still want. I still dream and I still love you. Oh God, how much!" Then, she closes the door to prepare for her suicide. It was just one incredible moment in a spine-tingling performance. When the National Academy of Television Arts and Sciences announced the nominations for the 1983 Emmy Awards in August, Stanwyck's performance was among those nominated as Best Performance by an Actress in a Dramatic Special.

Although Barbara was seventy-five years old when she made *The Thorn Birds*, the film's makeup artists found that they needed to apply plastic prosthesis to her face to make her look the seventy-five years the role called for. When asked the secret of her amazing fitness and enduring beauty, her response was simple: "I eat the right things and retire early. I never go out at night when I'm working, and I walk half a mile uphill on the treadmill in my bedroom every morning."

Asked about her reluctance to grant interviews, Barbara exclaimed, "I'm not a yesterday's woman. I'm a tomorrow's woman. If I don't have a job, what am I going to give interviews about? 'And then I did . . . and then I did . . .' Who the hell cares!?" Then, speaking of the state of her life, she went on, "I'm accustomed to living alone now. It was tough at first, especially those first two years, but now I doubt if I could live with anyone else. I'm too set in my ways. Too dull, some people might say."

Just a few months before starting work on *The Thorn Birds*, Barbara Stanwyck received what was probably the greatest tribute in her fifty-six-year film career. One of her few great career disappointments had been her failure to win an Academy Award. Just a year earlier, at the time of her Lincoln Center Tribute, she had confessed the disappointment to Rex Reed when she told him: "Happiness is within yourself. Get ready for the dream to fade. So I'm no longer in demand, but so what? I see no reason to go into a decline or hit the bottle or sink into a melancholy depression. I've had my time and it was lovely. And I'm very grateful for it. But now I move over and make room for somebody else. I'm not jealous of anybody. Well, I take it back. Maybe Miss Hepburn, because she won three Academy Awards. But seriously, sing no sad songs for Barbara Stanwyck. What the hell. Whatever I had, it worked, didn't it?"

Then, in February of 1982, the Academy of Motion Picture Arts and Sciences announced that it would present Barbara Stanwyck with a special award for lifetime achievement at the annual awards ceremony on March 29, 1982.

The evening of the awards, John Travolta, one of Barbara's newest friends, took center stage and told the star-studded crowd:

> Four years ago, William Holden and Barbara Stanwyck came up on this stage to present an award. When they did, Mr. Holden departed from the script to speak from his heart. He said that his career derived from the lady standing next to him. All he was came from her generosity, her support, and her abiding belief in him. Barbara was completely surprised by this. She listened, her public face letting her private face show, but just for an instant. The actress in control, and that's the very essence of Barbara Stanwyck's eminence and that hold she has on the audience. She's reality. She's professional and when she walks across the screen, it's beauty and confidence. She's always the woman she plays and yet always herself.

Then, Travolta introduced a beautifully crafted montage of scenes from Barbara's best films. There she was again as Lady Eve, as Annie Oakley, and with Ronald Reagan as Sierra Nevada Jones. Mollie Monahan rode the rails again, Phyllis Dietrichson died in Fred Mac-Murray's arms, and Leona Stevenson screamed into her phone for help. Finally, Lorna Moon glowed again as she tried to spur her Golden Boy on to greater heights, and Stella Dallas walked away from her daughter's marriage with a triumphant gleam in her eye. It was this last clip that induced the entire audience to spontaneous applause and put tears in their eyes, just as it had done almost fifty years before.

Following the completion of the clips, Travolta simply announced, "Ladies and gentlemen, Miss Barbara Stanwyck." And as she strode to the microphone, sure as a twenty-year-old and incandescently beautiful in a red sequinned gown, the audience stood. It was a long ovation and a sentimental one, led by such Stanwyck admirers and peers as Jane Fonda, Diane Keaton, Jack Nicholson, Maureen Stapleton, and a broadly beaming Burt Lancaster.

Barbara was overcome by the emotion shown by the audience, and it was obvious that she had been unable to hold back her tears. Struggling subtly with her composure, she spoke in that strong, husky voice, made even more vulnerable by her tears:

> Thank you. Thank you very much. I'd like to thank the Board of Governors of the Academy for giving me this special award. I . . . I tried many times to get it, but I didn't make it. So this is indeed very special to me. You don't get them alone. There were writers, directors, producers—all their kindnesses to me through the many years. And the people backstage. The remarkable crews that we have the privilege of working with. The electricians, the property men, the stage hands . . . oh . . . camera . . . they're just marvelous. And MY wonderful group, the stunt men and women who taught me so well. I'm grateful to them and I thank them very much.

Continuing, Barbara said, "A few years ago, I stood on this stage with William Holden, as a presenter. I loved him very much, and I miss him." Her speech grew unsteady as she attempted to swallow her tears, but she went on, "He always wished that I would get an Oscar, and so tonight, my Golden Boy, you got your wish."

As Barbara held her treasured Oscar aloft, and the audience responded to her heartfelt sentiments, you could almost hear William Holden's voice from the beyond, "I love you, Queen. It's about time!"

It was indeed about time.

BARBARA STANWYCK ON FILM

BROADWAY NIGHTS   1927. First National.
   CAST: Lois Wilson, Sam Hardy, Louis John Bartels, Philip Strange, Barbara Stanwyck (Dancer), Bunny Weldon, Sylvia Sidney.
   CREDITS: *Producer*—Robert Kane; *Director*—Joseph C. Boyle; *Screenplay*—Forrest Halsey from a story by Norman Houston; *Photography*—Ernest Haller.

THE LOCKED DOOR   1930. United Artists. *74 minutes.*
   CAST: Rod La Rocque, Barbara Stanwyck (Ann Carter), William Boyd, Betty Bronson, Harry Stubbs, Harry Mestayer, Mack Swain, ZaSu Pitts, George Bunny.
   CREDITS: *Producer-Director*—George Fitzmaurice; *Screenplay*—C. Gardner Sullivan from the play *The Sign on the Door* by Channing Pollock; *Editor*—Hal Kern.

MEXICALI ROSE   1930. Columbia. *62 minutes.*
   CAST: Barbara Stanwyck (Mexicali Rose), Sam Hardy, William Janney, Louis Natheaux, Arthur Rankin, Harry Vejar, Louis King, Julia Beharano.
   CREDITS: *Producer*—Harry Cohn; *Director*—Erle C. Kenton; *Screenplay*—Gladys Lehman; *Editor*—Leon Barsha.

LADIES OF LEISURE 1930. Columbia. *98 minutes.*

CAST: Barbara Stanwyck (Kay Arnold), Lowell Sherman, Ralph Graves, Marie Provost, Nance O'Neil, George Fawcett, Juliette Compton, Johnnie Walker.

CREDITS: *Producer*—Harry Cohn; *Director*—Frank Capra; *Screenplay*—Jo Swerling from the play *Ladies of the Evening* by Milton Herbert Gropper; *Editor*—Maurice Wright.

ILLICIT 1931. Warner Brothers. *81 minutes.*

CAST: Barbara Stanwyck (Anne Vincent), James Rennie, Ricardo Cortez, Natalie Moorhead, Charles Butterworth, Joan Blondell, Claude Gillingwater.

CREDITS: *Director*—Archie Mayo; *Screenplay*—Harvey Thew from the play by Edith Fitzgerald and Robert Riskin; *Editor*—William Holmes.

TEN CENTS A DANCE 1931. Columbia. *80 minutes.*

CAST: Barbara Stanwyck (Barbara O'Neil), Ricardo Cortez, Monroe Owsley, Sally Blane, Blanche Friderici, Martha Sleeper, David Newell, Victor Potel, Sidney Bracey.

CREDITS: *Producer*—Harry Cohn; *Director*—Lionel Barrymore; *Screenplay*—Jo Swerling; *Editor*—Arthur Huffsmith; *Music*—Abe Lyman and his band; *Music director*—Bakaleinikoff.

NIGHT NURSE 1931. Warner Brothers. *73 minutes.*

CAST: Barbara Stanwyck (Lora Hart), Ben Lyon, Joan Blondell, Clark Gable, Blanche Friderici, Charlotte Merriam, Charles Winninger, Edward Nugent, Vera Lewis, Ralf Harolde, Walter McGrail, Allan Lane, Marcia Mae Jones, Betty Jane Graham.

CREDITS: *Director*—William A. Wellman; *Screenplay*—Oliver H. P. Garrett from the novel by Dora Macy; *Editor*—Edward M. McDermott.

THE MIRACLE WOMAN 1931. Columbia. *90 minutes.*

CAST: Barbara Stanwyck (Florence Fallon), David Manners, Sam Hardy, Beryl Mercer, Russell Hopton, Charles Middleton, Eddie Boland, Thelma Hill.

CREDITS: *Producer*—Harry Cohn; *Director*—Frank Capra; *Screenplay*—Jo Swerling from the play *Bless You, Sister* by John Meehan and Robert Riskin; *Editor*—Maurice Wright.

FORBIDDEN 1932. Columbia. *85 minutes.*

CAST: Barbara Stanwyck (Lulu Smith), Adolphe Menjou, Ralph Bellamy,

Dorothy Peterson, Thomas Jefferson, Myrna Fresholt, Charlotte V. Henry, Oliver Eckhardt.

CREDITS: *Producer*—Harry Cohn; *Director*—Frank Capra; *Story*—Frank Capra; *Editor*—Maurice Wright.

SHOPWORN   1932. Columbia. *72 minutes.*

CAST: Barbara Stanwyck (Kitty Lane), Regis Toomey, ZaSu Pitts, Lucien Littlefield, Clara Blandick, Robert Alden, Oscar Apfel, Maude Turner Gordon, Albert Conti.

CREDITS: *Director*—Nicholas Grinde; *Story*—Sarah Y. Mason; *Editor*—Gene Havlick.

SO BIG   1932. Warner Brothers. *80 minutes.*

CAST: Barbara Stanwyck (Selina Peake), George Brent, Dickie Moore, Guy Kibbee, Bette Davis, Mae Madison, Hardie Albright, Robert Warwick, Arthur Stone, Earle Foxe, Alan Hale, Dorothy Peterson, Dawn O'Day, Dick Winslow, Harry Beresford, Eulalie Jensen, Elizabeth Patterson, Rita LeRoy, Blanche Friderici, Willard Robertson, Harry Holman, Lionel Belmore.

CREDITS: *Director*—William A. Wellman; *Screenplay*—J. Grubb Alexander and Robert Lord from the novel by Edna Ferber; *Editor*—William Holmes.

THE PURCHASE PRICE   1932. Warner Brothers. *68 minutes.*

CAST: Barbara Stanwyck (Joan Gordon), George Brent, Lyle Talbot, Hardie Albright, David Landau, Murray Kinnell, Leila Bennett, Matt McHugh, Clarence Wilson, Lucille Ward, Dawn O'Day, Victor Potel, Adele Watson, Snub Pollard.

CREDITS: *Director*—William A. Wellman; *Screenplay*—Robert Lord from the story "The Mud Lark" by Arthur Stringer; *Editor*—William Holmes.

THE BITTER TEA OF GENERAL YEN   1933. Columbia. *90 minutes.*

CAST: Barbara Stanwyck (Megan Davis), Nils Asther, Toshia Mori, Walther Connolly, Gavin Gordon, Lucien Littlefield, Richard Loo, Helen Jerome Eddy, Emmett Corrigan.

CREDITS: *Producer*—Walter Wanger; *Director*—Frank Capra; *Screenplay*—Edward Paramore from the story by Grace Zaring Stone; *Editor*—Edward Curtis; *Costumes*—Edward Stevenson; *Music*—W. Frank Harling.

LADIES THEY TALK ABOUT   1933. Warner Brothers. *69 minutes.*

CAST: Barbara Stanwyck (Nan Taylor), Preston Foster, Lyle Talbot, Dorothy Burgess, Lillian Roth, Maude Eburne, Harold Huber, Ruth Donnelly, Robert Warwick, Helen Ware, DeWitt Jennings, Robert McWade, Cecil

Cunningham, Helen Mann, Grace Cunard, Mme. Sul-Te-Wan, Harold Healy, Harry Gribbon.

CREDITS: *Directors*—Howard Bretherton, William Keighley; *Screenplay*— Sidney Sutherland and Brown Holmes from the play *Women in Prison* by Dorothy Mackaye and Carlton Miles; *Editor*—Basil Wrangel; *Art director*— Esdras Hartley; *Costumes*—Orry-Kelly.

BABY FACE   1933. Warner Brothers. *70 minutes.*

CAST: Barbara Stanwyck (Lily Powers), George Brent, Donald Cook, Alphonse Ethier, Henry Kolker, Margaret Lindsay, Arthur Hohl, John Wayne, Robert Barrat, Douglas Dumbrille, Theresa Harris.

CREDITS: *Director*—Alfred E. Green; *Screenplay*—Gene Markey and Kathryn Scola from a story by Mark Canfield; *Editor*—Howard Bretherton; *Costumes*—Orry-Kelly.

EVER IN MY HEART   1933. Warner Brothers. *68 minutes.*

CAST: Barbara Stanwyck (Mary Archer), Otto Kruger, Ralph Bellamy, Ruth Donnelly, Frank Albertson, George Cooper, Wallis Clark, Florence Roberts, Laura Hope Crews, Ronnie Crosby, Frank Reicher, Clara Blandick, Elizabeth Patterson, Willard Robertson, Nella Walker, Harry Beresford, Virginia Howell, Ethel Wales.

CREDITS: *Director*—Archie Mayo; *Screenplay*—Bertram Milhauser from a story by Milhauser and Beulah Marie Dix; *Editor*—Owen Marks; *Costumes*— Earl Luick.

GAMBLING LADY   1934. Warner Brothers. *66 minutes.*

CAST: Barbara Stanwyck (Lady Lee), Joel McCrea, Pat O'Brien, Claire Dodd, C. Aubrey Smith, Robert Barrat, Arthur Vinton, Phillip Reed, Philip Faversham, Robert Elliott, Ferdinand Gottschalk, Willard Robertson, Huey White.

CREDITS: *Director*—Archie Mayo; *Screenplay*—Ralph Block and Doris Malloy from a story by Malloy; *Editor*—Harold McLernon; *Costumes*—Orry-Kelly.

A LOST LADY   1934. First National. *61 minutes.*

CAST: Barbara Stanwyck (Marian Ormsby), Frank Morgan, Ricardo Cortez, Lyle Talbot, Phillip Reed, Hobart Cavanaugh, Henry Kolker, Rafaela Ottiano, Edward McWade, Walter Walker, Samuel Hinds, Willie Fung, Jameson Thomas.

CREDITS: *Director*—Alfred E. Green; *Screenplay*—Gene Markey and Kathryn Scola from the novel by Willa Cather; *Editor*—Owen Marks; *Costumes*— Orry-Kelly.

216

THE SECRET BRIDE   1935. Warner Brothers. *64 minutes.*
CAST: Barbara Stanwyck (Ruth Vincent), Warren William, Glenda Farrell, Grant Mitchell, Arthur Byron, Henry O'Neill, Douglas Dumbrille, Arthur Aylesworth, Willard Robertson, William Davidson.
CREDITS: *Director*—William Dieterle; *Screenplay*—Tom Buckingham, F. Hugh Herbert, Mary McCall, Jr., from the play by Leonard Ide; *Editor*—Owen Marks; *Costumes*—Orry-Kelly.

THE WOMAN IN RED   1935. First National. *68 minutes.*
CAST: Barbara Stanwyck (Shelby Barret), Gene Raymond, Genevieve Tobin, John Eldredge, Phillip Reed, Dorothy Tree, Russell Hicks, Nella Walker, Claude Gillingwater, Doris Lloyd, Hale Hamilton, Arthur Treacher.
CREDITS: *Director*—Robert Florey; *Screenplay*—Mary McCall, Jr., and Peter Milne from the novel *North Shore* by Wallace Irwin; *Editor*—Terry Morse; *Costumes*—Orry-Kelly.

RED SALUTE (RUNAWAY DAUGHTER)   1935. United Artists. *78 minutes.*
CAST: Barbara Stanwyck (Drue Van Allen), Robert Young, Hardie Albright, Cliff Edwards, Ruth Donnelly, Gordon Jones, Paul Stanton, Purnell Pratt, Nella Walker, Arthur Vinton, Edward McWade, Henry Kolker, Henry Otho.
CREDITS: *Producer*—Edward Small; *Director*—Sidney Lanfield; *Screenplay*—Humphrey Pearson and Manuel Seff from a story by Pearson; *Editor*—Grant Whytock.

ANNIE OAKLEY   1935. RKO. *90 minutes.*
CAST: Barbara Stanwyck (Annie Oakley), Preston Foster, Melvyn Douglas, Moroni Olsen, Pert Kelton, Andy Clyde, Chief Thunder Bird, Margaret Armstrong, Delmar Watson, Adeline Craig.
CREDITS: *Associate producer*—Cliff Reid; *Director*—George Stevens; *Screenplay*—Joel Sayre and John Twist from a story by Joseph A. Fields and Ewart Adamson; *Editor*—Jack Hively.

A MESSAGE TO GARCIA   1936. Twentieth Century–Fox. *86 minutes.*
CAST: Wallace Beery, Barbara Stanwyck (Señorita Raphaelita Maderos), John Boles, Alan Hale, Herbert Mundin, Mona Barrie, Enrique Acosta, Juan Torena, Martin Garralaga, Blanca Vischer, Jose Luis Tortosa.
CREDITS: *Producer*—Darryl F. Zanuck; *Associate producer*—Raymond Griffith; *Director*—George Marshall; *Screenplay*—W. P. Lipscomb and Gene Fowler,

suggested by Elbert Hubbard's essay and Lieutenant Andrew S. Rowan's book, *Editor*—Herbert Levy.

THE BRIDE WALKS OUT   1936. RKO. *81 minutes.*

CAST: Barbara Stanwyck (Carolyn Martin), Gene Raymond, Robert Young, Ned Sparks, Helen Broderick, Willie Best, Robert Warwick, Billy Gilbert, Wade Boteler, Hattie McDaniel, Irving Bacon.

CREDITS: *Producer*—Edward Small; *Director*—Leigh Jason; *Screenplay*—P. J. Wolfson and Philip G. Epstein from a story by Howard Emmett Rogers; *Editor*—Arthur Roberts; *Costumes*—Bernard Newman.

HIS BROTHER'S WIFE   1936. Metro-Goldwyn-Mayer. *90 minutes.*

CAST: Barbara Stanwyck (Rita Wilson), Robert Taylor, Jean Hersholt, Joseph Calleia, John Eldredge, Samuel S. Hinds, Leonard Mudie, Jed Prouty, Pedro De Cordoba, Rafael Corio, William Stack, Edgar Edwards.

CREDITS: *Producer*—Lawrence Weingarten; *Director*—W. S. Van Dyke; *Screenplay*—Leon Gordon and John Meehan from a story by George Auerbach; *Editor*—Conrad A. Nervig; *Costumes*—Dolly Tree.

BANJO ON MY KNEE   1936. Twentieth Century–Fox. *95 minutes.*

CAST: Barbara Stanwyck (Pearl), Joel McCrea, Walter Brennan, Buddy Ebsen, Helen Westley, Walter Catlett, Anthony Martin, Katherine de Mille, Victor Kilian, Minna Gombell, Spencer Charters, Hall Johnson Choir.

CREDITS: *Producer*—Darryl F. Zanuck; *Associate producer*—Nunnally Johnson; *Director*—John Cromwell; *Screenplay*—Nunnally Johnson from the novel by Harry Hamilton; *Photography*—Ernest Palmer; *Editor*—Hansen Fritch; *Costumes*—Gwen Wakeling; *Music director*—Arthur Lange.

THE PLOUGH AND THE STARS   1937. RKO. *72 minutes.*

CAST: Barbara Stanwyck (Nora Clitheroe), Preston Foster, Barry Fitzgerald, Denis O'Dea, Eileen Crow, F. J. McCormick, Arthur Shields, Una O'Connor, Moroni Olsen, J. M. Kerrigan, Bonita Granville, Erin O'Brien-Moore.

CREDITS: *Associate producers*—Cliff Reid, Robert Sisk; *Director*—John Ford, assisted by Arthur Shields of the Abbey Theatre; *Screenplay*—Dudley Nichols from the play by Sean O'Casey; *Editor*—George Hively; *Costumes*—Walter Plunkett; *Music*—Roy Webb; *Music director*—Nathaniel Shilkret.

INTERNES CAN'T TAKE MONEY   1937. Paramount. *75 minutes.*

CAST: Barbara Stanwyck (Janet Haley), Joel McCrea, Lloyd Nolan, Stanley Ridges, Lee Bowman, Barry Macollum, Irving Bacon, Gaylord Pendleton,

Pierre Watkin, Charles Lane, Priscilla Lawson, James Bush, Nick Lukats, Anthony Nace, Fay Holden, Frank Bruno, Sarah Padden.
CREDITS: *Producer*—Benjamin Glazer; *Director*—Alfred Santell; *Screenplay*—Rian James and Theodore Reeves from a story by Max Brand; *Editor*—Doane Harrison; *Costumes*—Travis Banton.

THIS IS MY AFFAIR   1937. Twentieth Century–Fox. *100 minutes.*
CAST: Robert Taylor, Barbara Stanwyck (Lil Duryea), Victor McLaglen, Brian Donlevy, Sidney Blackmer, John Carradine, Alan Dinehart, Douglas Fowley, Robert McWade, Frank Conroy, Sig Rumann, Marjorie Weaver, J. C. Nugent.
CREDITS: *Producer*—Darryl F. Zanuck; *Associate producer*—Kenneth Macgowan; *Director*—William A. Seiter; *Screenplay*—Allen Rivkin, Lamar Trotti; *Editor*—Allen McNeil; *Costumes*—Royer.

STELLA DALLAS   1937. United Artists. *105 minutes.*
CAST: Barbara Stanwyck (Stella Dallas), John Boles, Anne Shirley, Barbara O'Neil, Alan Hale, Marjorie Main, George Walcott, Ann Shoemaker, Tim Holt, Nella Walker, Bruce Satterlee, Jimmy Butler, Jack Egger, Dickie Jones, Al Shean.
CREDITS: *Producer*—Samuel Goldwyn; *Associate producer*—Merritt Hulburd; *Director*—King Vidor; *Screenplay*—Sarah Y. Mason and Victor Heerman from the novel by Olive Higgins Prouty; *Editor*—Sherman Todd; *Costumes*—Omar Kiam.

BREAKFAST FOR TWO   1937. RKO. *65 minutes.*
CAST: Barbara Stanwyck (Valentine Ransom), Herbert Marshall, Glenda Farrell, Eric Blore, Donald Meek, Etienne Girardot, Frank M. Thomas, Pierre Watkin.
CREDITS: *Producer*—Edward Kaufman; *Director*—Alfred Santell; *Screenplay*—Charles Kaufman, Paul Yawitz and Viola Brothers Shore from a story by David Garth; *Editor*—George Hively; *Costumes*—Edward Stevenson.

ALWAYS GOODBYE   1938. Twentieth Century–Fox. *75 minutes.*
CAST: Barbara Stanwyck (Margot Weston), Herbert Marshall, Ian Hunter, Cesar Romero, Lynn Bari, Binnie Barnes, Johnnie Russell, Mary Forbes, Albert Conti, Marcelle Corday, Franklyn Pangborn, George Davis, Ben Welden.
CREDITS: *Producer*—Darryl F. Zanuck; *Associate producer*—Raymond Griffith; *Director*—Sidney Lanfield; *Screenplay*—Kathryn Scola and Edith Skouras

from a story by Gilbert Emery and Douglas Doty; *Editor*—Robert Simpson; *Costumes*—Royer.

THE MAD MISS MANTON   1938. RKO. *80 minutes.*

CAST: Barbara Stanwyck (Melsa Manton), Henry Fonda, Sam Levene, Frances Mercer, Stanley Ridges, Whitney Bourne, Vicki Lester, Ann Evers, Catherine O'Quinn, Linda Terry, Eleanor Hansen, Hattie McDaniel, James Burke, Paul Guilfoyle, Penny Singleton, Leona Maricle, Kay Sutton, Miles Mander, John Qualen, Grady Sutton, Olin Howland.

CREDITS: *Producer*—Pandro S. Berman; *Associate producer*—P. J. Wolfson; *Director*—Leigh Jason; *Screenplay*—Philip G. Epstein from a story by Wilson Collison; *Editor*—George Hively; *Costumes*—Edward Stevenson.

UNION PACIFIC   1939. Paramount. *135 minutes.*

CAST: Barbara Stanwyck (Mollie Monahan), Joel McCrea, Akim Tamiroff, Lynne Overman, Robert Preston, Brian Donlevy, Anthony Quinn, Evelyn Keyes, Stanley Ridges, Regis Toomey, Syd Saylor, J. M. Kerrigan, William Haade, Harry Woods, Fuzzy Knight, Francis MacDonald, Henry Kolker, Richard Lane, Hugh McDonald.

CREDITS: *Producer-director*—Cecil B. DeMille; *Associate producer*—William H. Pine; *Second unit director*—Arthur Rosson; *Screenplay*—Walter DeLeon, C. Gardner Sullivan and Jesse Lasky, Jr., from an adaptation by Jack Cunningham of a story by Ernest Haycox; *Editor*—Anne Bauchens; *Costumes*—Natalie Visart.

GOLDEN BOY   1939. Columbia. *99 minutes.*

CAST: Barbara Stanwyck (Lorna Moon), Adolphe Menjou, William Holden, Lee J. Cobb, Joseph Calleia, Sam Levene, Edward S. Brophy, Beatrice Blinn, William H. Strauss, Don Beddoe.

CREDITS: *Producer*—William Perlberg; *Director*—Rouben Mamoulian; *Screenplay*—Lewis Meltzer, Daniel Taradash, Sarah Y. Mason, Victor Heerman from the play by Clifford Odets; *Editor*—Otto Meyer; *Costumes*—Kalloch.

REMEMBER THE NIGHT   1940. Paramount. *94 minutes.*

CAST: Barbara Stanwyck (Lee Leander), Fred MacMurray, Beulah Bondi, Elizabeth Patterson, Sterling Holloway, Willard Robertson, Charles Waldron, Paul Guilfoyle, Charlie Arnt, John Wray, Thomas W. Ross, Snowflake, Tom Kennedy, Georgia Caine, Virginia Brissac, Spencer Charters.

CREDITS: *Producer-Director*—Mitchell Leisen; *Screenplay*—Preston Sturges; *Editor*—Doane Harrison; *Stanwyck costumes*—Edith Head.

THE LADY EVE 1941. Paramount. *97 minutes.*

CAST: Barbara Stanwyck (Jean Harrington), Henry Fonda, Charles Coburn, Eugene Pallette, William Demarest, Eric Blore, Melville Cooper, Martha O'Driscoll, Janet Beecher, Robert Greig, Dora Clement, Luis Alberni.

CREDITS: *Producer*—Paul Jones; *Director*—Preston Sturges; *Screenplay*—Preston Sturges from a story by Monckton Hoffe; *Editor*—Stuart Gilmore; *Costumes*—Edith Head.

MEET JOHN DOE 1941. Warner Brothers/Frank Capra Productions. *123 minutes.*

CAST: Gary Cooper, Barbara Stanwyck (Ann Mitchell), Edward Arnold, Walter Brennan, Spring Byington, James Gleason, Gene Lockhart, Rod La Rocque, Irving Bacon, Regis Toomey, J. Farrell MacDonald, Warren Hymer, Harry Holman, Andrew Tombes, Pierre Watkin, Stanley Andrews, Mitchell Lewis, Charles Wilson, Vaughan Glaser, Sterling Holloway, Mike Frankovich, Knox Manning, John B. Hughes, Hall Johnson Choir.

CREDITS: *Producer-director*—Frank Capra; *Screenplay*—Robert Riskin from a story by Richard Connell and Robert Presnell; *Editor*—Daniel Mandell; *Costumes*—Natalie Visart.

YOU BELONG TO ME 1941. Columbia. *94 minutes.*

CAST: Barbara Stanwyck (Helen Hunt), Henry Fonda, Edgar Buchanan, Roger Clark, Ruth Donnelly, Melville Cooper, Ralph Peters, Maude Eburne, Renie Riano, Ellen Lowe, Mary Treen, Gordon Jones.

CREDITS: *Producer-director*—Wesley Ruggles; *Screenplay*—Claude Binyon from a story by Dalton Trumbo; *Photography*—Joseph Walker; *Editor*—Viola Lawrence; *Art director*—Lionel Banks; *Costumes*—Edith Head; *Music*—Frederick Hollander; *Music director*—M. W. Stoloff.

BALL OF FIRE 1942. RKO. *111 minutes.*

CAST: Gary Cooper, Barbara Stanwyck (Sugarpuss O'Shea), Oscar Homolka, Henry Travers, S. Z. Sakall, Tully Marshall, Leonid Kinskey, Richard Haydn, Aubrey Mather, Allen Jenkins, Dana Andrews, Dan Duryea, Ralph Peters, Kathleen Howard, Mary Field, Charles Lane, Charles Arnt, Elisha Cook, Alan Rhein, Eddie Foster, Aldrich Bowker, Addison Richards, Pat West, Kenneth Howell, Tommy Ryan, Tim Ryan, Will Lee, Gene Krupa and his orchestra.

CREDITS: *Producer*—Samuel Goldwyn; *Director*—Howard Hawks; *Screenplay*—Charles Brackett and Billy Wilder from a story "From A to Z" by

Wilder and Thomas Monroe; *Editor*—Daniel Mandell; *Stanwyck costumes*—
Edith Head.

THE GREAT MAN'S LADY   1942. Paramount. *90 minutes*.
CAST: Barbara Stanwyck (Hannah Sempler), Joel McCrea, Brian Donlevy,
Katharine Stevens, Thurston Hall, Lloyd Corrigan, Etta McDaniel, Frank
M. Thomas, William B. Davidson, Lillian Yarbo, Helen Lynd, Lucien
Littlefield, John Hamilton.
CREDITS: *Producer-Director*—William A. Wellman; *Screenplay*—W. L. River;
Original story by Adela Rogers St. John and Seena Owen from a short story
by Viña Delmar; *Photography*—William C. Mellor; *Editor*—Thomas Scott;
Costumes—Edith Head.

THE GAY SISTERS   1942. Warner Brothers. *110 minutes*.
CAST: Barbara Stanwyck (Fiona Gaylord), George Brent, Geraldine
Fitzgerald, Donald Crisp, Gig Young, Nancy Coleman, Gene Lockhart,
Larry Simms, Donald Woods, Grant Mitchell, William T. Orr, Anne
Revere, Helene Thimig, George Lessey, Charles D. Waldron, Frank
Reicher, David Clyde, Mary Thomas, Hank Mann.
CREDITS: *Producer*—Henry Blanke; *Director*—Irving Rapper; *Screenplay*—
Lenore Coffee from the novel by Stephen Longstreet; *Editor*—Warren Low;
Stanwyck costumes—Edith Head.

LADY OF BURLESQUE   1943. United Artists. *91 minutes*.
CAST: Barbara Stanwyck (Dixie Daisy), Michael O'Shea, J. Edward Brom-
berg, Iris Adrian, Gloria Dickson, Victoria Faust, Stephanie Bachelor,
Charles Dingle, Marion Martin, Eddie Gordon, Frank Fenton, Pinky Lee,
Frank Conroy, Lew Kelly, Claire Carleton, Janis Carter, Gerald Mohr, Bert
Hanlon, Sid Marion, Lou Lubin.
CREDITS: *Producer*—Hunt Stromberg; *Director*—William A. Wellman; *Screen-
play*—James Gunn from the novel *The G-String Murders* by Gypsy Rose Lee;
Editor—James E. Newcome; *Stanwyck costumes*—Edith Head.

FLESH AND FANTASY   1943. Universal. *93 minutes*.
CAST: Edward G. Robinson, Charles Boyer, Barbara Stanwyck (Joan Stan-
ley), Betty Field, Robert Cummings, Thomas Mitchell, Charles Winninger,
Anna Lee, Dame May Whitty, C. Aubrey Smith, Robert Benchley, Edgar
Barrier, David Hoffman.
CREDITS: *Producers*—Charles Boyer, Julien Duvivier; *Director*—Julien Duvi-
vier; *Screenplay*—Ernest Pascal, Samuel Hoffenstein, Ellis St. Joseph from

222

stories by St. Joseph, Oscar Wilde, and Laslo Vadnay; *Editor*—Arthur Hilton; *Stanwyck costumes*—Edith Head.

DOUBLE INDEMNITY   1944. Paramount. *107 minutes.*
CAST: Fred MacMurray, Barbara Stanwyck (Phyllis Dietrichson), Edward G. Robinson, Porter Hall, Jean Heather, Tom Powers, Byron Barr, Richard Gaines, Fortunio Bonanova, John Philliber, Betty Farrington.
CREDITS: *Producer*—Joseph Sistrom; *Director*—Billy Wilder; *Screenplay*—Billy Wilder and Raymond Chandler from a James M. Cain short story in his book *Three Of a Kind*; *Editor*—Doane Harrison; *Costumes*—Edith Head.

HOLLYWOOD CANTEEN   1944. Warner Brothers. *123 minutes.*
CAST: Joan Leslie, Robert Hutton, Dane Clark, Janis Paige. Guest appearances by Barbara Stanwyck and many other Warner stars.
CREDITS: *Producer*—Alex Gottlieb; *Director and screenplay*—Delmer Daves; *Editor*—Christian Nyby.

CHRISTMAS IN CONNECTICUT   1945. Warner Brothers. *101 minutes.*
CAST: Barbara Stanwyck (Elizabeth Lane), Dennis Morgan, Sydney Greenstreet, Reginald Gardiner, S. Z. Sakall, Robert Shayne, Una O'Connor, Frank Jenks, Joyce Compton, Dick Elliott, Charles Arnt.
CREDITS: *Producer*—William Jacobs; *Director*—Peter Godfrey; *Screenplay*—Lionel Houser and Adele Commandini from a story by Aileen Hamilton; *Editor*—Frank Magee; *Costumes*—Edith Head.

MY REPUTATION   1946. Warner Brothers. *96 minutes.*
CAST: Barbara Stanwyck (Jessica Drummond), George Brent, Warner Anderson, Lucile Watson, John Ridgely, Eve Arden, Jerome Cowan, Esther Dale, Scotty Beckett, Bobby Cooper, Leona Maricle, Mary Servoss, Cecil Cunningham, Janis Wilson, Ann Todd.
CREDITS: *Producer*—Henry Blanke; *Director*—Curtis Bernhardt; *Screenplay*—Catherine Turney from the novel *Instruct My Sorrows* by Clare Jaynes; *Editor*—David Weisbart; *Stanwyck costumes*—Edith Head.

THE BRIDE WORE BOOTS   1946. Paramount. *86 minutes.*
CAST: Barbara Stanwyck (Sally Warren), Robert Cummings, Diana Lynn, Patric Knowles, Peggy Wood, Robert Benchley, Willie Best, Natalie Wood, Gregory Muradian, Mary Young.
CREDITS: *Producer*—Seton I. Miller; *Director*—Irving Pichel; *Screenplay*—Dwight Mitchell Wiley from a story by Wiley and a play by Harry Segall; *Editor*—Ellsworth Hoagland; *Costumes*—Edith Head.

THE STRANGE LOVE OF MARTHA IVERS 1946. Paramount. *116 minutes.*
  CAST: Barbara Stanwyck (Martha Ivers), Van Heflin, Lizabeth Scott, Kirk Douglas, Judith Anderson, Roman Bohnen, Darryl Hickman, Janis Wilson, Ann Doran, Frank Orth, James Flavin, Mickey Kuhn, Charles D. Brown.
  CREDITS: *Producer*—Hal B. Wallis; *Director*—Lewis Milestone; *Screenplay*— Robert Rossen from a story by Jack Patrick; *Editor*—Archie Marshek; *Costumes*—Edith Head.

CALIFORNIA 1947. Paramount. *98 minutes.*
  CAST: Ray Milland, Barbara Stanwyck (Lily Bishop), Barry Fitzgerald, George Coulouris, Albert Dekker, Anthony Quinn, Frank Faylen, Gavin Muir, James Burke, Eduardo Ciannelli, Roman Bohnen, Argentina Brunetti, Howard Freeman, Julia Faye.
  CREDITS: *Producer*—Seton I. Miller; *Director*—John Farrow; *Screenplay*—Frank Butler and Theodore Strauss from a story by Boris Ingster; *Editor*—Eda Warren; *Women's costumes*—Edith Head.

THE TWO MRS. CARROLLS 1947. Warner Brothers. *99 minutes.*
  CAST: Humphrey Bogart, Barbara Stanwyck (Sally), Alexis Smith, Nigel Bruce, Isobel Elsom, Pat O'Moore, Ann Carter, Anita Bolster, Barry Bernard, Colin Campbell, Peter Godfrey.
  CREDITS: *Producer*—Mark Hellinger; *Director*—Peter Godfrey; *Screenplay*— Thomas Job from the play by Martin Vale; *Editor*—Frederick Richards; *Stanwyck costumes*—Edith Head.

THE OTHER LOVE 1947. United Artists. *96 minutes.*
  CAST: Barbara Stanwyck (Karen Duncan), David Niven, Richard Conte, Gilbert Roland, Joan Lorring, Lenore Aubert, Maria Palmer, Natalie Schafer, Edward Ashley, Richard Hale, Michael Romanoff, Jimmy Horne, Mary Forbes, Ann Codee, Kathleen Williams.
  CREDITS: *Producer*—David Lewis; *Director*—André de Toth; *Screenplay*— Harry Brown and Ladislas Fodor from the short story "Beyond" by Erich Maria Remarque; *Editor*—Walter Thompson; *Stanwyck costumes*—Edith Head.

CRY WOLF 1947. Warner Brothers. *84 minutes.*
  CAST: Errol Flynn, Barbara Stanwyck (Sandra Demarest), Geraldine Brooks, Richard Basehart, Jerome Cowan, John Ridgely, Patricia White, Rory Mallinson, Helen Thimig, Paul Stanton, Barry Bernard.
  CREDITS: *Producer*—Henry Blanke; *Director*—Peter Godfrey; *Screenplay*—

Catherine Turney from the novel by Marjorie Carleton; *Editor*—Folmar Blangsted; *Stanwyck costumes*—Edith Head.

VARIETY GIRL   1947. Paramount. *93 minutes.*
CAST: Brief appearance by Bing Crosby, Bob Hope, Gary Cooper, Ray Milland, Alan Ladd, Barbara Stanwyck, Paulette Goddard, Dorothy Lamour, and most of the Paramount lot.
CREDITS: *Producer*—Daniel Dare; *Director*—George Marshall; *Screenplay*—Edmund Hartmann, Frank Tashlin, Robert Welch, Monte Brice; *Editor*—LeRoy Stone; *Stars' costumes*—Edith Head.

B. F.'S DAUGHTER   1948. Metro-Goldwyn-Mayer. *108 minutes.*
CAST: Barbara Stanwyck (Polly Fulton), Van Heflin, Charles Coburn, Richard Hart, Keenan Wynn, Margaret Lindsay, Spring Byington, Marshall Thompson, Barbara Laage, Thomas E. Breen, Fred Nurney.
CREDITS: *Producer*—Edwin H. Knopf; *Director*—Robert Z. Leonard; *Screenplay*—Luther Davis from the novel by John P. Marquand; *Editor*—George White; *Women's costumes*—Irene.

SORRY, WRONG NUMBER   1948. Paramount. *89 minutes.*
CAST: Barbara Stanwyck (Leona Stevenson), Burt Lancaster, Ann Richards, Wendell Corey, Harold Vermilyea, Ed Begley, Leif Erickson, William Conrad, John Bromfield, Jimmy Hunt, Dorothy Neumann, Paul Fierro.
CREDITS: *Producers*—Hal B. Wallis, Anatole Litvak; *Director*—Anatole Litvak; *Screenplay*—Lucille Fletcher from her radio play; *Editor*—Warren Low; *Costumes*—Edith Head.

THE LADY GAMBLES   1949. Universal. *99 minutes.*
CAST: Barbara Stanwyck (Joan Boothe), Robert Preston, Stephen McNally, Edith Barrett, John Hoyt, Elliott Sullivan, John Harmon, Phil Van Zandt, Leif Erickson, Curt Conway, Houseley Stevenson, Don Beddoe, Nana Bryant, Anthony Curtis, Peter Leeds.
CREDITS: *Producer*—Michel Kraike; *Director*—Michael Gordon; *Screenplay*—Roy Huggins; *Adaptation*—Halsted Welles; *Story*—Lewis Meltzer, Oscar Saul; *Editor*—Milton Carruth; *Stanwyck costumes*—Orry-Kelly.

EAST SIDE, WEST SIDE   1949. Metro-Goldwyn-Mayer. *108 minutes.*
CAST: Barbara Stanwyck (Jessie Bourne), James Mason, Van Heflin, Ava Gardner, Cyd Charisse, Nancy Davis, Gale Sondergaard, William Conrad, Raymond Greenleaf, Douglas Kennedy, Beverly Michaels, William Frawley, Lisa Golm, Tom Powers.

CREDITS: *Producer*—Voldemar Vetluguin; *Director*—Mervyn LeRoy; *Screenplay*—Isobel Lennart from the novel by Marcia Davenport; *Editor*—Harold F. Kress; *Women's costumes*—Helen Rose.

THE FILE ON THELMA JORDAN 1950. Paramount. *100 minutes.*
CAST: Barbara Stanwyck (Thelma Jordan), Wendell Corey, Paul Kelly, Joan Tetzel, Stanley Ridges, Richard Rober, Minor Watson, Barry Kelley, Laura Elliot, Basil Ruysdael, Jane Novak, Gertrude W. Hoffman, Harry Antrim, Geraldine Wall.
CREDITS: *Producer*—Hal B. Wallis; *Director*—Robert Siodmak; *Screenplay*—Ketti Frings from a story by Marty Holland; *Editor*—Warren Low; *Costumes*—Edith Head.

NO MAN OF HER OWN 1950. Paramount. *98 minutes.*
CAST: Barbara Stanwyck (Helen Ferguson, Patrice Harkness), John Lund, Jane Cowl, Phyllis Thaxter, Lyle Bettger, Henry O'Neill, Richard Denning, Carole Mathews, Harry Antrim, Catherine Craig, Esther Dale, Milburn Stone, Griff Barnett, Georgia Backus.
CREDITS: *Producer*—Richard Maibaum; *Director*—Mitchell Leisen; *Screenplay*—Sally Benson, Catherine Turney from the novel *I Married a Dead Man* by William Irish; *Editor*—Alma Macrorie; *Costumes*—Edith Head.

THE FURIES 1950. Paramount. *109 minutes.*
CAST: Barbara Stanwyck (Vance Jeffords), Wendell Corey, Walter Huston, Judith Anderson, Gilbert Roland, Thomas Gomez, Beulah Bondi, Albert Dekker, John Bromfield, Wallace Ford, Blanche Yurka, Louis Jean Heydt, Frank Ferguson.
CREDITS: *Producer*—Hal B. Wallis; *Director*—Anthony Mann; *Screenplay*—Charles Schnee from a novel by Niven Busch; *Editor*—Archie Marshek; *Costumes*—Edith Head.

TO PLEASE A LADY 1950. Metro-Goldwyn-Mayer. *91 minutes.*
CAST: Clark Gable, Barbara Stanwyck (Regina Forbes), Adolphe Menjou, Will Geer, Roland Winters, William C. McGaw, Lela Bliss, Emory Parnell, Frank Jenks, Helen Spring, Bill Hickman, Lew Smith, Ted Husing.
CREDITS: *Producer-Director*—Clarence Brown; *Screenplay*—Barré Lyndon and Marge Decker; *Editor*—Robert J. Kern; *Costumes*—Helen Rose.

THE MAN WITH A CLOAK 1951. Metro-Goldwyn-Mayer. *81 minutes.*
CAST: Joseph Cotten, Barbara Stanwyck (Lorna Bounty), Louis Calhern, Leslie Caron, Joe DeSantis, Jim Backus, Margaret Wycherly, Richard Hale, Nicholas Joy, Roy Roberts, Mitchell Lewis.

CREDITS: *Producer*—Stephen Ames; *Director*—Fletcher Markle; *Screenplay*—Frank Fenton from a story by John Dickson Carr; *Editor*—Newell P. Kimlin; *Women's costumes*—Walter Plunkett.

CLASH BY NIGHT 1952. RKO. *105 minutes.*
CAST: Barbara Stanwyck (Mae Doyle), Paul Douglas, Robert Ryan, Marilyn Monroe, J. Carrol Naish, Keith Andes, Silvio Minciotti.
CREDITS: *Executive producers*—Jerry Wald, Norman Krasna; *Producer*—Harriet Parsons; *Director*—Fritz Lang; *Screenplay*—Alfred Hayes from the play by Clifford Odets; *Editor*—George J. Amy; *Costumes*—Michael Woulfe.

JEOPARDY 1953. Metro-Goldwyn-Mayer. *69 minutes.*
CAST: Barbara Stanwyck (Helen Stilwin), Barry Sullivan, Ralph Meeker, Lee Aaker.
CREDITS: *Producer*—Sol Baer Fielding; *Director*—John Sturges; *Screenplay*—Mel Dinelli from a story by Maurice Zimm; *Editor*—Newell P. Kimlin; *Costumes*—Helen Rose.

TITANIC 1953. Twentieth Century–Fox. *98 minutes.*
CAST: Clifton Webb, Barbara Stanwyck (Julia Sturges), Audrey Dalton, Harper Carter, Robert Wagner, Brian Aherne, Thelma Ritter, Richard Basehart, Allyn Joslyn, James Todd, Frances Bergen, William Johnstone.
CREDITS: *Producer*—Charles Brackett; *Director*—Jean Negulesco; *Screenplay*—Charles Brackett, Walter Reisch, Richard Breen; *Editor*—Louis Loeffler; *Costumes*—Dorothy Jeakins.

ALL I DESIRE 1953. Universal. *79 minutes.*
CAST: Barbara Stanwyck (Naomi Murdoch), Richard Carlson, Lyle Bettger, Marcia Henderson, Lori Nelson, Maureen O'Sullivan, Richard Long, Billy Gray, Lotte Stein, Dayton Lummis, Fred Nurney.
CREDITS: *Producer*—Ross Hunter; *Director*—Douglas Sirk; *Screenplay*—James Gunn, Robert Blees from the novel *Stopover* by Carol Brink; *Adaptation*—Gina Kaus; *Editor*—Milton Carruth; *Costumes*—Rosemary Odell.

THE MOONLIGHTER 1953. Warner Brothers. *77 minutes.*
CAST: Barbara Stanwyck (Rela), Fred MacMurray, Ward Bond, William Ching, John Dierkes, Morris Ankrum, Jack Elam, Charles Halton, Norman Leavitt, Sam Flint, Myra Marsh.
CREDITS: *Producer*—Joseph Bernhard; *Director*—Roy Rowland; *Screenplay*—Niven Busch; *Editor*—Terry Morse; *Costumes*—Joe King, Ann Peck.

BLOWING WILD   1953. Warner Brothers. *90 minutes.*
CAST: Gary Cooper, Barbara Stanwyck (Marina), Ruth Roman, Anthony Quinn, Ward Bond, Ian MacDonald, Richard Karlan.
CREDITS: *Producer*—Milton Sperling; *Director*—Hugo Fregonese; *Screenplay*—Philip Yordan; *Editor*—Alan Crosland, Jr.

WITNESS TO MURDER   1954. United Artists. *83 minutes.*
CAST: Barbara Stanwyck (Cheryl Draper), George Sanders, Gary Merrill, Jesse White, Harry Shannon, Claire Carleton, Lewis Martin, Dick Elliott, Harry Tyler, Juanita Moore, Joy Hallward, Adeline DeWalt Reynolds, Gertrude Graner.
CREDITS: *Producer*—Chester Erskine; *Director*—Roy Rowland; *Screenplay*—Chester Erskine; *Editor*—Robert Swink; *Costumes*—Jack Masters, Irene Caine.

EXECUTIVE SUITE   1954. Metro-Goldwyn-Mayer. *104 minutes.*
CAST: William Holden, June Allyson, Barbara Stanwyck (Julia Tredway), Fredric March, Walter Pidgeon, Shelley Winters, Paul Douglas, Louis Calhern, Dean Jagger, Nina Foch, Tim Considine, William Phipps, Lucille Knoch, Edgar Stehli, Mary Adams, Virginia Brissac, Harry Shannon.
CREDITS: *Producer*—John Houseman; *Director*—Robert Wise; *Screenplay*—Ernest Lehman from the novel by Cameron Hawley; *Editor*—Ralph E. Winters; *Women's costumes*—Helen Rose.

CATTLE QUEEN OF MONTANA   1955. RKO. *88 minutes.*
CAST: Barbara Stanwyck (Sierra Nevada Jones), Ronald Reagan, Gene Evans, Lance Fuller, Anthony Caruso, Jack Elam, Yvette Dugay, Morris Ankrum, Chubby Johnson, Myron Healey, Rod Redwing.
CREDITS: *Producer*—Benedict Bogeaus; *Director*—Allan Dwan; *Screenplay*—Howard Estabrook and Robert Blees from a story by Thomas Blackburn; *Editor*—Carl Lodato; *Costumes*—Gwen Wakeling.

THE VIOLENT MEN   1955. Columbia. *96 minutes.*
CAST: Glenn Ford, Barbara Stanwyck (Martha Wilkison), Edward G. Robinson, Dianne Foster, Brian Keith, May Wynn, Warner Anderson, Basil Ruysdael, Lita Milan, Richard Jaeckel, James Westerfield, Jack Kelly, Willis Bouchey, Harry Shannon.
CREDITS: *Producer*—Lewis J. Rachmil; *Director*—Rudolph Maté; *Screenplay*—Harry Kleiner from a novel by Donald Hamilton; *Editor*—Jerome Thoms; *Costumes*—Jean Louis.

ESCAPE TO BURMA   1955. RKO. *88 minutes.*
CAST: Barbara Stanwyck (Gwen Moore), Robert Ryan, David Farrar, Murvyn Vye, Lisa Montell, Robert Warwick, Reginald Denny, Peter Coe, Alex Montoya, Robert Cabal, Anthony Numkema, Lala Chand Mehra.
CREDITS: *Producer*—Benedict Bogeaus; *Director*—Allan Dwan; *Screenplay*—Talbot Jennings and Hobart Donavan from a story "Bow Tamely to Me" by Kenneth Perkins; *Editor*—James Leicester; *Costumes*—Gwen Wakeling.

THERE'S ALWAYS TOMORROW   1956. Universal. *84 minutes.*
CAST: Barbara Stanwyck (Norma Miller), Fred MacMurray, Joan Bennett, Pat Crowley, William Reynolds, Gigi Perreau, Judy Nugent, Jane Darwell.
CREDITS: *Producer*—Ross Hunter; *Director*—Douglas Sirk; *Screenplay*—Bernard C. Schoenfeld from a story by Ursula Parrott; *Editor*—William M. Morgan; *Costumes*—Jay Morley, Jr.

THE MAVERICK QUEEN   1956. Republic. *92 minutes.*
CAST: Barbara Stanwyck (Kit Banion), Barry Sullivan, Scott Brady, Mary Murphy, Wallace Ford, Howard Petrie, Jim Davis, Emile Meyer, Walter Sande, George Keymas, John Doucette, Taylor Holmes, Pierre Watkin.
CREDITS: *Associate producer-director*—Joe Kane; *Screenplay*—Kenneth Gamet and DeVallon Scott from the novel by Zane Grey; *Editor*—Richard L. Van Enger; *Costumes*—Adele Palmer.

THESE WILDER YEARS   1956. Metro-Goldwyn-Mayer. *91 minutes.*
CAST: James Cagney, Barbara Stanwyck (Ann Dempster), Walter Pidgeon, Betty Lou Keim, Don Dubbins, Edward Andrews, Basil Ruysdael, Grandon Rhodes.
CREDITS: *Producer*—Jules Schermer; *Director*—Roy Rowland; *Screenplay*—Frank Fenton from a story by Ralph Wheelwright; *Editor*—Ben Lewis; *Costumes*—Helen Rose.

CRIME OF PASSION   1957. United Artists. *84 minutes.*
CAST: Barbara Stanwyck (Kathy), Sterling Hayden, Raymond Burr, Fay Wray, Royal Dano, Virginia Grey, Dennis Cross, Robert Griffin, Jay Adler, Malcolm Atterbury, John S. Launer.
CREDITS: *Executive producer*—Bob Goldstein; *Producer*—Herman Cohen; *Director*—Gerd Oswald; *Screenplay*—Joe Eisinger; *Editor*—Marjorie Fowler; *Costumes*—Grace Houston.

TROOPER HOOK   1957. United Artists. *81 minutes.*
CAST: Joel McCrea, Barbara Stanwyck (Cora), Earl Holliman, Edward

Andrews, John Dehner, Susan Kohner, Royal Dano, Terry Lawrence, Celia Lovsky, Rudolfo Acosta.

CREDITS: *Producer*—Sol Baer Fielding; *Director*—Charles Marquis Warren; *Screenplay*—Warren, David Victor and Herbert Little, Jr., from a story by Jack Schaefer; *Editor*—Fred Berger; *Women's costumes*—Voulee Giokaris.

FORTY GUNS 1957. Twentieth Century–Fox. *80 minutes.*

CAST: Barbara Stanwyck (Jessica Drummond), Barry Sullivan, Dean Jagger, John Ericson, Gene Barry, Robert Dix, Jidge Carroll, Paul Dubov, Gerald Milton, Ziva Rodann, Hank Worden, Neyle Morrow, Eve Brent.

CREDITS: *Producer, Director, Screenplay*—Samuel Fuller; *Editor*—Gene Fowler, Jr.; *Costumes*—Charles LeMaire, Leah Rhodes.

WALK ON THE WILD SIDE 1962. Columbia. *114 minutes.*

CAST: Laurence Harvey, Capucine, Jane Fonda, Anne Baxter, Barbara Stanwyck (Jo Courtney), Joanna Moore, Richard Rust, Karl Swenson, Donald Barry, Juanita Moore, John Anderson, Ken Lynch, Todd Armstrong, Lillian Bronson, Adrienne Marden, Sherry O'Neil, John Bryant, Kathryn Card.

CREDITS: *Producer*—Charles K. Feldman; *Director*—Edward Dmytryk; *Screenplay*—John Fante and Edmund Morris from the novel by Nelson Algren; *Editor*—Harry Gerstad; *Costumes*—Charles Lemaire.

ROUSTABOUT 1964. Paramount. *101 minutes.*

CAST: Elvis Presley, Barbara Stanwyck (Maggie Morgan), Joan Freeman, Leif Erickson, Sue Ane Langdon, Pat Buttram, Joan Staley, Dabbs Greer, Steve Brodie, Norman Grabowski, Jack Albertson, Jane Dulo.

CREDITS: *Producer*—Hal B. Wallis; *Director*—John Rich; *Screenplay*—Anthony Lawrence and Allan Weiss from a story by Weiss; *Editor*—Warren Low; *Costumes*—Edith Head.

THE NIGHT WALKER 1965. Universal. *86 minutes.*

CAST: Robert Taylor, Barbara Stanwyck (Irene Trent), Judith Meredith, Hayden Rorke, Rochelle Hudson, Marjorie Bennett, Jess Barker, Tetsu Kumal, Ted Durant, Lloyd Bochner.

CREDITS: *Producer-Director*—William Castle; *Screenplay*—Robert Bloch; *Editor*—Edwin H. Bryant; *Costumes*—Helen Colvig.

THE HOUSE THAT WOULDN'T DIE 1970. ABC Movie of the Week. *73 minutes.*

CAST: Barbara Stanwyck (Ruth Bennett), Richard Egan, Michael Anderson Jr., Katherine Winn, Doreen Lang, Mabel Albertson.

CREDITS: *Producer*—Aaron Spelling; *Director*—John Llewellyn Moxey; *Teleplay*—Henry Farrell from the novel *Ammie, Come Home* by Barbara Michaels; *Editor*—Art Seid; *Stanwyck costumes*—Nolan Miller.

A TASTE OF EVIL   1971. ABC Movie of the Week. *74 minutes.*
CAST: Barbara Stanwyck (Miriam Jennings), Barbara Parkins, Roddy McDowall, William Windom, Arthur O'Connell, Bing Russell, Dawn Frame.
CREDITS: *Producer*—Aaron Spelling; *Director*—John Llewellyn Moxey; *Teleplay*—Jimmy Sangster; *Editor*—Art Seid; *Stanwyck costumes*—Nolan Miller.

THE LETTERS   1973. ABC Movie of the Week. *74 minutes.*
CAST: Story 1—John Forsythe, Jane Powell, Lesley Warren. Story 2—Barbara Stanwyck (Geraldine Parkington), Leslie Nielsen, Dina Merrill. Story 3—Ida Lupino, Ben Murphy, Pamela Franklin.
CREDITS: *Executive producers*—Aaron Spelling, Leonard Goldberg; *Producer*—Paul Junger Witt; *Credits for Stanwyck story*—*Director*—Gene Nelson; *Teleplay*—Ellis Marcus, Hal Sitowitz from a story by Marcus; *Editor*—Carroll Sax; *Stanwyck costumes*—Nolan Miller.

THE THORN BIRDS   1982. ABC. *472 minutes.*
CAST: Richard Chamberlain, Rachel Ward, Jean Simmons, Ken Howard, Mare Winningham, Piper Laurie, Richard Kiley, Earl Holliman, Bryan Brown, Philip Anglim, Christopher Plummer, Allyn Ann McLerie, and Barbara Stanwyck (Mary Carson).
CREDITS: *Executive producers*—David L. Wolper, Edward Lewis; *Producer*—Stan Margulies; *Director*—Daryl Duke; *Teleplay*—Carmen Culver based on the novel by Colleen McCullough; *Editor*—Robert F. Shugrue; *Costumes*—Travilla.